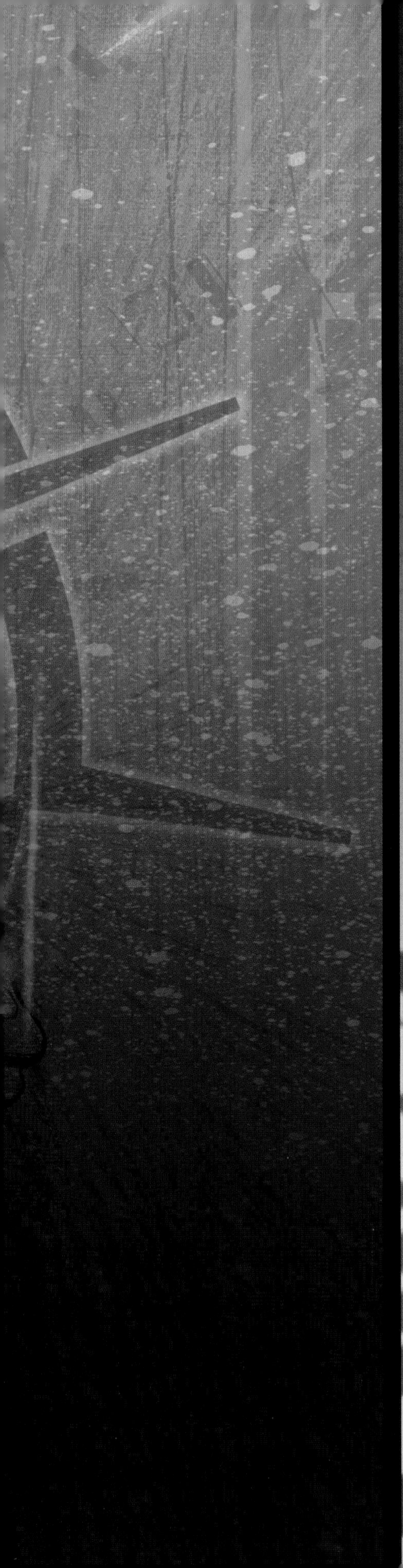

THE FANTASTIC FOUR

1. A team — and a family — of adventurers, explorers and imaginauts, the Fantastic Four lead lives both ordinary — and extraordinary. As of today:

2. Following several turbulent months, the Richards family has finally regained much of its footing... on a very slippery slope...

3. ...with the team's fame and fortune badly undercut. Together, they must start from scratch to rebuild their finances and their public image. It can be done...

4. ...but New York is a tough town.

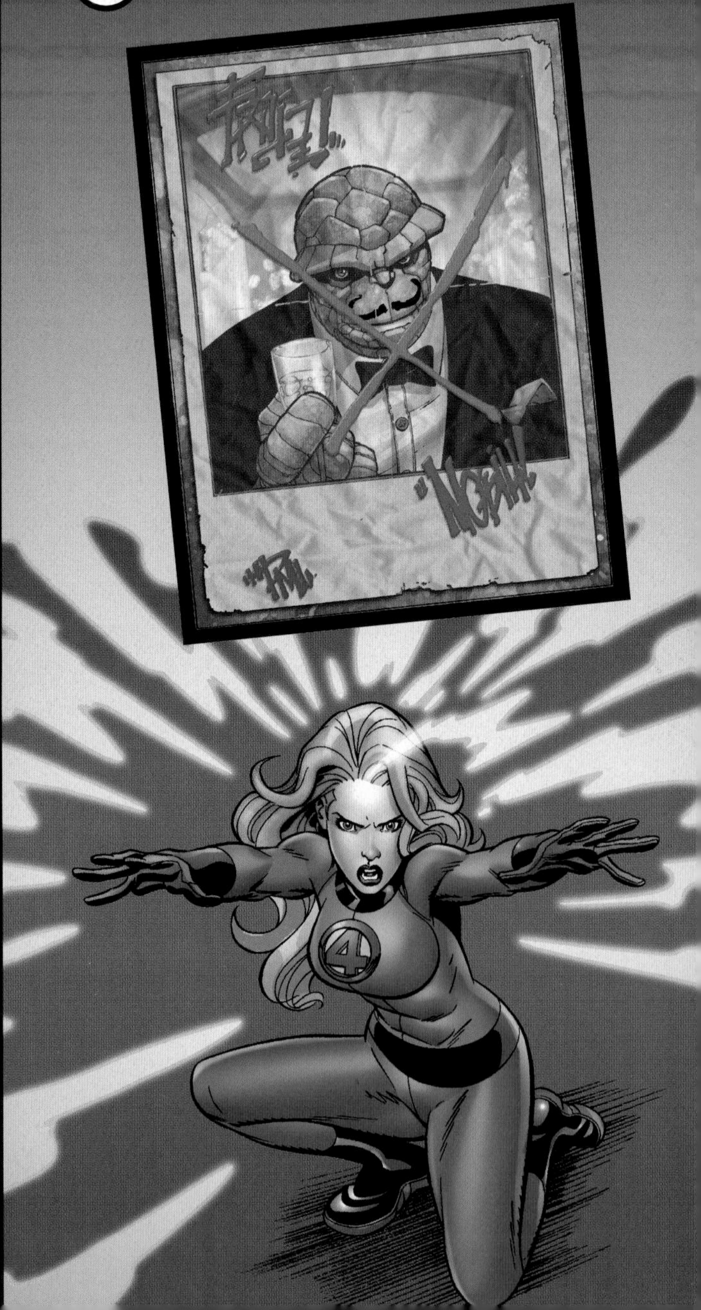

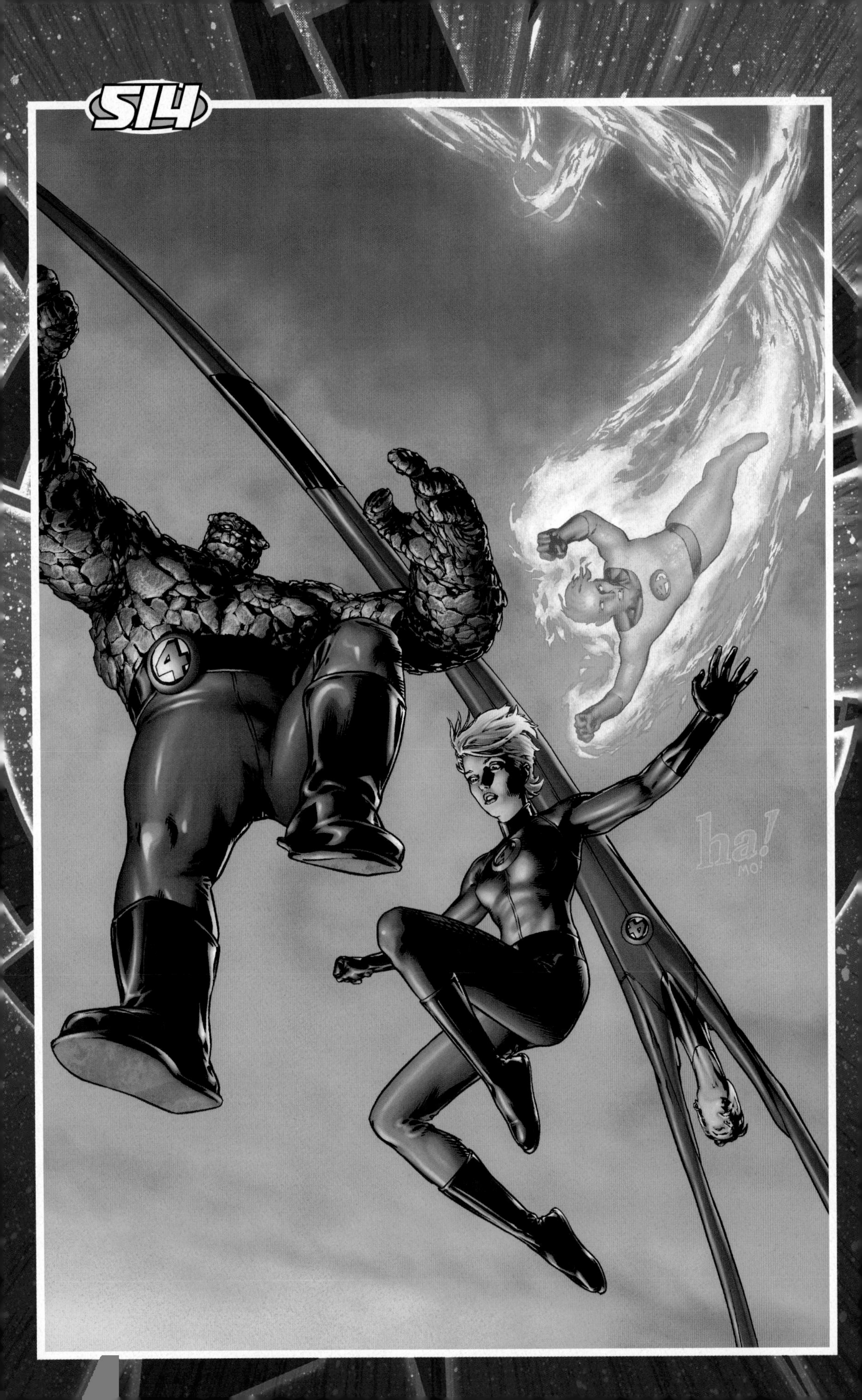
514

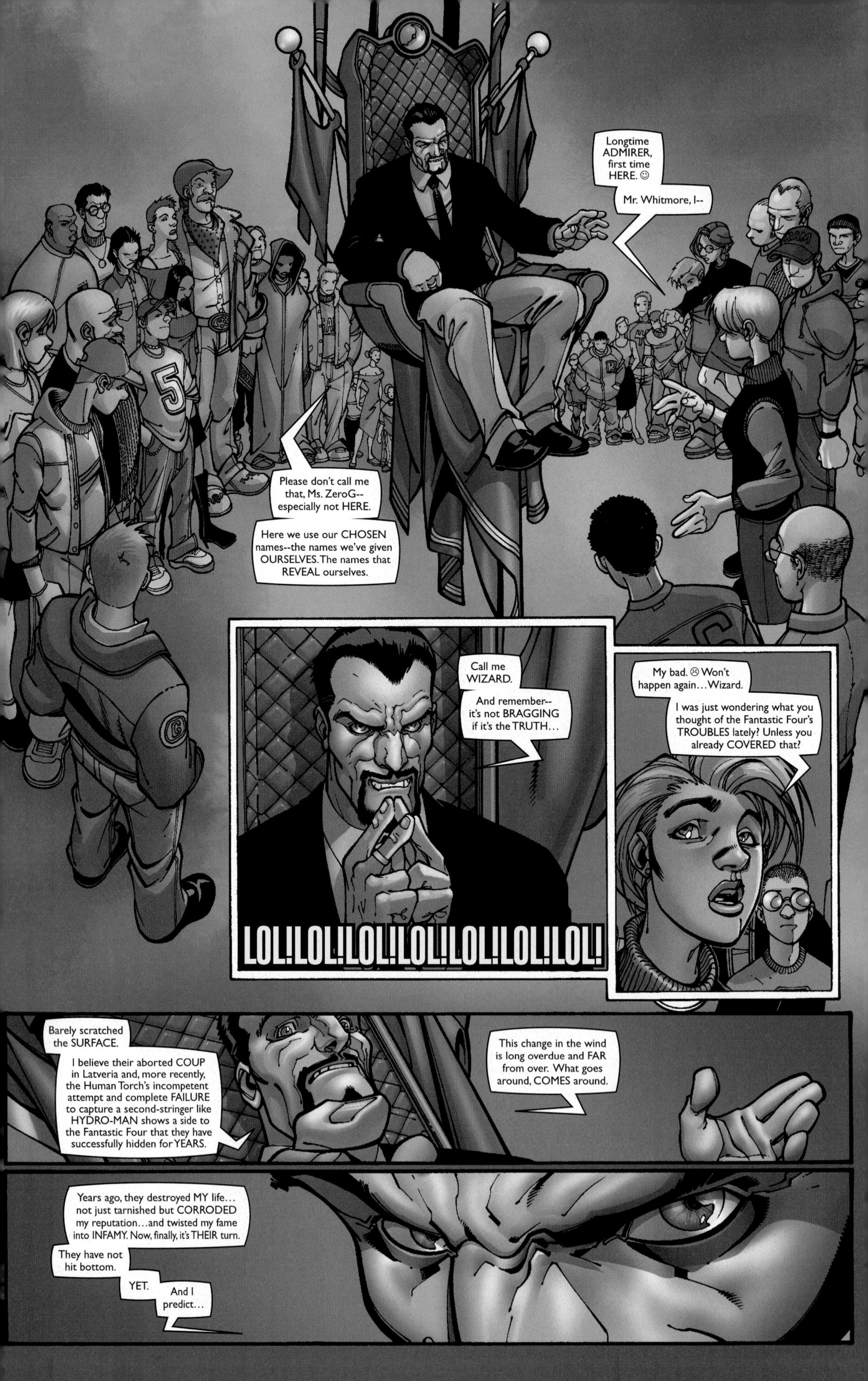
Longtime ADMIRER, first time HERE. ☺
Mr. Whitmore, I--
Please don't call me that, Ms. ZeroG-- especially not HERE.
Here we use our CHOSEN names--the names we've given OURSELVES. The names that REVEAL ourselves.
Call me WIZARD.
And remember-- it's not BRAGGING if it's the TRUTH...
LOL!LOL!LOL!LOL!LOL!LOL!LOL!
My bad. ☹ Won't happen again...Wizard.
I was just wondering what you thought of the Fantastic Four's TROUBLES lately? Unless you already COVERED that?
Barely scratched the SURFACE.
I believe their aborted COUP in Latveria and, more recently, the Human Torch's incompetent attempt and complete FAILURE to capture a second-stringer like HYDRO-MAN shows a side to the Fantastic Four that they have successfully hidden for YEARS.
This change in the wind is long overdue and FAR from over. What goes around, COMES around.
Years ago, they destroyed MY life... not just tarnished but CORRODED my reputation...and twisted my fame into INFAMY. Now, finally, it's THEIR turn.
They have not hit bottom.
YET.
And I predict...

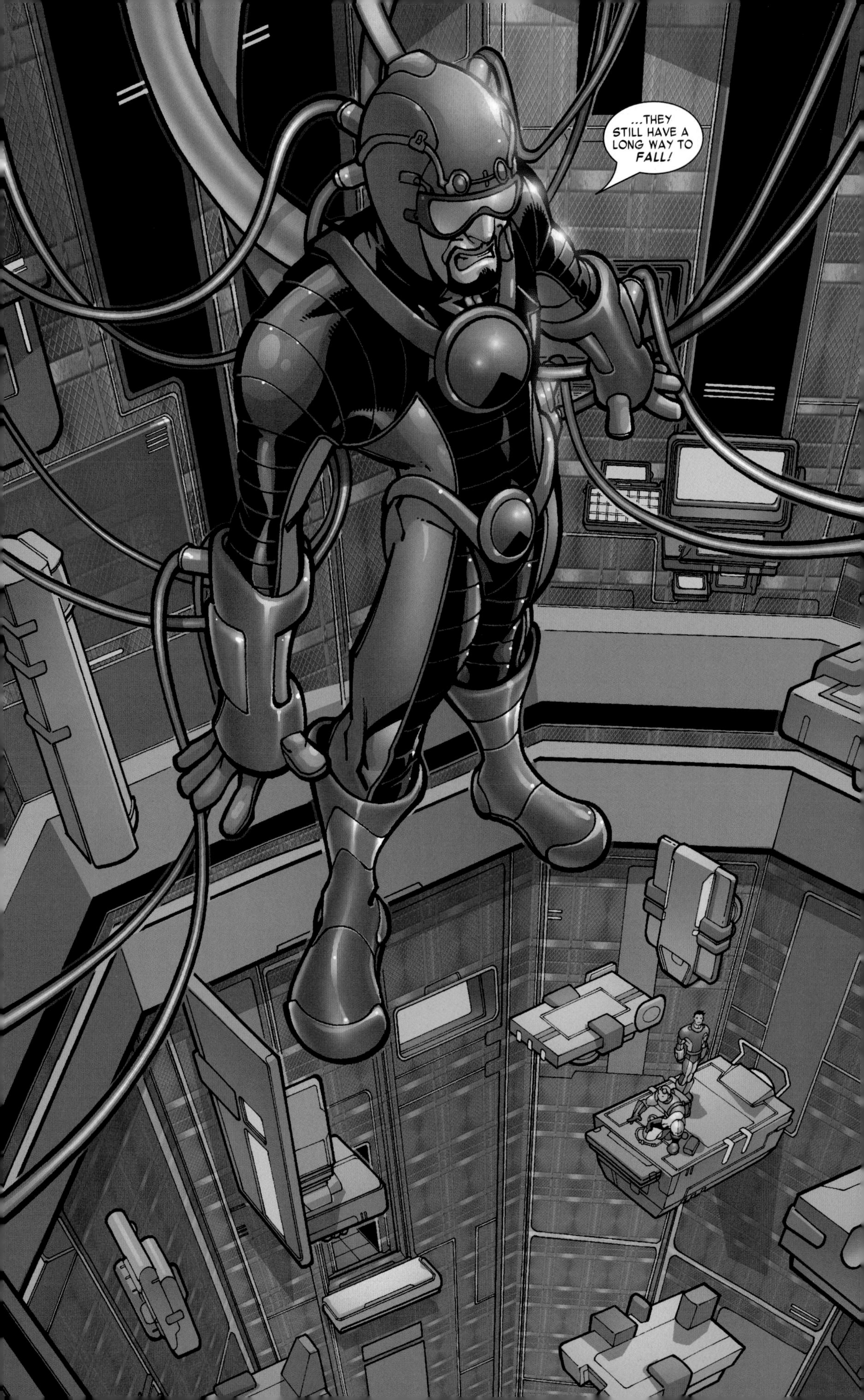
...THEY STILL HAVE A LONG WAY TO FALL!

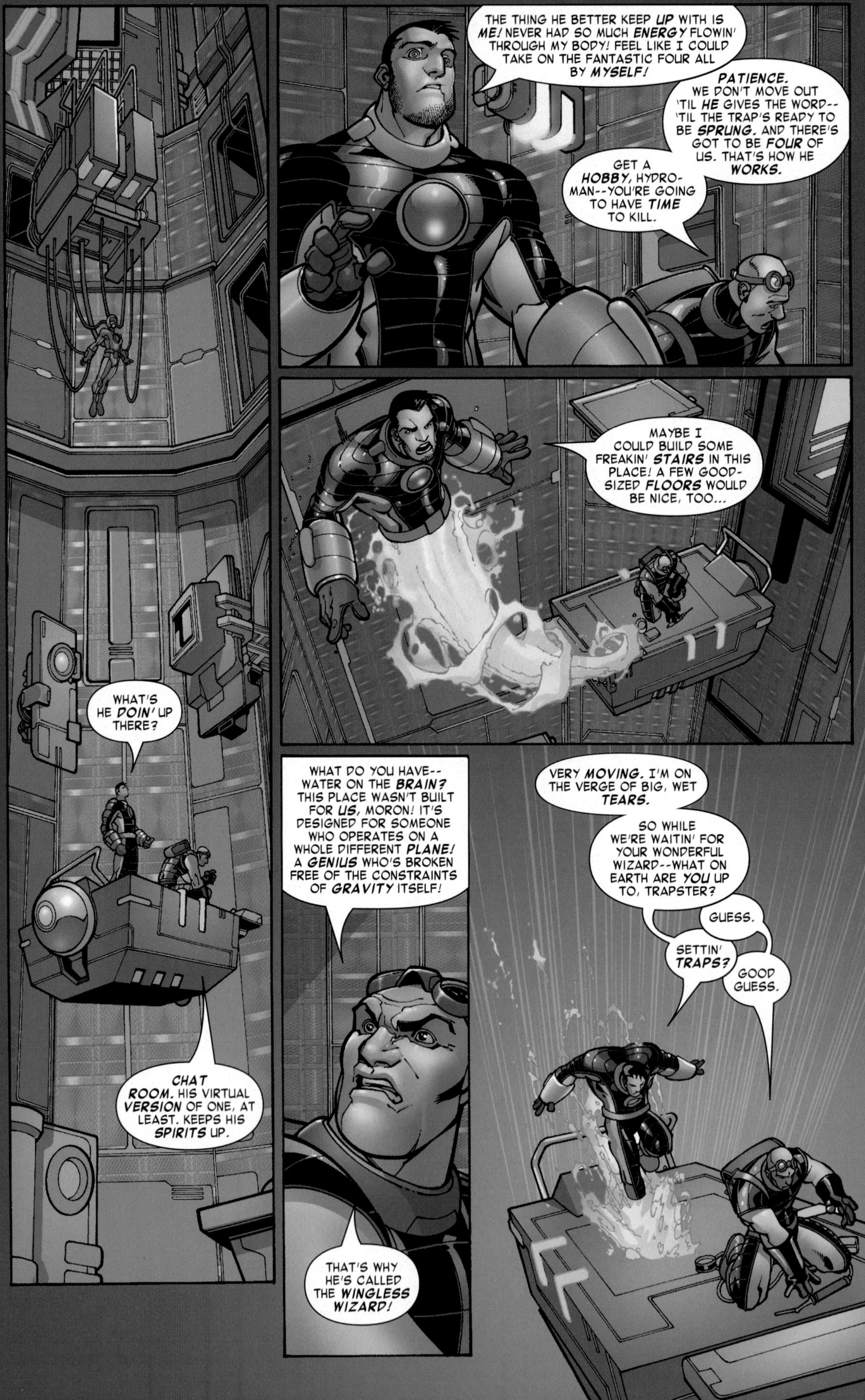
THE THING HE BETTER KEEP UP WITH IS ME! NEVER HAD SO MUCH ENERGY FLOWIN' THROUGH MY BODY! FEEL LIKE I COULD TAKE ON THE FANTASTIC FOUR ALL BY MYSELF!
PATIENCE. WE DON'T MOVE OUT 'TIL HE GIVES THE WORD-- 'TIL THE TRAP'S READY TO BE SPRUNG. AND THERE'S GOT TO BE FOUR OF US. THAT'S HOW HE WORKS.
GET A HOBBY, HYDRO-MAN--YOU'RE GOING TO HAVE TIME TO KILL.
WHAT'S HE DOIN' UP THERE?
CHAT ROOM. HIS VIRTUAL VERSION OF ONE, AT LEAST. KEEPS HIS SPIRITS UP.
MAYBE I COULD BUILD SOME FREAKIN' STAIRS IN THIS PLACE! A FEW GOOD-SIZED FLOORS WOULD BE NICE, TOO...
WHAT DO YOU HAVE-- WATER ON THE BRAIN? THIS PLACE WASN'T BUILT FOR US, MORON! IT'S DESIGNED FOR SOMEONE WHO OPERATES ON A WHOLE DIFFERENT PLANE! A GENIUS WHO'S BROKEN FREE OF THE CONSTRAINTS OF GRAVITY ITSELF!
THAT'S WHY HE'S CALLED THE WINGLESS WIZARD!
VERY MOVING. I'M ON THE VERGE OF BIG, WET TEARS.
SO WHILE WE'RE WAITIN' FOR YOUR WONDERFUL WIZARD--WHAT ON EARTH ARE YOU UP TO, TRAPSTER?
GUESS.
SETTIN' TRAPS?
GOOD GUESS.

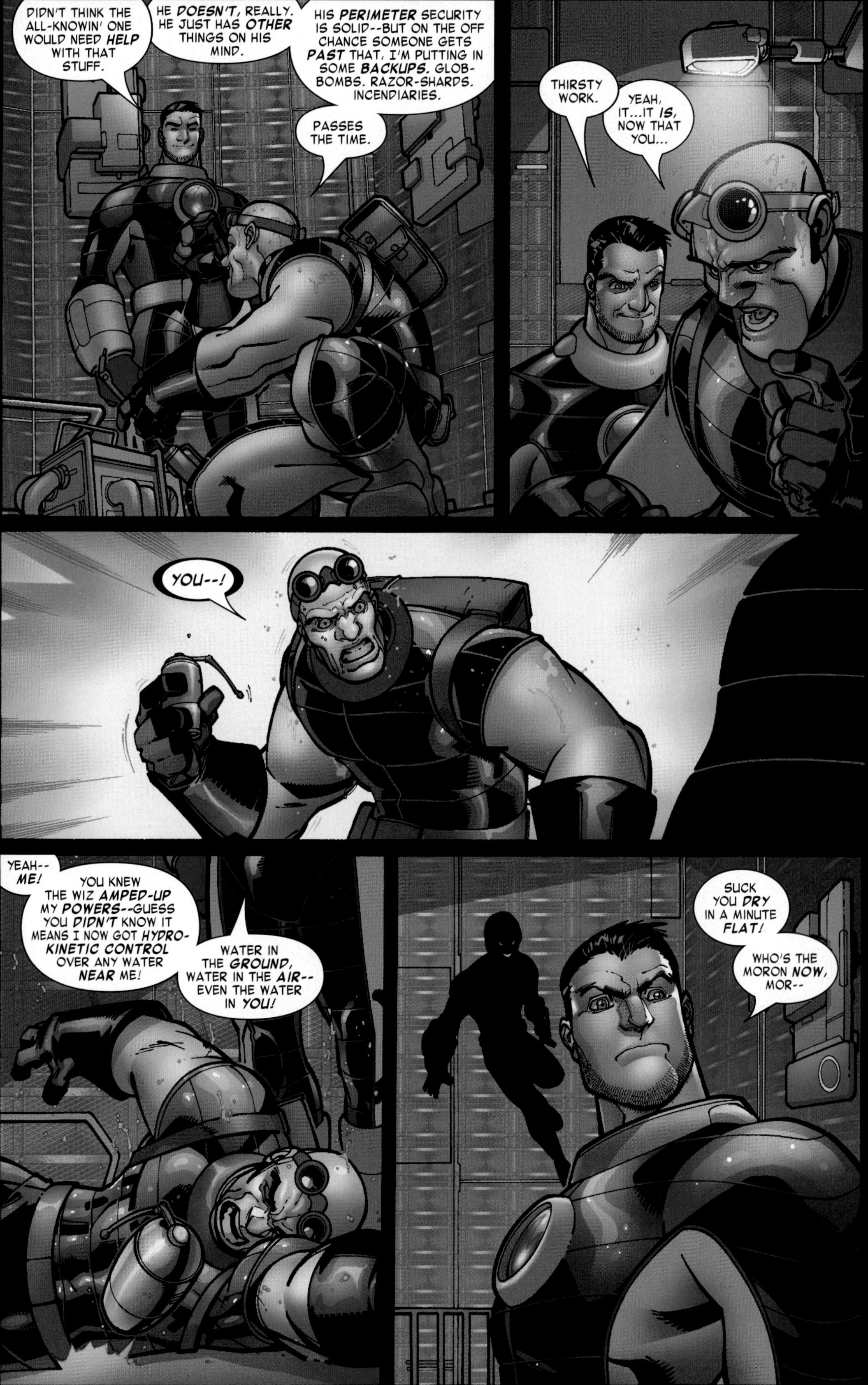
DIDN'T THINK THE ALL-KNOWIN' ONE WOULD NEED **HELP** WITH THAT STUFF.
HE **DOESN'T**, REALLY. HE JUST HAS **OTHER** THINGS ON HIS MIND.
HIS **PERIMETER** SECURITY IS SOLID--BUT ON THE OFF CHANCE SOMEONE GETS **PAST** THAT, I'M PUTTING IN SOME **BACKUPS.** GLOB-BOMBS. RAZOR-SHARDS. INCENDIARIES.
PASSES THE TIME.
THIRSTY WORK.
YEAH, IT...IT **IS**, NOW THAT YOU...
YOU--!
YEAH-- **ME!**
YOU KNEW THE WIZ **AMPED-UP** MY **POWERS**--GUESS YOU **DIDN'T** KNOW IT MEANS I NOW GOT **HYDRO-KINETIC CONTROL** OVER ANY WATER **NEAR** ME!
WATER IN THE **GROUND**, WATER IN THE **AIR**--EVEN THE WATER IN **YOU!**
SUCK YOU **DRY** IN A MINUTE **FLAT!**
WHO'S THE MORON **NOW**, MOR--

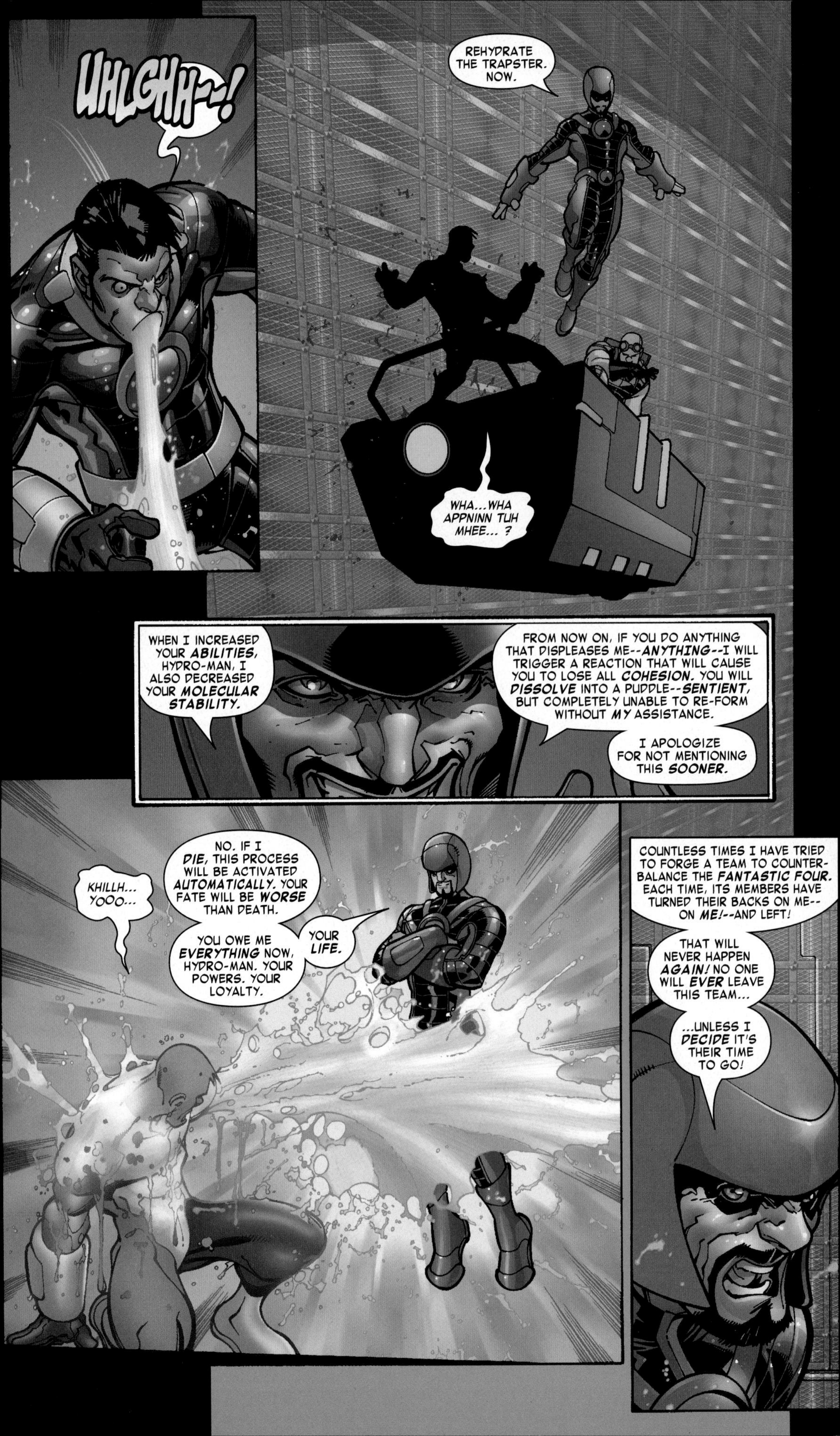
UHLGHH--!
REHYDRATE THE TRAPSTER. NOW.
WHA...WHA APPNINN TUH MHEE... ?
WHEN I INCREASED YOUR ABILITIES, HYDRO-MAN, I ALSO DECREASED YOUR MOLECULAR STABILITY.
FROM NOW ON, IF YOU DO ANYTHING THAT DISPLEASES ME--ANYTHING--I WILL TRIGGER A REACTION THAT WILL CAUSE YOU TO LOSE ALL COHESION. YOU WILL DISSOLVE INTO A PUDDLE--SENTIENT, BUT COMPLETELY UNABLE TO RE-FORM WITHOUT MY ASSISTANCE.
I APOLOGIZE FOR NOT MENTIONING THIS SOONER.
KHILLH... YOOO...
NO. IF I DIE, THIS PROCESS WILL BE ACTIVATED AUTOMATICALLY. YOUR FATE WILL BE WORSE THAN DEATH.
YOU OWE ME EVERYTHING NOW, HYDRO-MAN. YOUR POWERS. YOUR LOYALTY.
YOUR LIFE.
COUNTLESS TIMES I HAVE TRIED TO FORGE A TEAM TO COUNTER-BALANCE THE FANTASTIC FOUR. EACH TIME, ITS MEMBERS HAVE TURNED THEIR BACKS ON ME--ON ME!--AND LEFT!
THAT WILL NEVER HAPPEN AGAIN! NO ONE WILL EVER LEAVE THIS TEAM...
...UNLESS I DECIDE IT'S THEIR TIME TO GO!

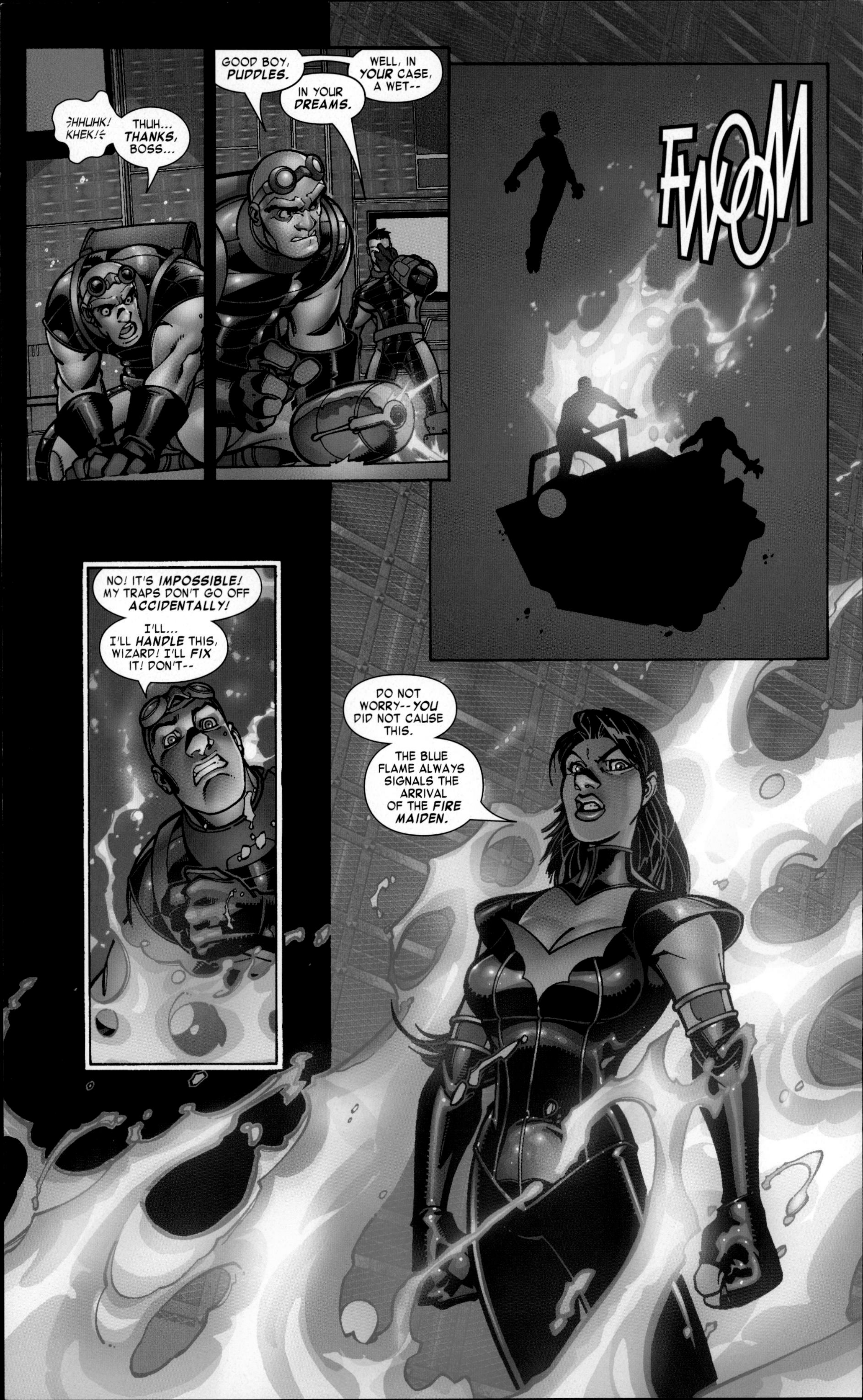

HHUHK! KHEK!
THUH... THANKS, BOSS...
GOOD BOY, PUDDLES.
IN YOUR DREAMS.
WELL, IN YOUR CASE, A WET--
FWOOM
NO! IT'S IMPOSSIBLE! MY TRAPS DON'T GO OFF ACCIDENTALLY!
I'LL... I'LL HANDLE THIS, WIZARD! I'LL FIX IT! DON'T--
DO NOT WORRY--YOU DID NOT CAUSE THIS.
THE BLUE FLAME ALWAYS SIGNALS THE ARRIVAL OF THE FIRE MAIDEN.

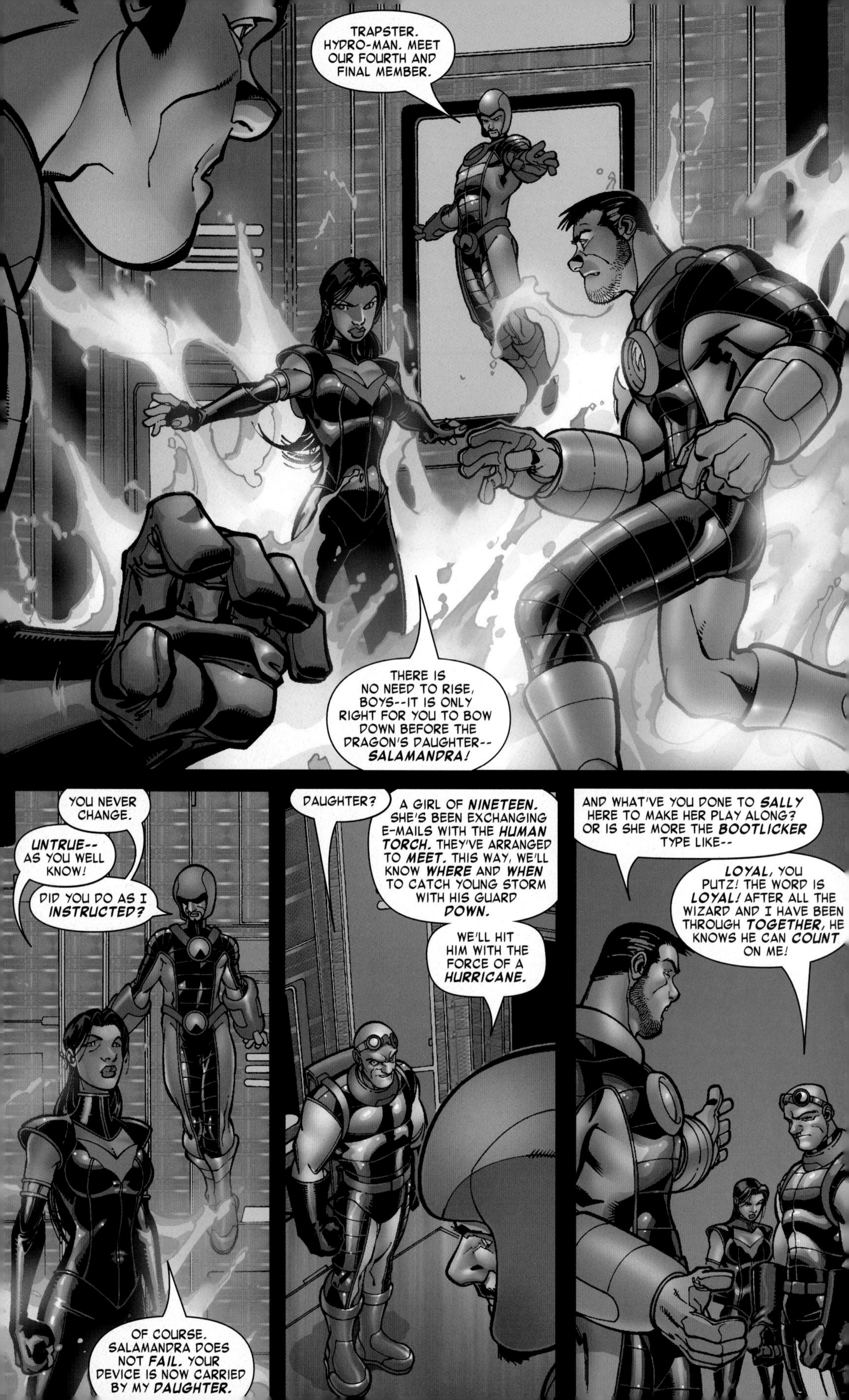
TRAPSTER. HYDRO-MAN. MEET OUR FOURTH AND FINAL MEMBER.
THERE IS NO NEED TO RISE, BOYS--IT IS ONLY RIGHT FOR YOU TO BOW DOWN BEFORE THE DRAGON'S DAUGHTER-- SALAMANDRA!
YOU NEVER CHANGE.
UNTRUE-- AS YOU WELL KNOW!
DID YOU DO AS I INSTRUCTED?
OF COURSE. SALAMANDRA DOES NOT FAIL. YOUR DEVICE IS NOW CARRIED BY MY DAUGHTER.
DAUGHTER?
A GIRL OF NINETEEN. SHE'S BEEN EXCHANGING E-MAILS WITH THE HUMAN TORCH. THEY'VE ARRANGED TO MEET. THIS WAY, WE'LL KNOW WHERE AND WHEN TO CATCH YOUNG STORM WITH HIS GUARD DOWN.
WE'LL HIT HIM WITH THE FORCE OF A HURRICANE.
AND WHAT'VE YOU DONE TO SALLY HERE TO MAKE HER PLAY ALONG? OR IS SHE MORE THE BOOTLICKER TYPE LIKE--
LOYAL, YOU PUTZ! THE WORD IS LOYAL! AFTER ALL THE WIZARD AND I HAVE BEEN THROUGH TOGETHER, HE KNOWS HE CAN COUNT ON ME!

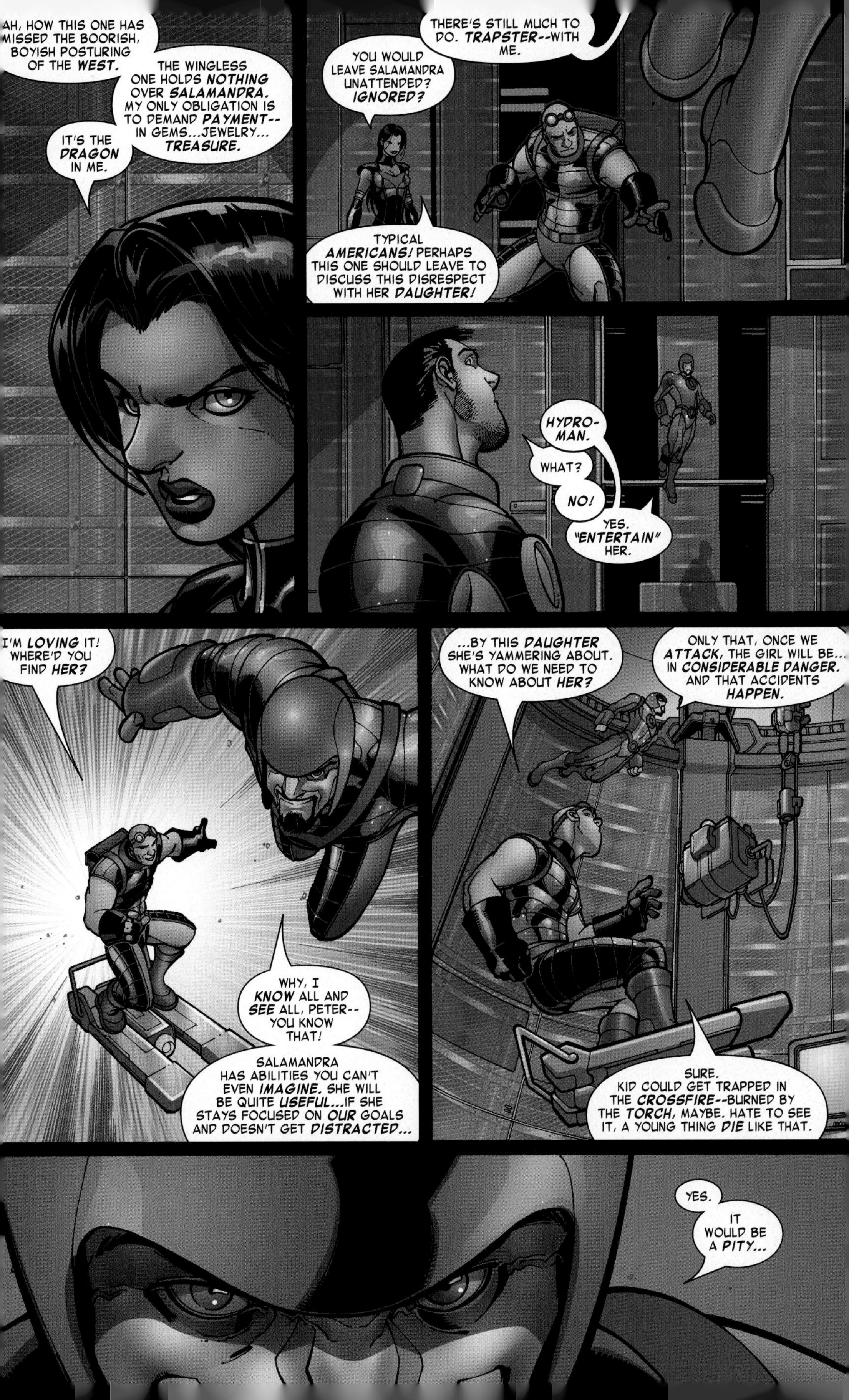
AH, HOW THIS ONE HAS MISSED THE BOORISH, BOYISH POSTURING OF THE WEST.
THE WINGLESS ONE HOLDS NOTHING OVER SALAMANDRA. MY ONLY OBLIGATION IS TO DEMAND PAYMENT--IN GEMS...JEWELRY... TREASURE.
IT'S THE DRAGON IN ME.
THERE'S STILL MUCH TO DO. TRAPSTER--WITH ME.
YOU WOULD LEAVE SALAMANDRA UNATTENDED? IGNORED?
TYPICAL AMERICANS! PERHAPS THIS ONE SHOULD LEAVE TO DISCUSS THIS DISRESPECT WITH HER DAUGHTER!
HYDRO-MAN.
WHAT?
NO!
YES. "ENTERTAIN" HER.
I'M LOVING IT! WHERE'D YOU FIND HER?
WHY, I KNOW ALL AND SEE ALL, PETER--YOU KNOW THAT!
SALAMANDRA HAS ABILITIES YOU CAN'T EVEN IMAGINE. SHE WILL BE QUITE USEFUL...IF SHE STAYS FOCUSED ON OUR GOALS AND DOESN'T GET DISTRACTED...
...BY THIS DAUGHTER SHE'S YAMMERING ABOUT. WHAT DO WE NEED TO KNOW ABOUT HER?
ONLY THAT, ONCE WE ATTACK, THE GIRL WILL BE... IN CONSIDERABLE DANGER. AND THAT ACCIDENTS HAPPEN.
SURE. KID COULD GET TRAPPED IN THE CROSSFIRE--BURNED BY THE TORCH, MAYBE. HATE TO SEE IT, A YOUNG THING DIE LIKE THAT.
YES.
IT WOULD BE A PITY...

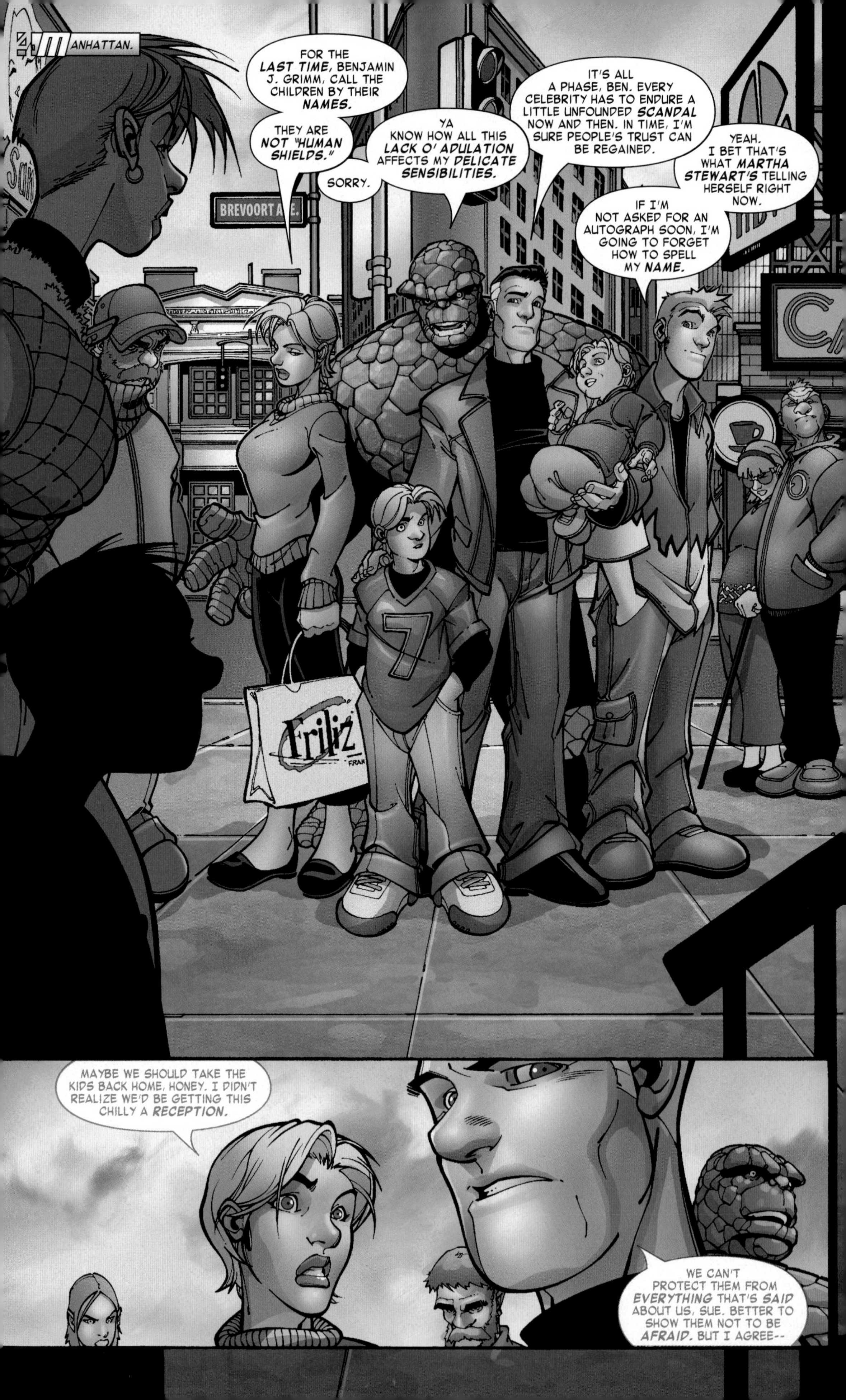
MANHATTAN.
FOR THE LAST TIME, BENJAMIN J. GRIMM, CALL THE CHILDREN BY THEIR NAMES.
THEY ARE NOT "HUMAN SHIELDS."
SORRY.
YA KNOW HOW ALL THIS LACK O' ADULATION AFFECTS MY DELICATE SENSIBILITIES.
IT'S ALL A PHASE, BEN. EVERY CELEBRITY HAS TO ENDURE A LITTLE UNFOUNDED SCANDAL NOW AND THEN. IN TIME, I'M SURE PEOPLE'S TRUST CAN BE REGAINED.
YEAH. I BET THAT'S WHAT MARTHA STEWART'S TELLING HERSELF RIGHT NOW.
IF I'M NOT ASKED FOR AN AUTOGRAPH SOON, I'M GOING TO FORGET HOW TO SPELL MY NAME.
BREVOORT AVE.
Friliz
MAYBE WE SHOULD TAKE THE KIDS BACK HOME, HONEY. I DIDN'T REALIZE WE'D BE GETTING THIS CHILLY A RECEPTION.
WE CAN'T PROTECT THEM FROM EVERYTHING THAT'S SAID ABOUT US, SUE. BETTER TO SHOW THEM NOT TO BE AFRAID. BUT I AGREE--

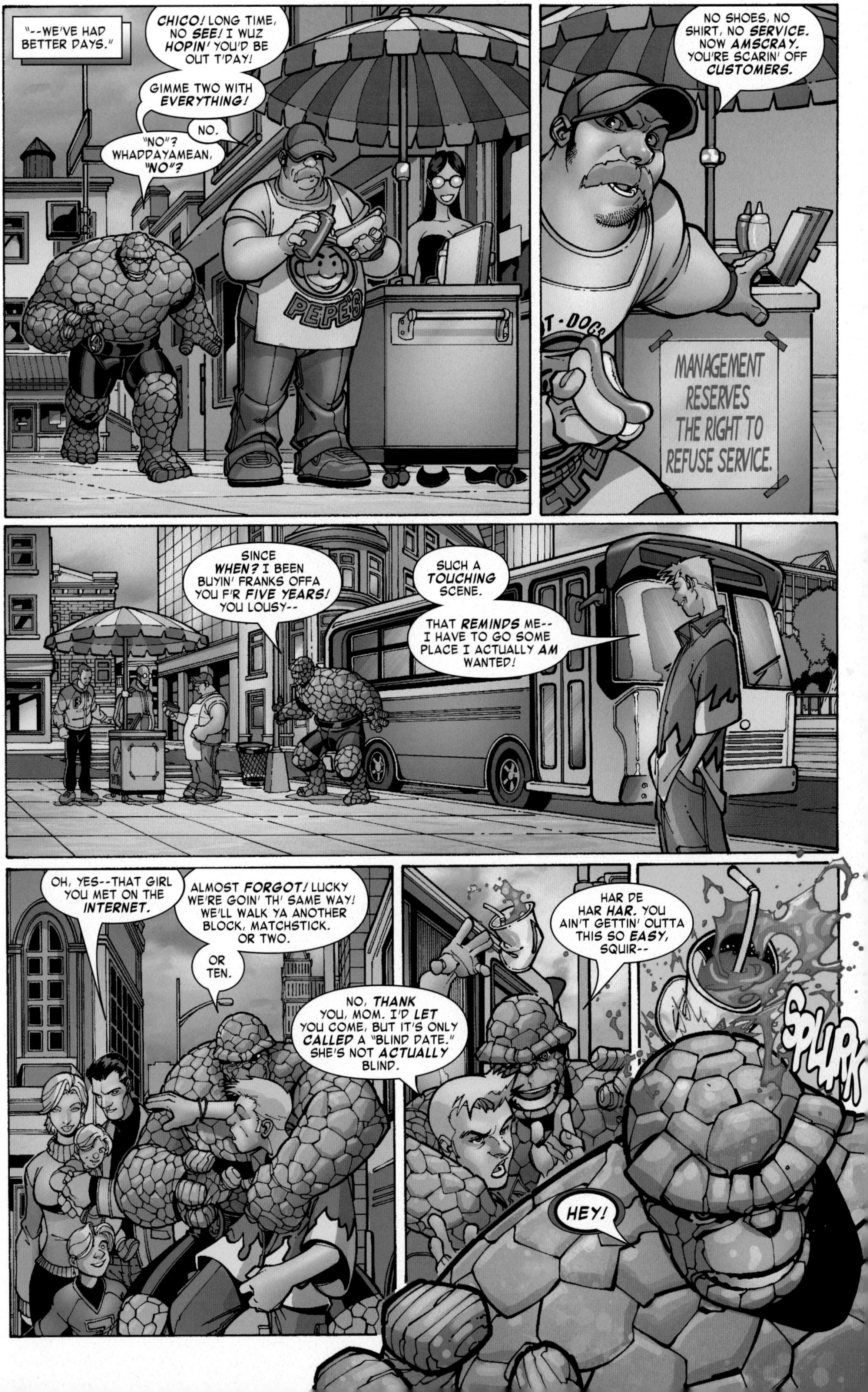
"--WE'VE HAD BETTER DAYS."
CHICO! LONG TIME, NO SEE! I WUZ HOPIN' YOU'D BE OUT T'DAY!
GIMME TWO WITH EVERYTHING!
NO.
"NO"? WHADDAYAMEAN, "NO"?
PEPE'S
NO SHOES, NO SHIRT, NO SERVICE. NOW AMSCRAY. YOU'RE SCARIN' OFF CUSTOMERS.
MANAGEMENT RESERVES THE RIGHT TO REFUSE SERVICE.
SINCE WHEN? I BEEN BUYIN' FRANKS OFFA YOU F'R FIVE YEARS! YOU LOUSY--
SUCH A TOUCHING SCENE.
THAT REMINDS ME-- I HAVE TO GO SOME PLACE I ACTUALLY AM WANTED!
OH, YES--THAT GIRL YOU MET ON THE INTERNET.
ALMOST FORGOT! LUCKY WE'RE GOIN' TH' SAME WAY! WE'LL WALK YA ANOTHER BLOCK, MATCHSTICK. OR TWO.
OR TEN.
NO, THANK YOU, MOM. I'D LET YOU COME, BUT IT'S ONLY CALLED A "BLIND DATE." SHE'S NOT ACTUALLY BLIND.
HAR DE HAR HAR. YOU AIN'T GETTIN' OUTTA THIS SO EASY, SQUIR--
SPLURK
HEY!

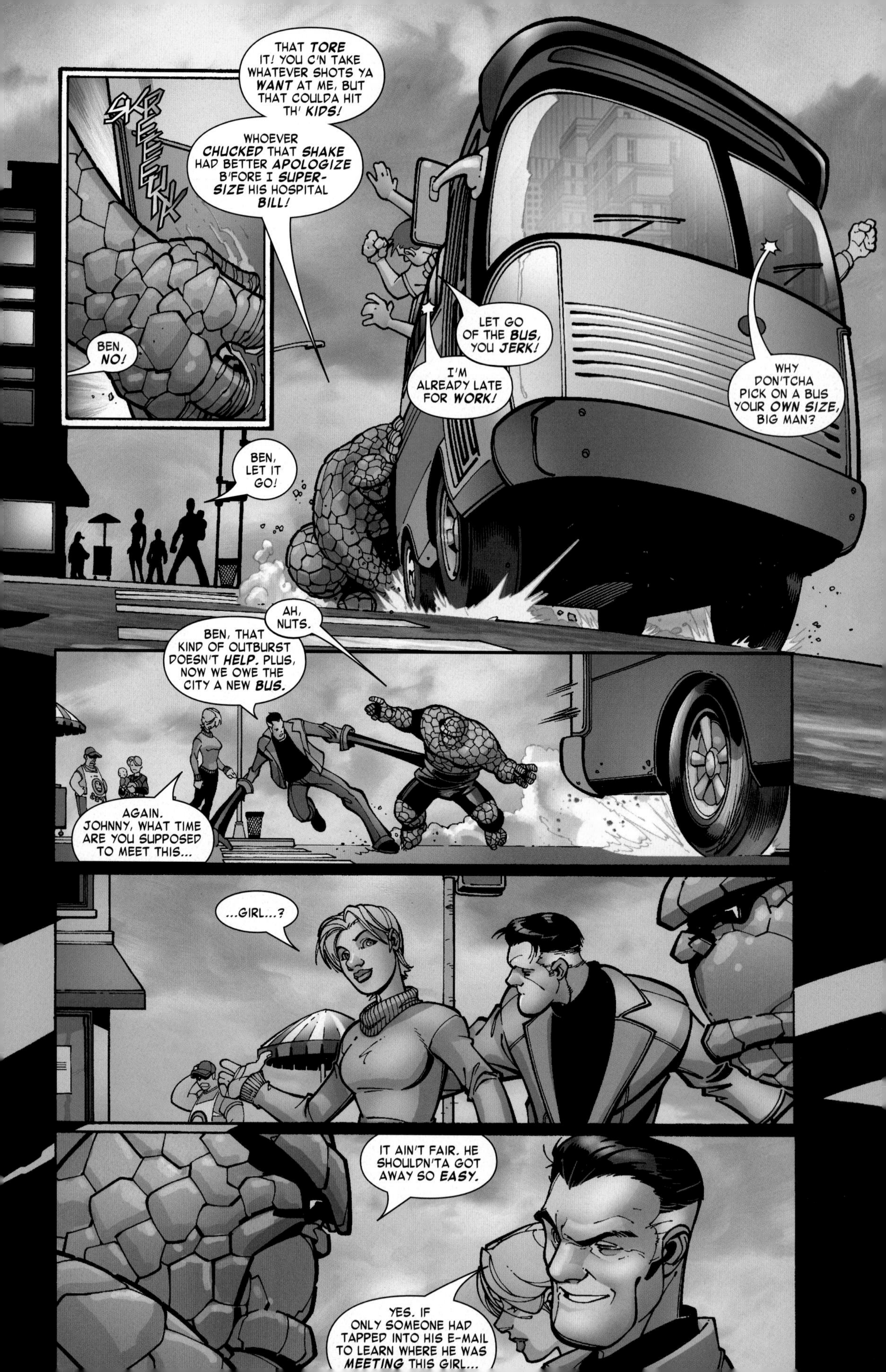
SKREEEENK
THAT TORE IT! YOU C'N TAKE WHATEVER SHOTS YA WANT AT ME, BUT THAT COULDA HIT TH' KIDS!
WHOEVER CHUCKED THAT SHAKE HAD BETTER APOLOGIZE B'FORE I SUPER-SIZE HIS HOSPITAL BILL!
BEN, NO!
LET GO OF THE BUS, YOU JERK!
I'M ALREADY LATE FOR WORK!
WHY DON'TCHA PICK ON A BUS YOUR OWN SIZE, BIG MAN?
BEN, LET IT GO!
AH, NUTS.
BEN, THAT KIND OF OUTBURST DOESN'T HELP. PLUS, NOW WE OWE THE CITY A NEW BUS.
AGAIN. JOHNNY, WHAT TIME ARE YOU SUPPOSED TO MEET THIS...
...GIRL...?
IT AIN'T FAIR. HE SHOULDN'TA GOT AWAY SO EASY.
YES. IF ONLY SOMEONE HAD TAPPED INTO HIS E-MAIL TO LEARN WHERE HE WAS MEETING THIS GIRL...

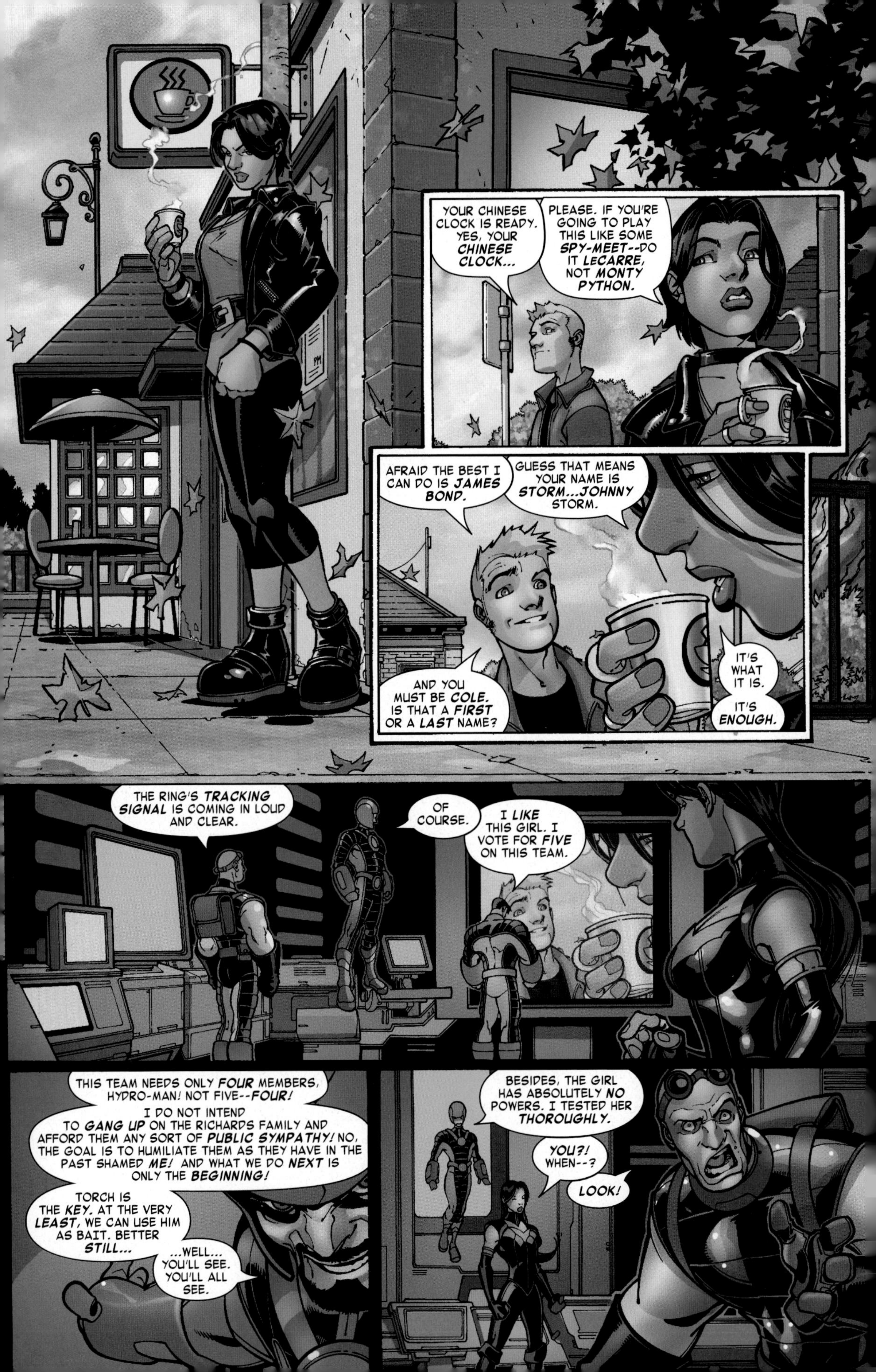
YOUR CHINESE CLOCK IS READY. YES, YOUR CHINESE CLOCK...
PLEASE. IF YOU'RE GOING TO PLAY THIS LIKE SOME SPY-MEET--DO IT LeCARRE, NOT MONTY PYTHON.
AFRAID THE BEST I CAN DO IS JAMES BOND.
GUESS THAT MEANS YOUR NAME IS STORM...JOHNNY STORM.
AND YOU MUST BE COLE. IS THAT A FIRST OR A LAST NAME?
IT'S WHAT IT IS.
IT'S ENOUGH.
THE RING'S TRACKING SIGNAL IS COMING IN LOUD AND CLEAR.
OF COURSE.
I LIKE THIS GIRL. I VOTE FOR FIVE ON THIS TEAM.
THIS TEAM NEEDS ONLY FOUR MEMBERS, HYDRO-MAN! NOT FIVE--FOUR!
I DO NOT INTEND TO GANG UP ON THE RICHARDS FAMILY AND AFFORD THEM ANY SORT OF PUBLIC SYMPATHY! NO, THE GOAL IS TO HUMILIATE THEM AS THEY HAVE IN THE PAST SHAMED ME! AND WHAT WE DO NEXT IS ONLY THE BEGINNING!
TORCH IS THE KEY. AT THE VERY LEAST, WE CAN USE HIM AS BAIT. BETTER STILL...
...WELL... YOU'LL SEE. YOU'LL ALL SEE.
BESIDES, THE GIRL HAS ABSOLUTELY NO POWERS. I TESTED HER THOROUGHLY.
YOU?! WHEN--?
LOOK!

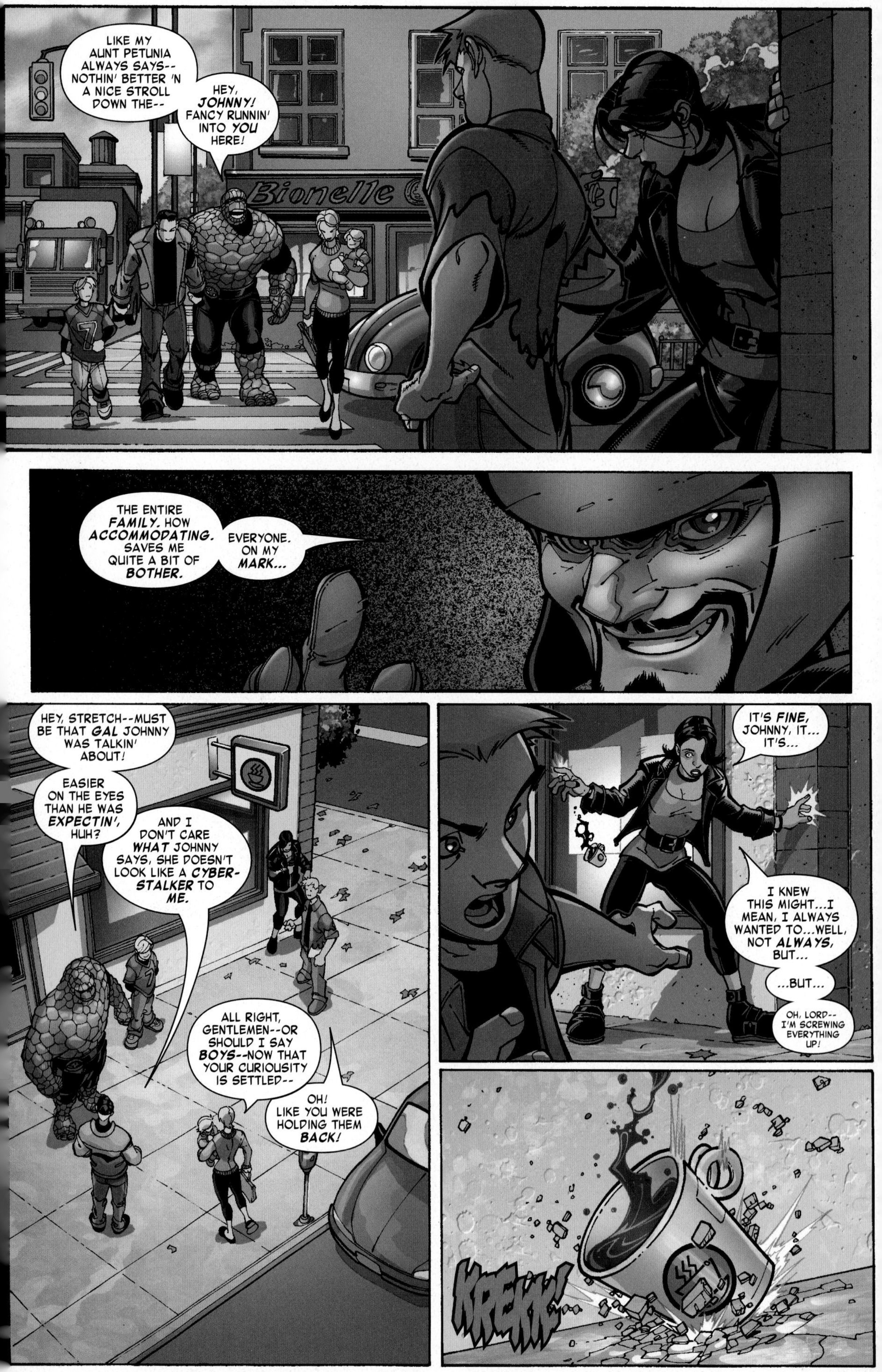
LIKE MY AUNT PETUNIA ALWAYS SAYS--NOTHIN' BETTER 'N A NICE STROLL DOWN THE--
HEY, JOHNNY! FANCY RUNNIN' INTO YOU HERE!
Bionelle
THE ENTIRE FAMILY. HOW ACCOMMODATING. SAVES ME QUITE A BIT OF BOTHER.
EVERYONE. ON MY MARK...
HEY, STRETCH--MUST BE THAT GAL JOHNNY WAS TALKIN' ABOUT!
EASIER ON THE EYES THAN HE WAS EXPECTIN', HUH?
AND I DON'T CARE WHAT JOHNNY SAYS, SHE DOESN'T LOOK LIKE A CYBER-STALKER TO ME.
ALL RIGHT, GENTLEMEN--OR SHOULD I SAY BOYS--NOW THAT YOUR CURIOUSITY IS SETTLED--
OH! LIKE YOU WERE HOLDING THEM BACK!
IT'S FINE, JOHNNY, IT... IT'S...
I KNEW THIS MIGHT...I MEAN, I ALWAYS WANTED TO...WELL, NOT ALWAYS, BUT...
...BUT...
OH, LORD--I'M SCREWING EVERYTHING UP!
KREKK!

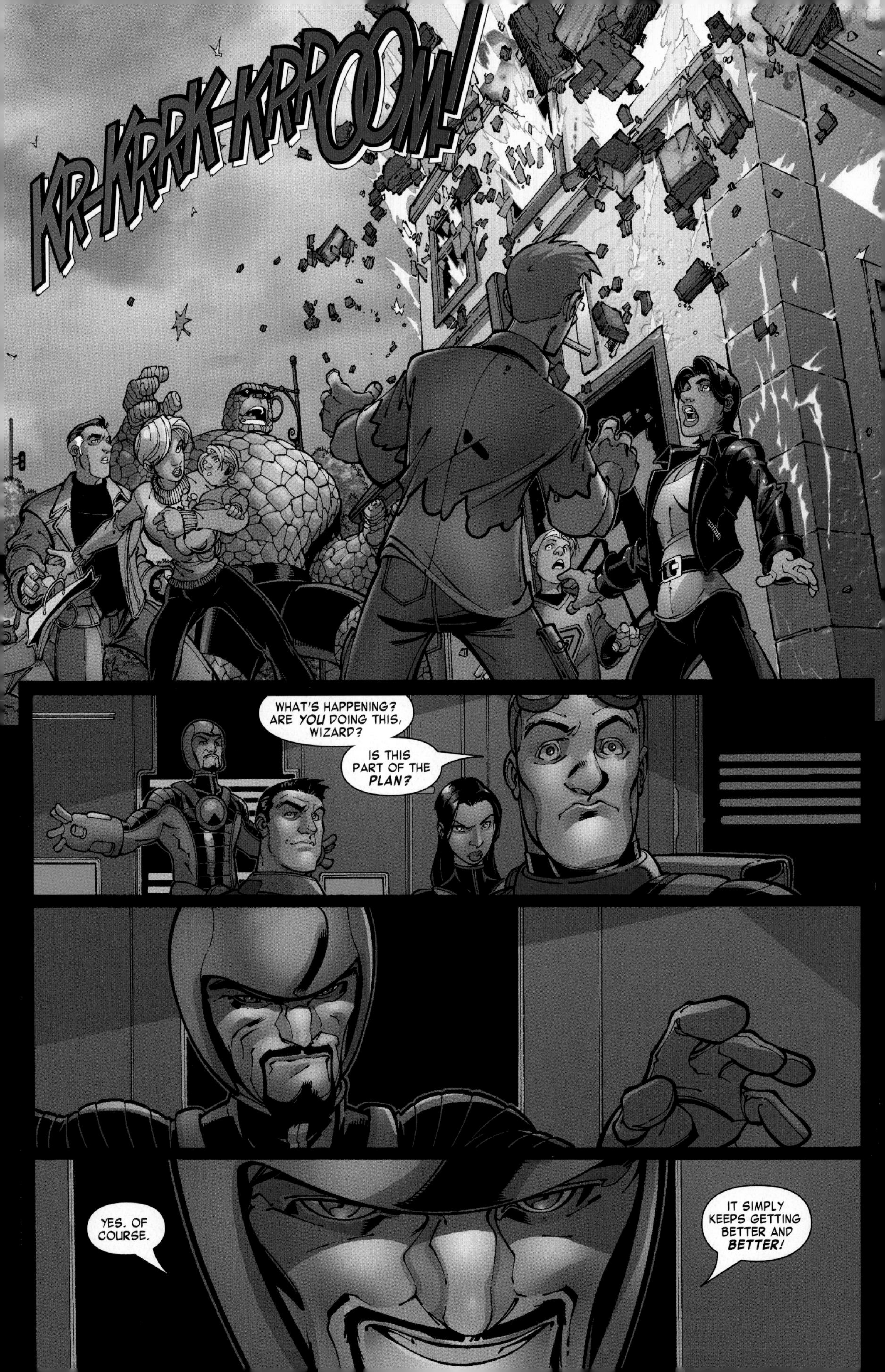
KR-KRRK-KRROOM!
WHAT'S HAPPENING? ARE YOU DOING THIS, WIZARD?
IS THIS PART OF THE PLAN?
YES. OF COURSE.
IT SIMPLY KEEPS GETTING BETTER AND BETTER!

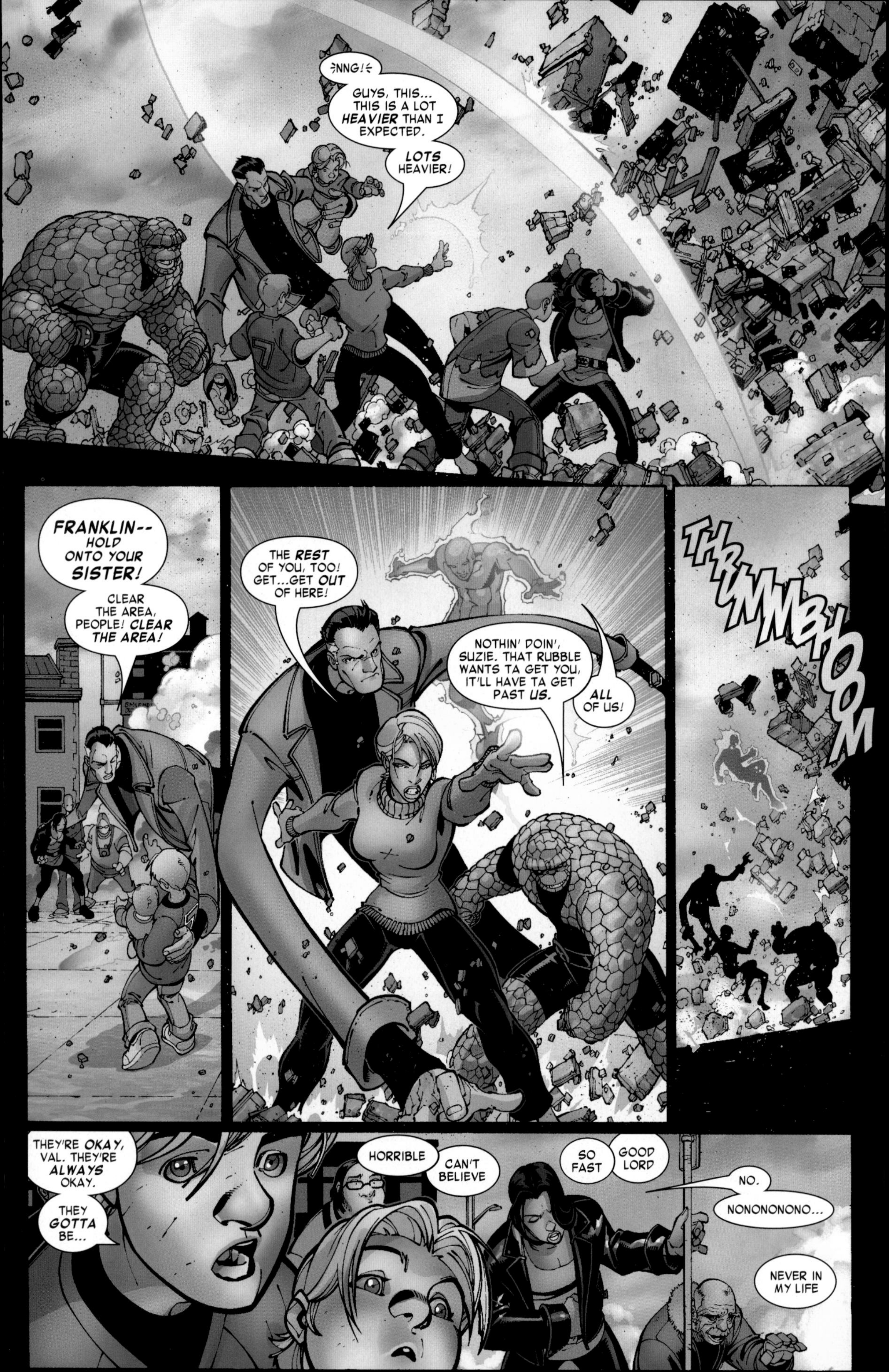

NNG!
GUYS, THIS... THIS IS A LOT HEAVIER THAN I EXPECTED.
LOTS HEAVIER!
FRANKLIN-- HOLD ONTO YOUR SISTER!
CLEAR THE AREA, PEOPLE! CLEAR THE AREA!
THE REST OF YOU, TOO! GET...GET OUT OF HERE!
NOTHIN' DOIN', SUZIE. THAT RUBBLE WANTS TA GET YOU, IT'LL HAVE TA GET PAST US.
ALL OF US!
THRUMMBHOOM
THEY'RE OKAY, VAL. THEY'RE ALWAYS OKAY.
THEY GOTTA BE...
HORRIBLE
CAN'T BELIEVE
SO FAST
GOOD LORD
NO.
NONONONONO...
NEVER IN MY LIFE

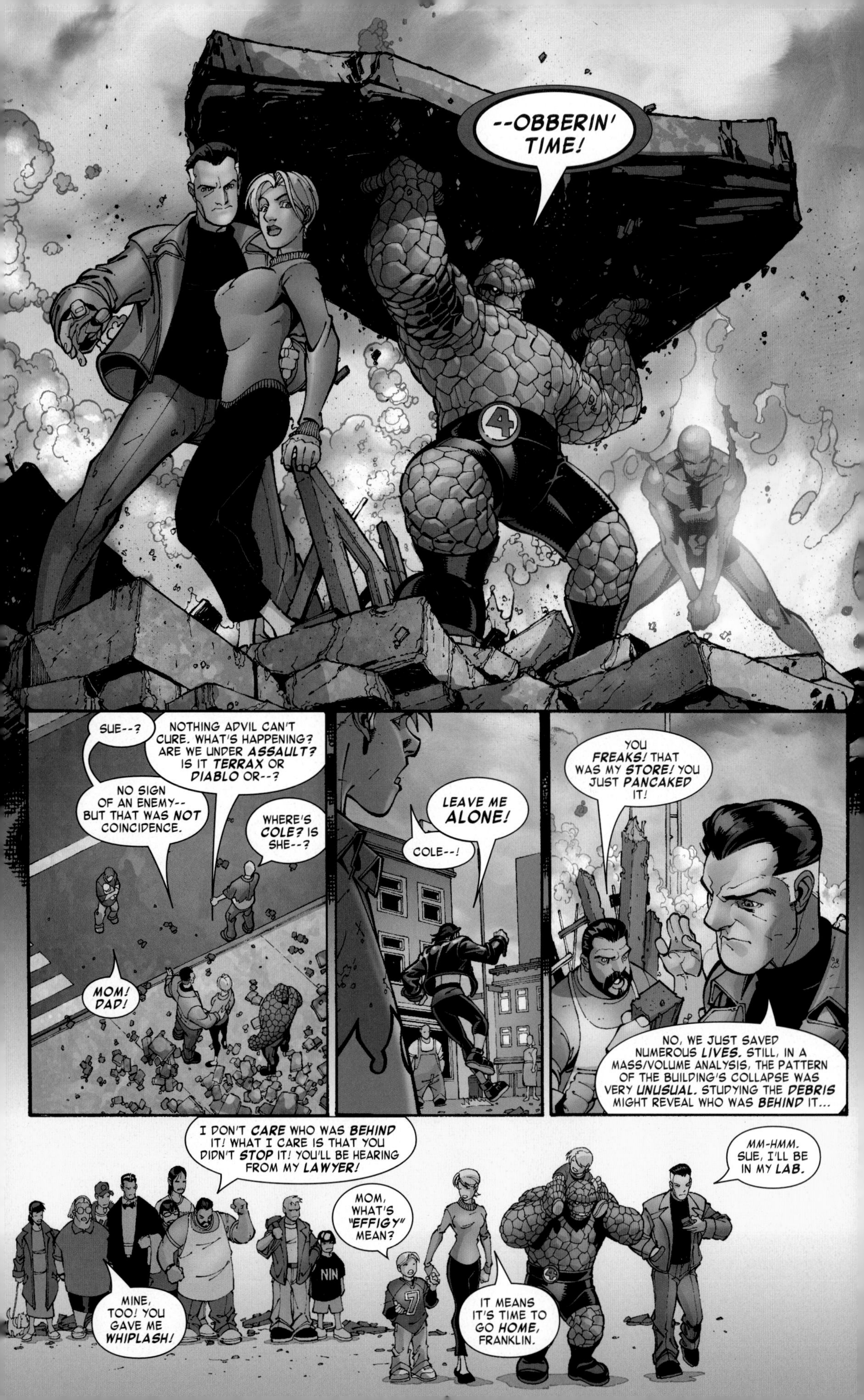
--OBBERIN' TIME!
SUE--?
NOTHING ADVIL CAN'T CURE. WHAT'S HAPPENING? ARE WE UNDER ASSAULT? IS IT TERRAX OR DIABLO OR--?
NO SIGN OF AN ENEMY-- BUT THAT WAS NOT COINCIDENCE.
WHERE'S COLE? IS SHE--?
MOM! DAD!
LEAVE ME ALONE!
COLE--!
YOU FREAKS! THAT WAS MY STORE! YOU JUST PANCAKED IT!
NO, WE JUST SAVED NUMEROUS LIVES. STILL, IN A MASS/VOLUME ANALYSIS, THE PATTERN OF THE BUILDING'S COLLAPSE WAS VERY UNUSUAL. STUDYING THE DEBRIS MIGHT REVEAL WHO WAS BEHIND IT...
I DON'T CARE WHO WAS BEHIND IT! WHAT I CARE IS THAT YOU DIDN'T STOP IT! YOU'LL BE HEARING FROM MY LAWYER!
MINE, TOO! YOU GAVE ME WHIPLASH!
MOM, WHAT'S "EFFIGY" MEAN?
IT MEANS IT'S TIME TO GO HOME, FRANKLIN.
MM-HMM. SUE, I'LL BE IN MY LAB.

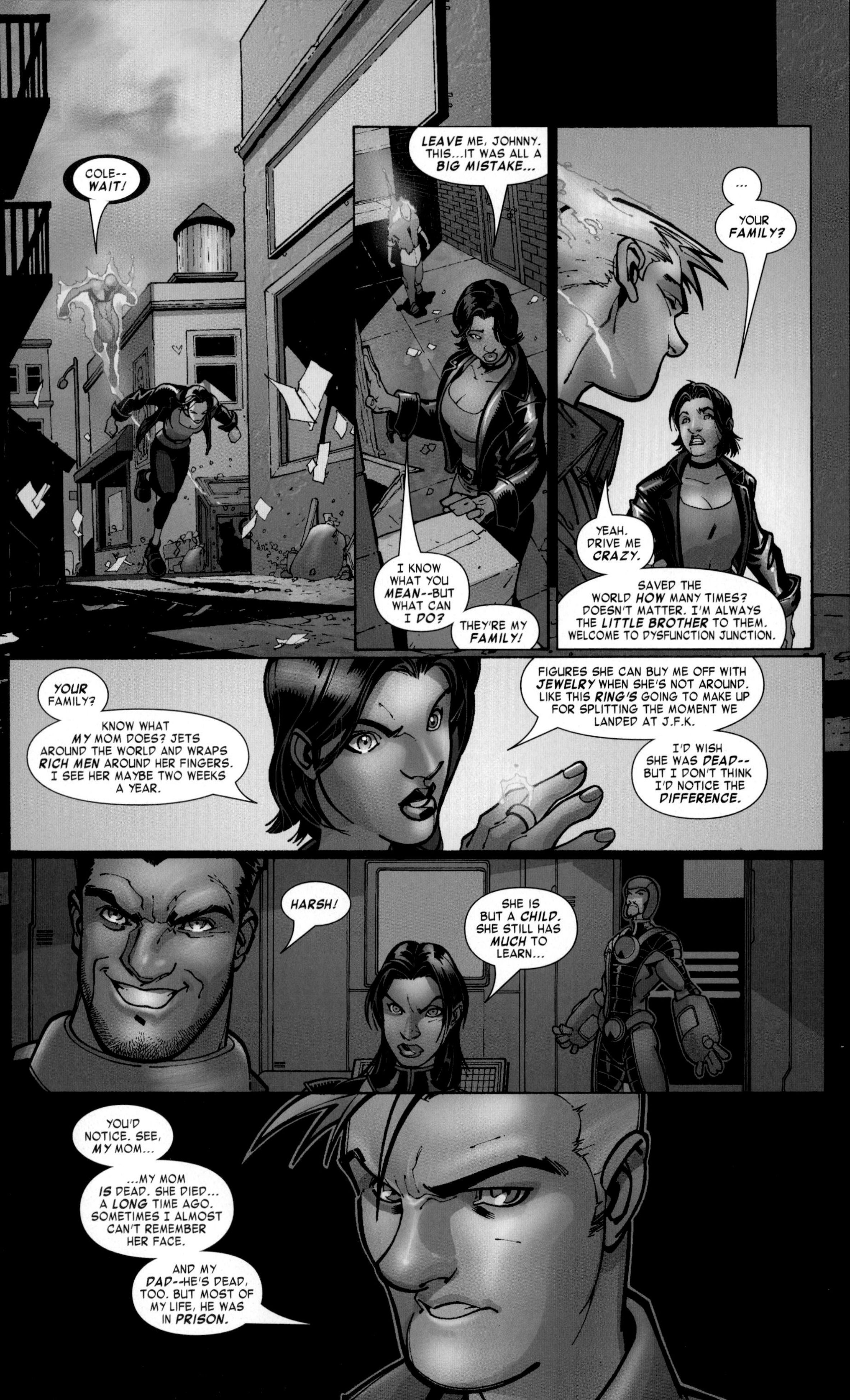

COLE-- WAIT!
LEAVE ME, JOHNNY. THIS...IT WAS ALL A BIG MISTAKE...
I KNOW WHAT YOU MEAN--BUT WHAT CAN I DO?
THEY'RE MY FAMILY!
...
YOUR FAMILY?
YEAH. DRIVE ME CRAZY.
SAVED THE WORLD HOW MANY TIMES? DOESN'T MATTER. I'M ALWAYS THE LITTLE BROTHER TO THEM. WELCOME TO DYSFUNCTION JUNCTION.
YOUR FAMILY?
KNOW WHAT MY MOM DOES? JETS AROUND THE WORLD AND WRAPS RICH MEN AROUND HER FINGERS. I SEE HER MAYBE TWO WEEKS A YEAR.
FIGURES SHE CAN BUY ME OFF WITH JEWELRY WHEN SHE'S NOT AROUND. LIKE THIS RING'S GOING TO MAKE UP FOR SPLITTING THE MOMENT WE LANDED AT J.F.K.
I'D WISH SHE WAS DEAD-- BUT I DON'T THINK I'D NOTICE THE DIFFERENCE.
HARSH!
SHE IS BUT A CHILD. SHE STILL HAS MUCH TO LEARN...
YOU'D NOTICE. SEE, MY MOM...
...MY MOM IS DEAD. SHE DIED... A LONG TIME AGO. SOMETIMES I ALMOST CAN'T REMEMBER HER FACE.
AND MY DAD--HE'S DEAD, TOO. BUT MOST OF MY LIFE, HE WAS IN PRISON.

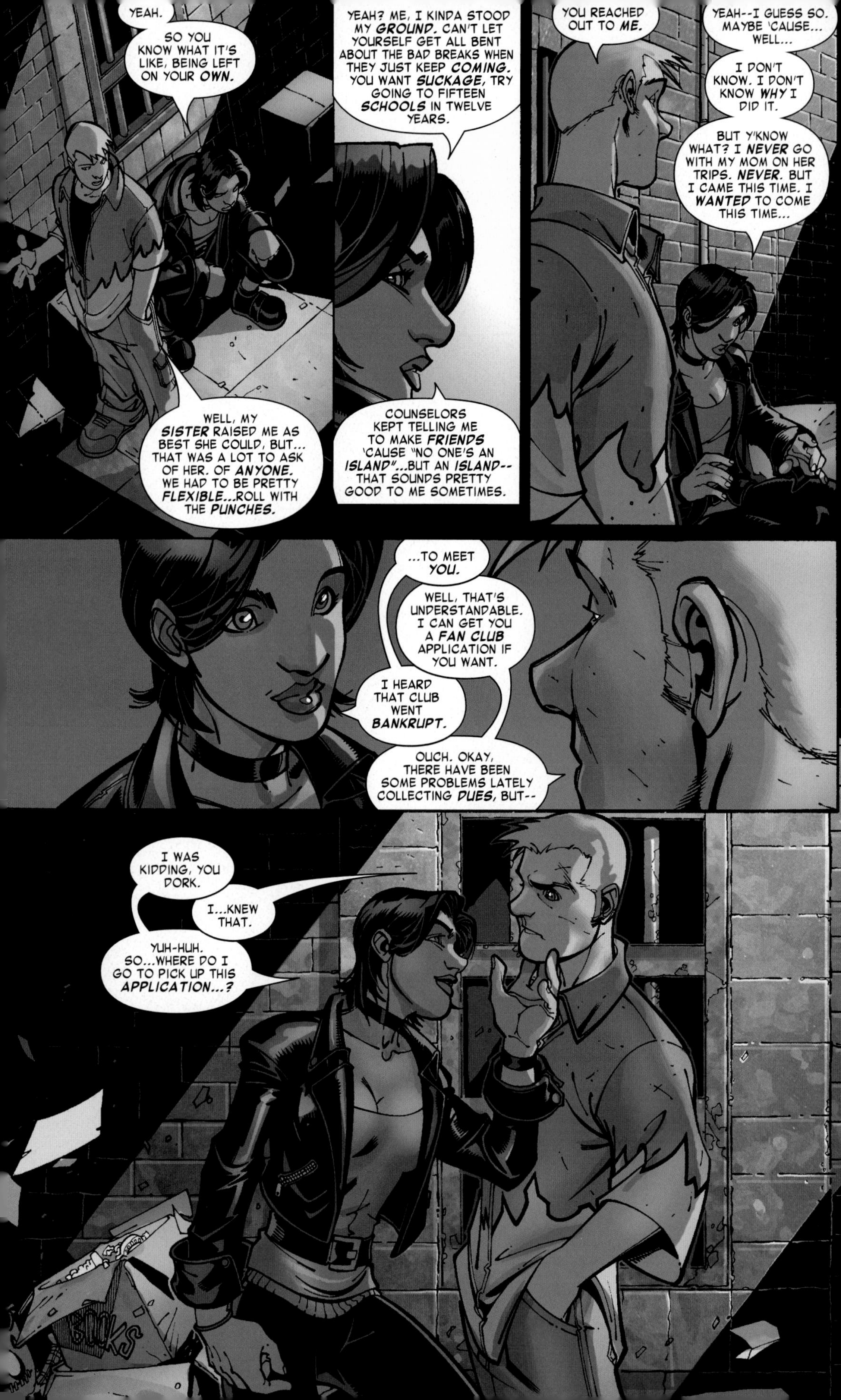
YEAH.
SO YOU KNOW WHAT IT'S LIKE, BEING LEFT ON YOUR OWN.
WELL, MY SISTER RAISED ME AS BEST SHE COULD, BUT... THAT WAS A LOT TO ASK OF HER. OF ANYONE. WE HAD TO BE PRETTY FLEXIBLE...ROLL WITH THE PUNCHES.
YEAH? ME, I KINDA STOOD MY GROUND. CAN'T LET YOURSELF GET ALL BENT ABOUT THE BAD BREAKS WHEN THEY JUST KEEP COMING. YOU WANT SUCKAGE, TRY GOING TO FIFTEEN SCHOOLS IN TWELVE YEARS.
COUNSELORS KEPT TELLING ME TO MAKE FRIENDS 'CAUSE "NO ONE'S AN ISLAND"...BUT AN ISLAND--THAT SOUNDS PRETTY GOOD TO ME SOMETIMES.
YOU REACHED OUT TO ME.
YEAH--I GUESS SO. MAYBE 'CAUSE... WELL...
I DON'T KNOW. I DON'T KNOW WHY I DID IT.
BUT Y'KNOW WHAT? I NEVER GO WITH MY MOM ON HER TRIPS. NEVER. BUT I CAME THIS TIME. I WANTED TO COME THIS TIME...
...TO MEET YOU.
WELL, THAT'S UNDERSTANDABLE. I CAN GET YOU A FAN CLUB APPLICATION IF YOU WANT.
I HEARD THAT CLUB WENT BANKRUPT.
OUCH. OKAY, THERE HAVE BEEN SOME PROBLEMS LATELY COLLECTING DUES, BUT--
I WAS KIDDING, YOU DORK.
I...KNEW THAT.
YUH-HUH. SO...WHERE DO I GO TO PICK UP THIS APPLICATION...?

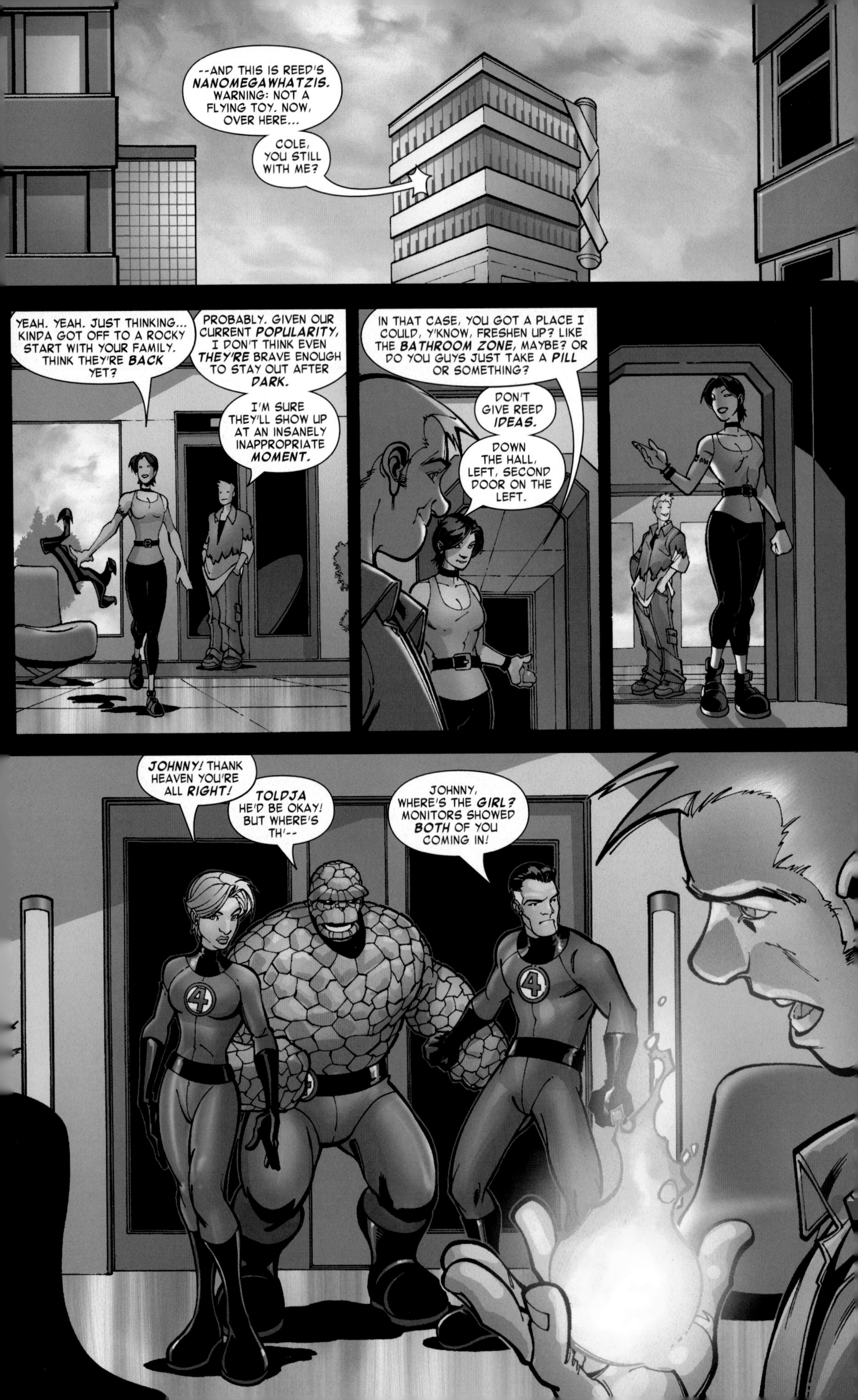

--AND THIS IS REED'S NANOMEGAWHATZIS. WARNING: NOT A FLYING TOY. NOW, OVER HERE...
COLE, YOU STILL WITH ME?
YEAH. YEAH. JUST THINKING... KINDA GOT OFF TO A ROCKY START WITH YOUR FAMILY. THINK THEY'RE BACK YET?
PROBABLY. GIVEN OUR CURRENT POPULARITY, I DON'T THINK EVEN THEY'RE BRAVE ENOUGH TO STAY OUT AFTER DARK.
I'M SURE THEY'LL SHOW UP AT AN INSANELY INAPPROPRIATE MOMENT.
IN THAT CASE, YOU GOT A PLACE I COULD, Y'KNOW, FRESHEN UP? LIKE THE BATHROOM ZONE, MAYBE? OR DO YOU GUYS JUST TAKE A PILL OR SOMETHING?
DON'T GIVE REED IDEAS.
DOWN THE HALL, LEFT, SECOND DOOR ON THE LEFT.
JOHNNY! THANK HEAVEN YOU'RE ALL RIGHT!
TOLDJA HE'D BE OKAY! BUT WHERE'S TH'--
JOHNNY, WHERE'S THE GIRL? MONITORS SHOWED BOTH OF YOU COMING IN!

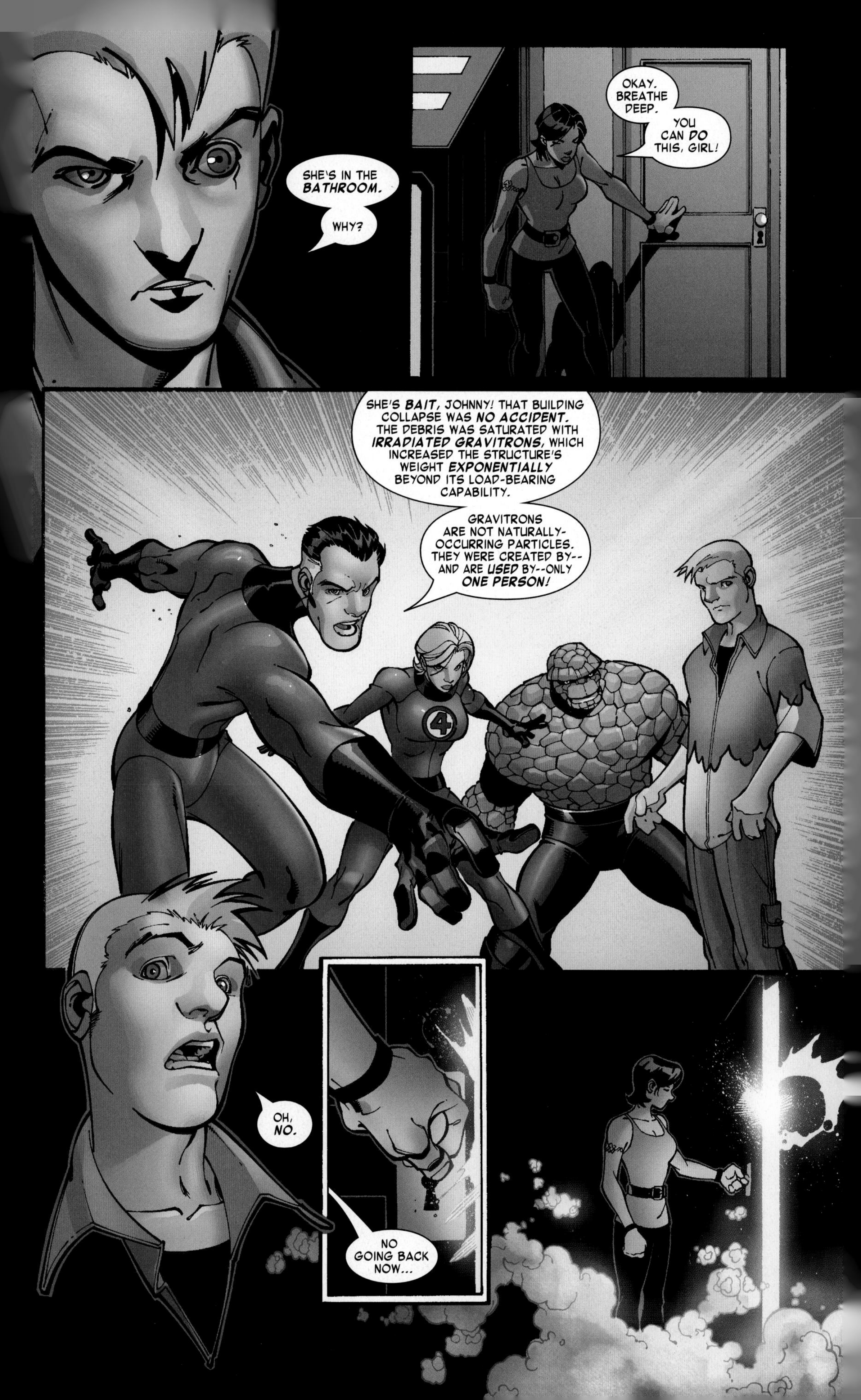
SHE'S IN THE BATHROOM.
WHY?
OKAY. BREATHE DEEP.
YOU CAN DO THIS, GIRL!
SHE'S BAIT, JOHNNY! THAT BUILDING COLLAPSE WAS NO ACCIDENT. THE DEBRIS WAS SATURATED WITH IRRADIATED GRAVITRONS, WHICH INCREASED THE STRUCTURE'S WEIGHT EXPONENTIALLY BEYOND ITS LOAD-BEARING CAPABILITY.
GRAVITRONS ARE NOT NATURALLY-OCCURRING PARTICLES. THEY WERE CREATED BY--AND ARE USED BY--ONLY ONE PERSON!
OH, NO.
NO GOING BACK NOW...

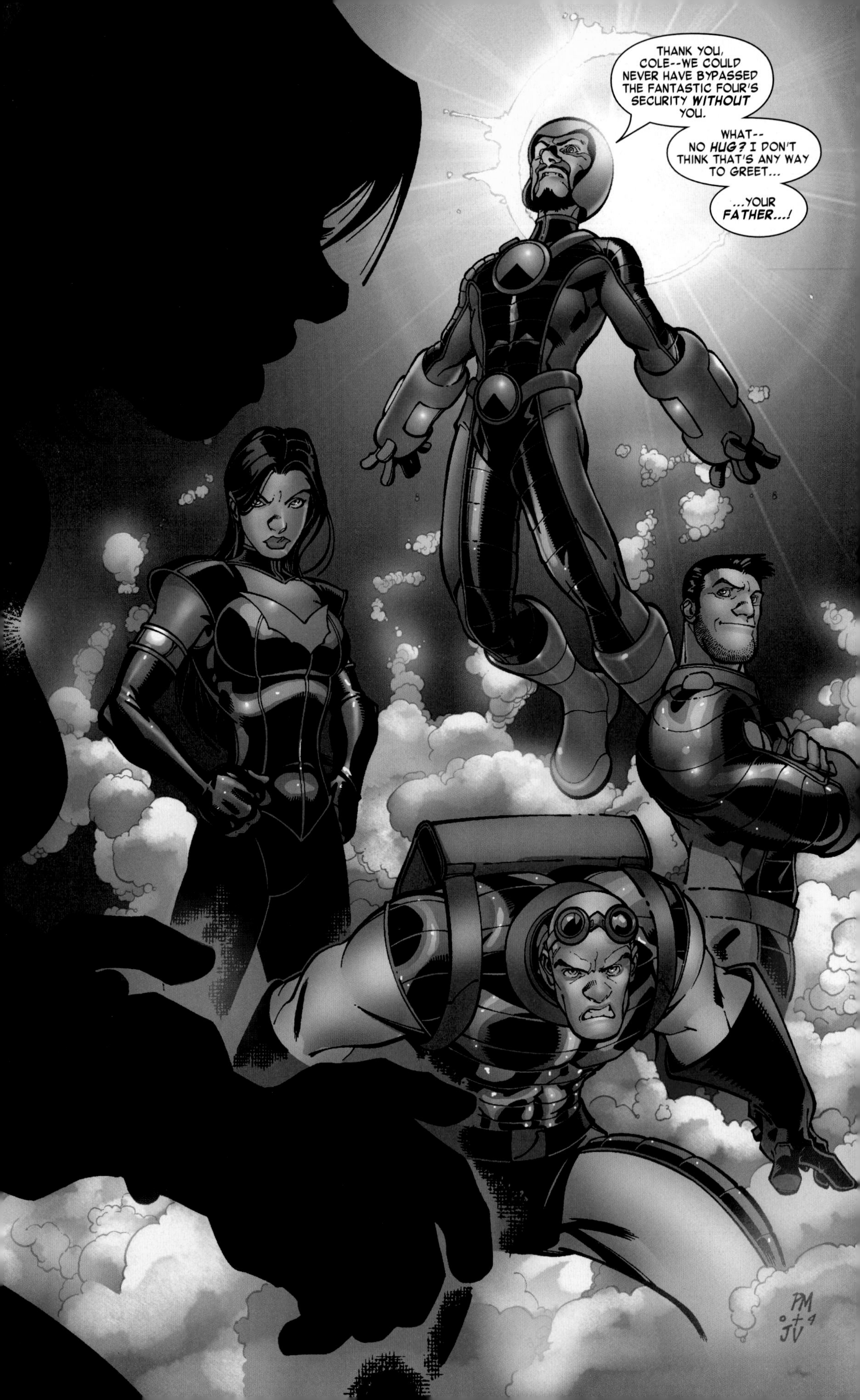
THANK YOU, COLE--WE COULD NEVER HAVE BYPASSED THE FANTASTIC FOUR'S SECURITY *WITHOUT* YOU.
WHAT-- NO *HUG?* I DON'T THINK THAT'S ANY WAY TO GREET...
...YOUR *FATHER...!*
PM + JV

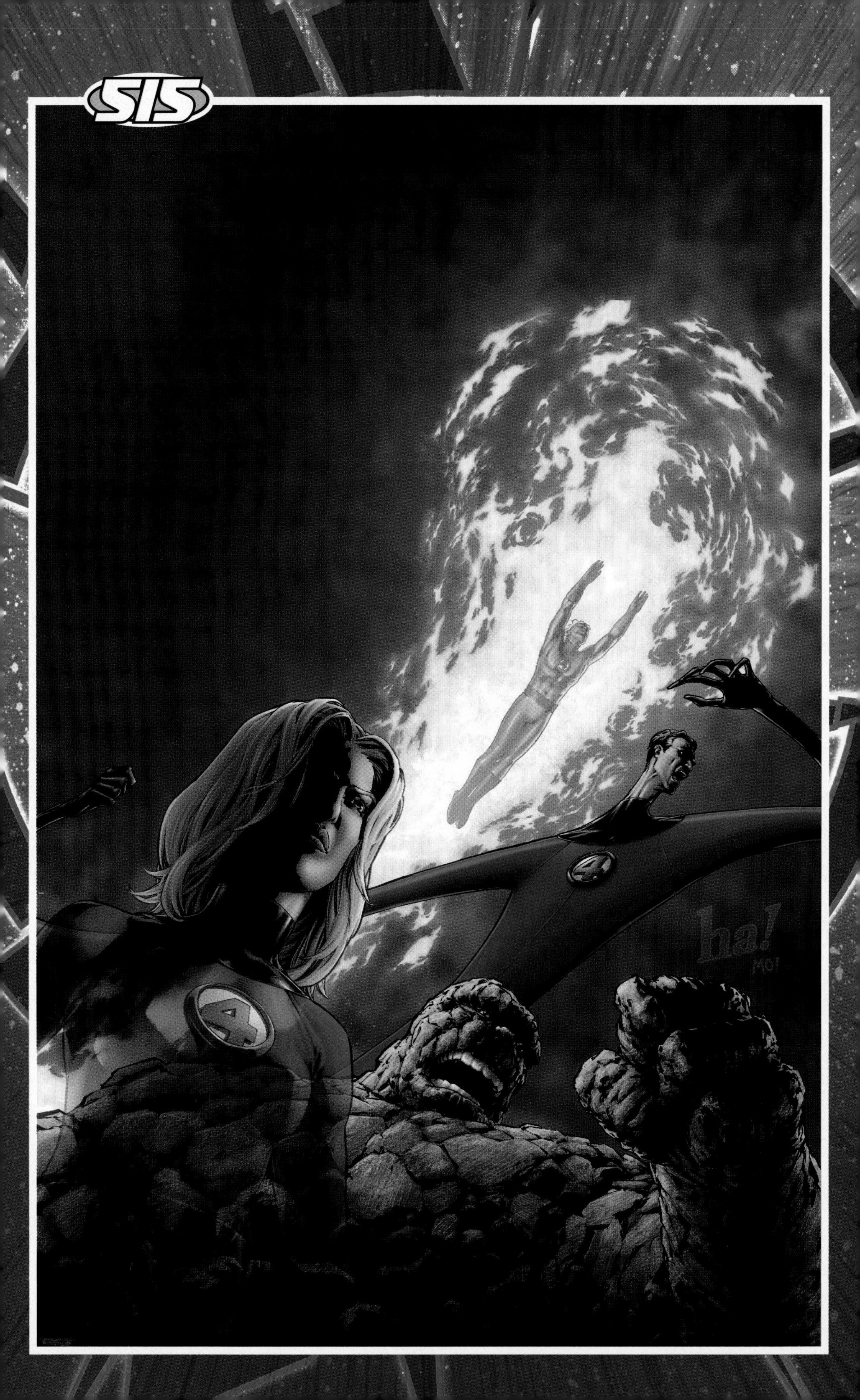
515
ha!
MO!

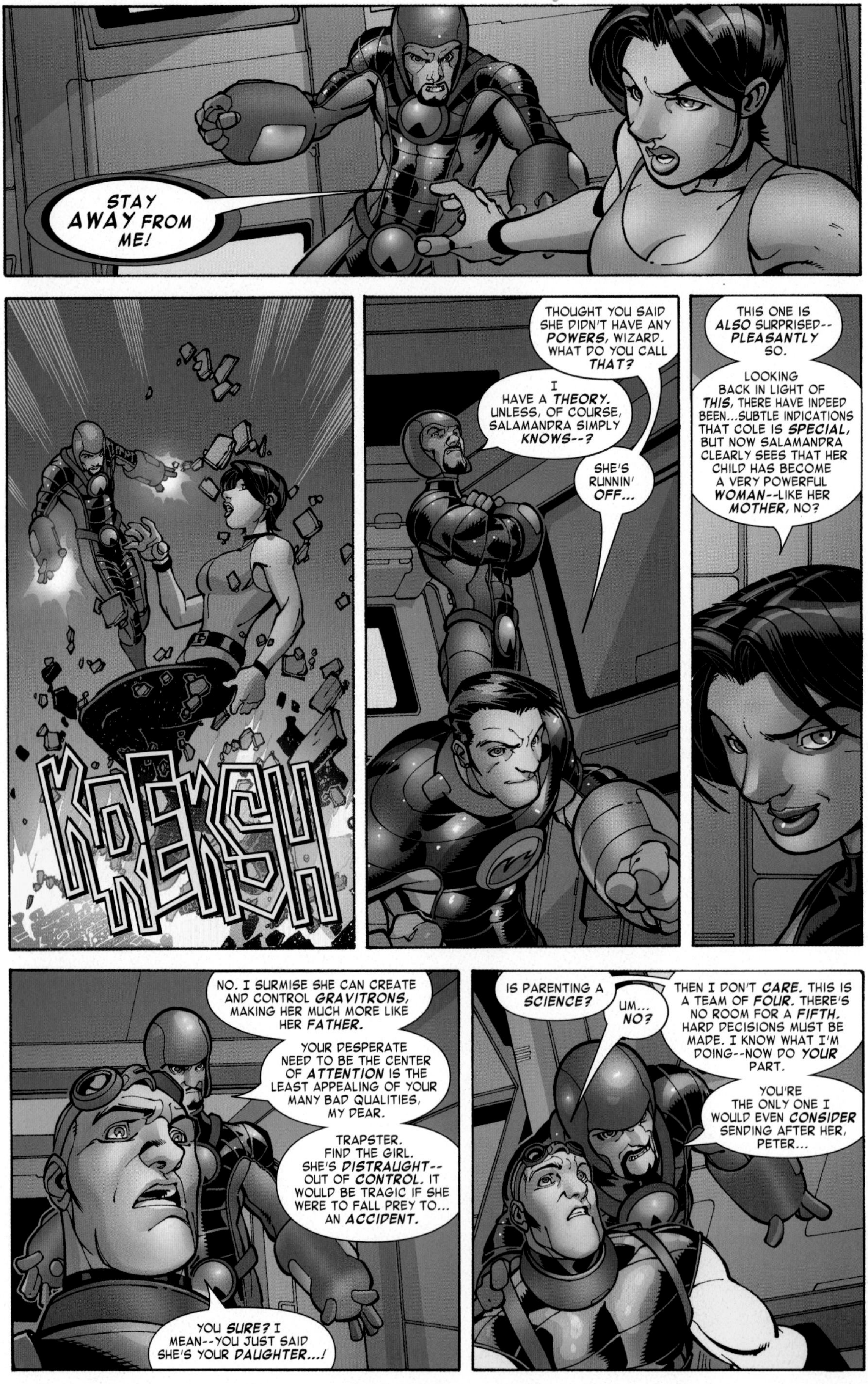
STAY AWAY FROM ME!
KRRESH
THOUGHT YOU SAID SHE DIDN'T HAVE ANY POWERS, WIZARD. WHAT DO YOU CALL THAT?
I HAVE A THEORY. UNLESS, OF COURSE, SALAMANDRA SIMPLY KNOWS--?
SHE'S RUNNIN' OFF...
THIS ONE IS ALSO SURPRISED-- PLEASANTLY SO.
LOOKING BACK IN LIGHT OF THIS, THERE HAVE INDEED BEEN...SUBTLE INDICATIONS THAT COLE IS SPECIAL, BUT NOW SALAMANDRA CLEARLY SEES THAT HER CHILD HAS BECOME A VERY POWERFUL WOMAN--LIKE HER MOTHER, NO?
NO. I SURMISE SHE CAN CREATE AND CONTROL GRAVITRONS, MAKING HER MUCH MORE LIKE HER FATHER.
YOUR DESPERATE NEED TO BE THE CENTER OF ATTENTION IS THE LEAST APPEALING OF YOUR MANY BAD QUALITIES, MY DEAR.
TRAPSTER. FIND THE GIRL. SHE'S DISTRAUGHT-- OUT OF CONTROL. IT WOULD BE TRAGIC IF SHE WERE TO FALL PREY TO... AN ACCIDENT.
YOU SURE? I MEAN--YOU JUST SAID SHE'S YOUR DAUGHTER...!
IS PARENTING A SCIENCE?
UM... NO?
THEN I DON'T CARE. THIS IS A TEAM OF FOUR. THERE'S NO ROOM FOR A FIFTH. HARD DECISIONS MUST BE MADE. I KNOW WHAT I'M DOING--NOW DO YOUR PART.
YOU'RE THE ONLY ONE I WOULD EVEN CONSIDER SENDING AFTER HER, PETER...

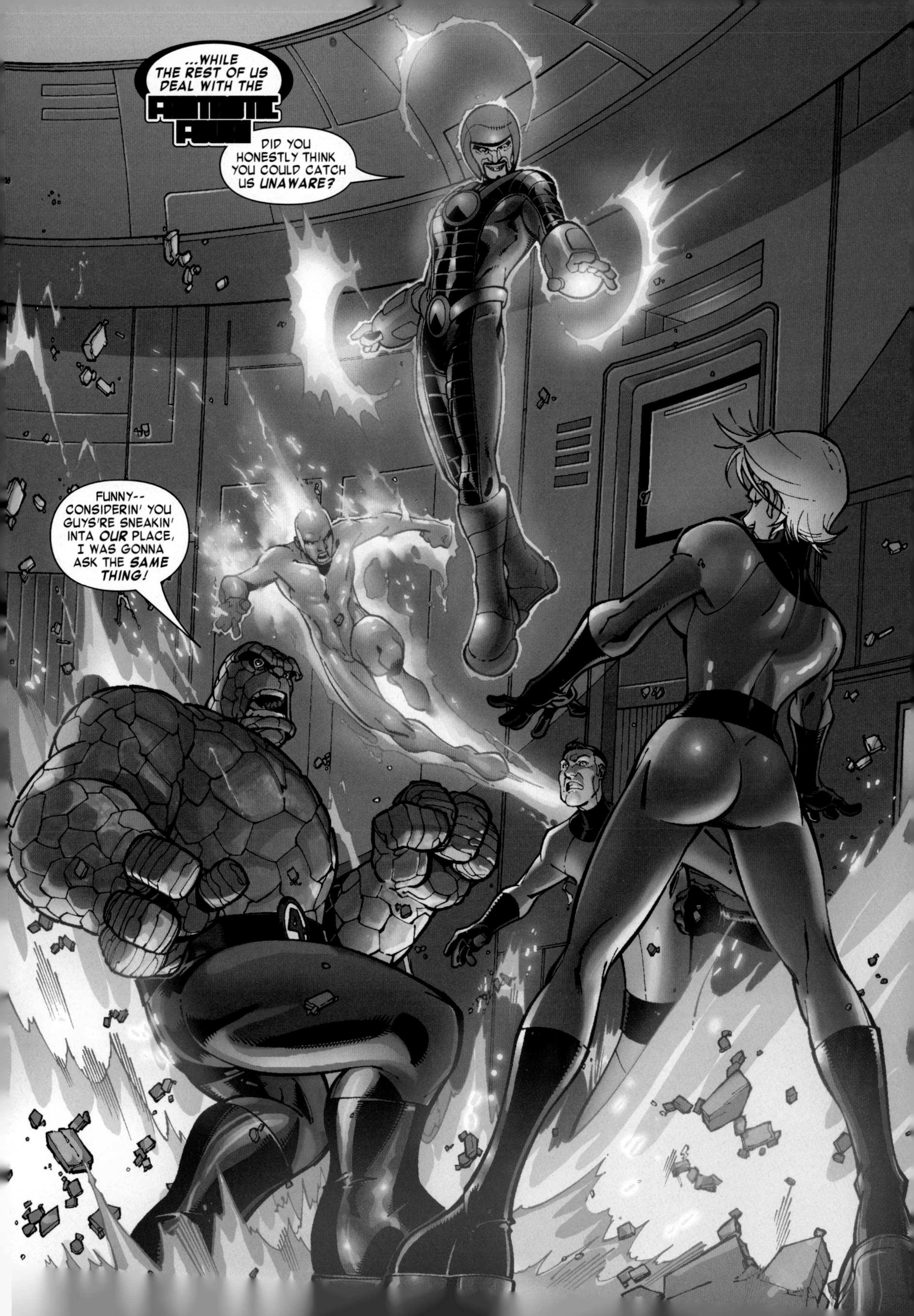
...WHILE THE REST OF US DEAL WITH THE
FANTASTIC FOUR
DID YOU HONESTLY THINK YOU COULD CATCH US UNAWARE?
FUNNY-- CONSIDERIN' YOU GUYS'RE SNEAKIN' INTA OUR PLACE, I WAS GONNA ASK THE SAME THING!

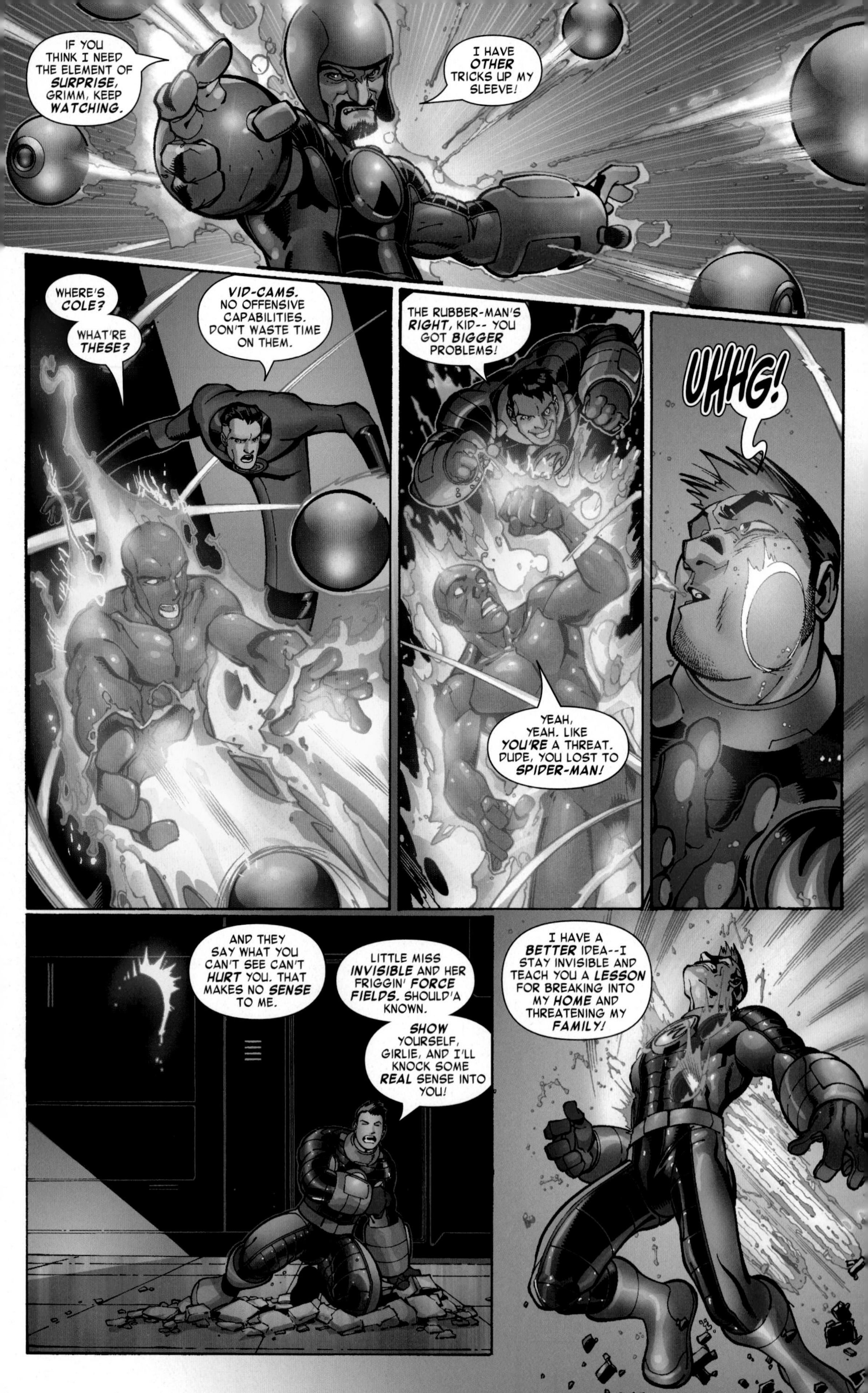

IF YOU THINK I NEED THE ELEMENT OF SURPRISE, GRIMM, KEEP WATCHING.
I HAVE OTHER TRICKS UP MY SLEEVE!
WHERE'S COLE?
WHAT'RE THESE?
VID-CAMS. NO OFFENSIVE CAPABILITIES. DON'T WASTE TIME ON THEM.
THE RUBBER-MAN'S RIGHT, KID-- YOU GOT BIGGER PROBLEMS!
YEAH, YEAH. LIKE YOU'RE A THREAT. DUDE, YOU LOST TO SPIDER-MAN!
UHHG!
AND THEY SAY WHAT YOU CAN'T SEE CAN'T HURT YOU. THAT MAKES NO SENSE TO ME.
LITTLE MISS INVISIBLE AND HER FRIGGIN' FORCE FIELDS. SHOULD'A KNOWN.
SHOW YOURSELF, GIRLIE, AND I'LL KNOCK SOME REAL SENSE INTO YOU!
I HAVE A BETTER IDEA--I STAY INVISIBLE AND TEACH YOU A LESSON FOR BREAKING INTO MY HOME AND THREATENING MY FAMILY!

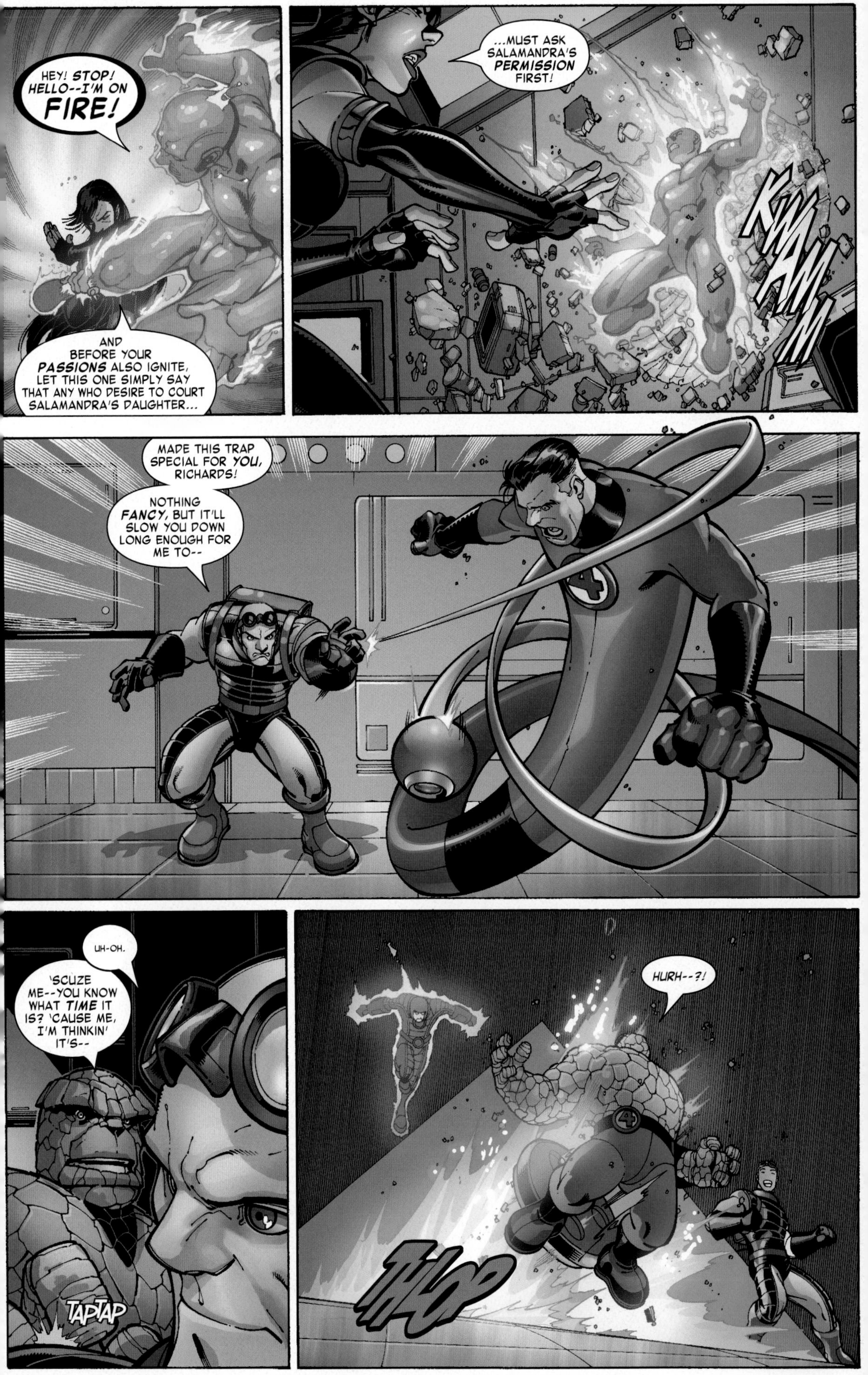
HEY! STOP! HELLO--I'M ON FIRE!
AND BEFORE YOUR PASSIONS ALSO IGNITE, LET THIS ONE SIMPLY SAY THAT ANY WHO DESIRE TO COURT SALAMANDRA'S DAUGHTER...
...MUST ASK SALAMANDRA'S PERMISSION FIRST!
KWAMM
MADE THIS TRAP SPECIAL FOR YOU, RICHARDS!
NOTHING FANCY, BUT IT'LL SLOW YOU DOWN LONG ENOUGH FOR ME TO--
UH-OH.
'SCUZE ME--YOU KNOW WHAT TIME IT IS? 'CAUSE ME, I'M THINKIN' IT'S--
TAPTAP
HURH--?!
THOP

WELL, I'D SAY IT'S *WOBBLIN' TIME!* HARD TO PACK A PUNCH WITH NO *LEVERAGE*, HUH, UGLY?

THANKS, WIZA--

YOU'RE WASTING *TIME*, YOU *TROLL!*

BUT... I WAS JUST *HELP--*

DON'T! DO AS YOU WERE *TOLD...*

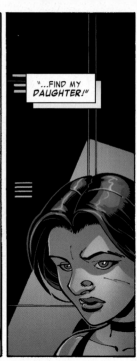

"...FIND MY *DAUGHTER!*"

OKAY, LADY, YOU WANNA PLAY WITH *FIRE--?!*

SUCH *INTENSITY!* THIS ONE CAN SEE WHY HER DAUGHTER IS *ATTRACTED* TO YOU.

STILL, *SALAMANDRA* GROWS *BORED...*

GIMME A *BREAK!* SUPER-STRONG, FIREPROOF, NOW-- *WHAT?*--INVISIBILITY? TELEPORTATION?

HOW MUCH CAN THIS LADY *DO?*

YOU THINK I'M THE SAME *LOSER* YOU FOUGHT *BEFORE?* I GOT NEW TRICKS, SWEETIE--LIKE *THIS* ONE!

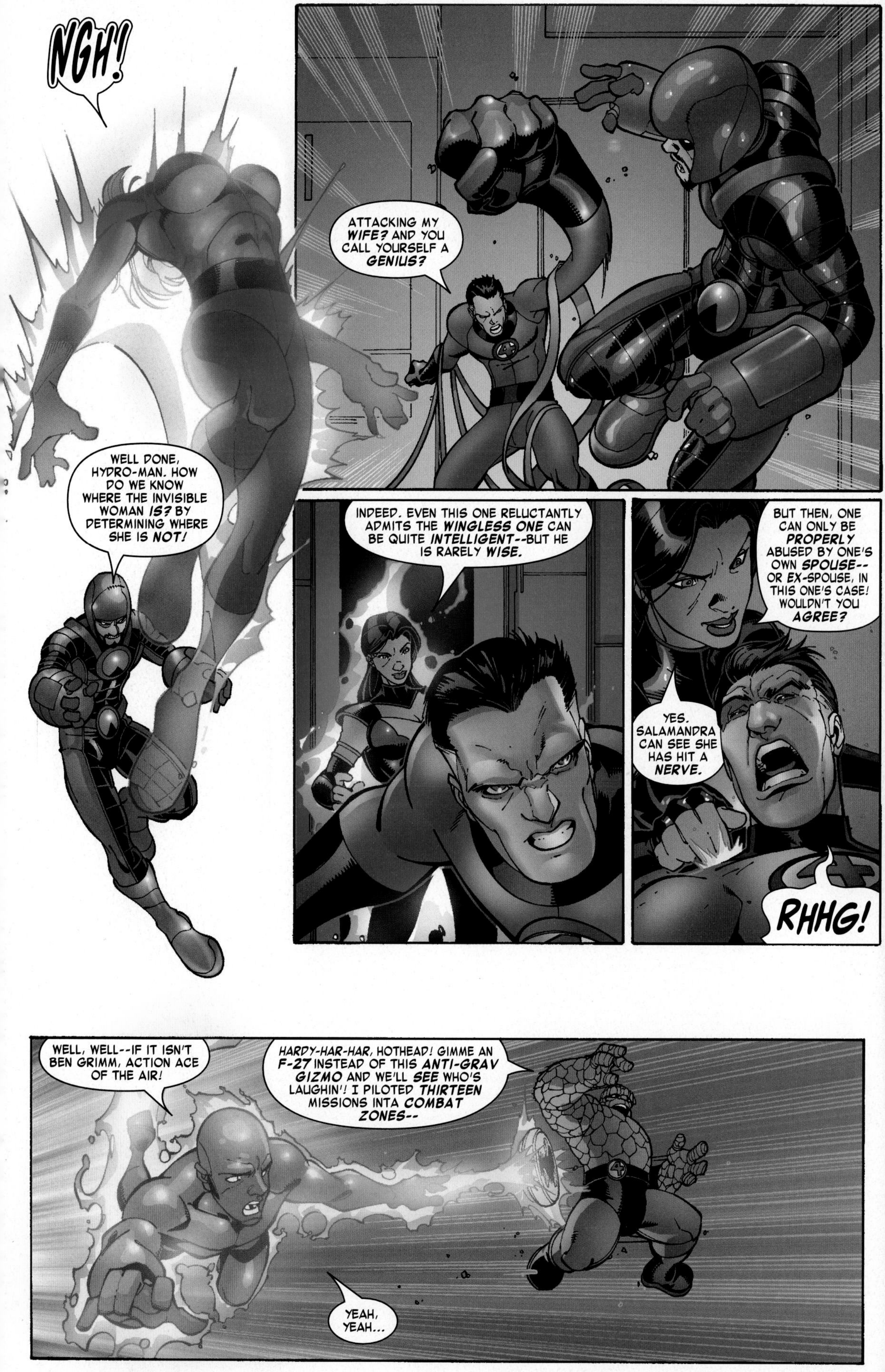
NGH!
ATTACKING MY WIFE? AND YOU CALL YOURSELF A GENIUS?
WELL DONE, HYDRO-MAN. HOW DO WE KNOW WHERE THE INVISIBLE WOMAN IS? BY DETERMINING WHERE SHE IS NOT!
INDEED. EVEN THIS ONE RELUCTANTLY ADMITS THE WINGLESS ONE CAN BE QUITE INTELLIGENT--BUT HE IS RARELY WISE.
BUT THEN, ONE CAN ONLY BE PROPERLY ABUSED BY ONE'S OWN SPOUSE--OR EX-SPOUSE, IN THIS ONE'S CASE! WOULDN'T YOU AGREE?
YES. SALAMANDRA CAN SEE SHE HAS HIT A NERVE.
RHHG!
WELL, WELL--IF IT ISN'T BEN GRIMM, ACTION ACE OF THE AIR!
HARDY-HAR-HAR, HOTHEAD! GIMME AN F-27 INSTEAD OF THIS ANTI-GRAV GIZMO AND WE'LL SEE WHO'S LAUGHIN'! I PILOTED THIRTEEN MISSIONS INTA COMBAT ZONES--
YEAH, YEAH...

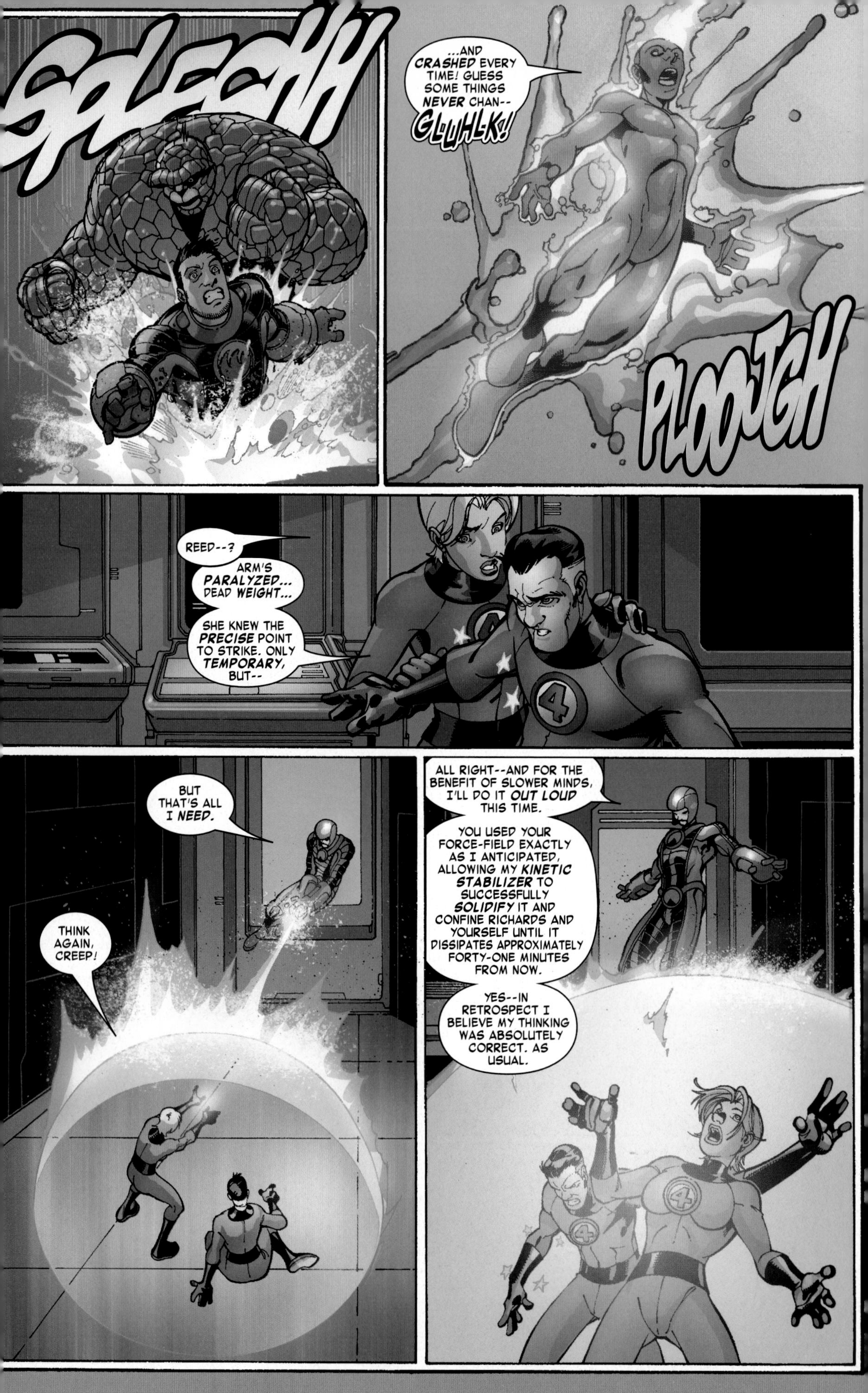
SPLOOSH
...AND CRASHED EVERY TIME! GUESS SOME THINGS NEVER CHAN--
GLUHLK!
PLOOUGH
REED--?
ARM'S PARALYZED... DEAD WEIGHT...
SHE KNEW THE PRECISE POINT TO STRIKE. ONLY TEMPORARY, BUT--
BUT THAT'S ALL I NEED.
THINK AGAIN, CREEP!
ALL RIGHT--AND FOR THE BENEFIT OF SLOWER MINDS, I'LL DO IT OUT LOUD THIS TIME.
YOU USED YOUR FORCE-FIELD EXACTLY AS I ANTICIPATED, ALLOWING MY KINETIC STABILIZER TO SUCCESSFULLY SOLIDIFY IT AND CONFINE RICHARDS AND YOURSELF UNTIL IT DISSIPATES APPROXIMATELY FORTY-ONE MINUTES FROM NOW.
YES--IN RETROSPECT I BELIEVE MY THINKING WAS ABSOLUTELY CORRECT. AS USUAL.

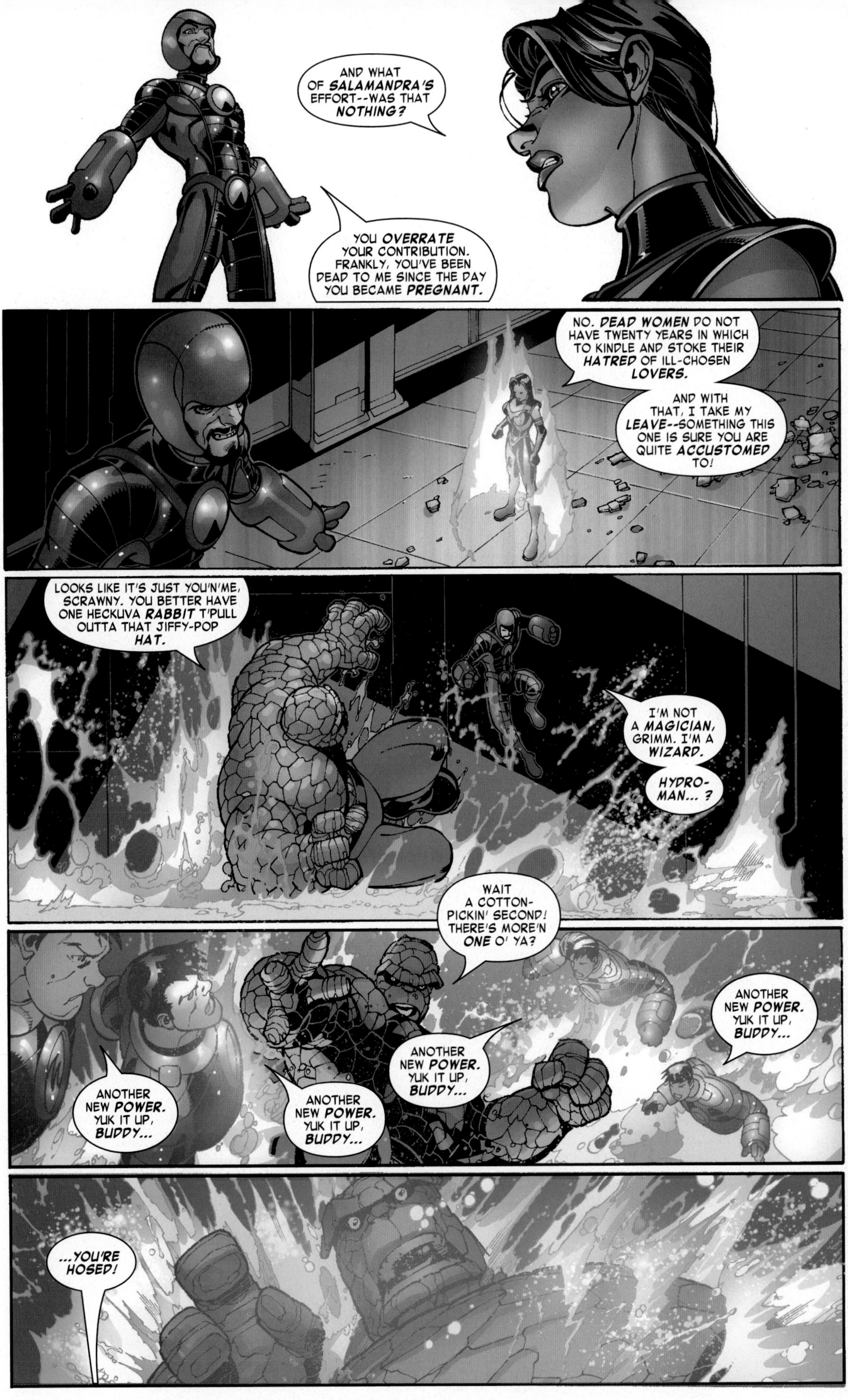
AND WHAT OF SALAMANDRA'S EFFORT--WAS THAT NOTHING?
YOU OVERRATE YOUR CONTRIBUTION. FRANKLY, YOU'VE BEEN DEAD TO ME SINCE THE DAY YOU BECAME PREGNANT.
NO. DEAD WOMEN DO NOT HAVE TWENTY YEARS IN WHICH TO KINDLE AND STOKE THEIR HATRED OF ILL-CHOSEN LOVERS.
AND WITH THAT, I TAKE MY LEAVE--SOMETHING THIS ONE IS SURE YOU ARE QUITE ACCUSTOMED TO!
LOOKS LIKE IT'S JUST YOU'N'ME, SCRAWNY. YOU BETTER HAVE ONE HECKUVA RABBIT T'PULL OUTTA THAT JIFFY-POP HAT.
I'M NOT A MAGICIAN, GRIMM. I'M A WIZARD.
HYDRO-MAN... ?
WAIT A COTTON-PICKIN' SECOND! THERE'S MORE'N ONE O' YA?
ANOTHER NEW POWER. YUK IT UP, BUDDY...
ANOTHER NEW POWER. YUK IT UP, BUDDY...
ANOTHER NEW POWER. YUK IT UP, BUDDY...
ANOTHER NEW POWER. YUK IT UP, BUDDY...
...YOU'RE HOSED!

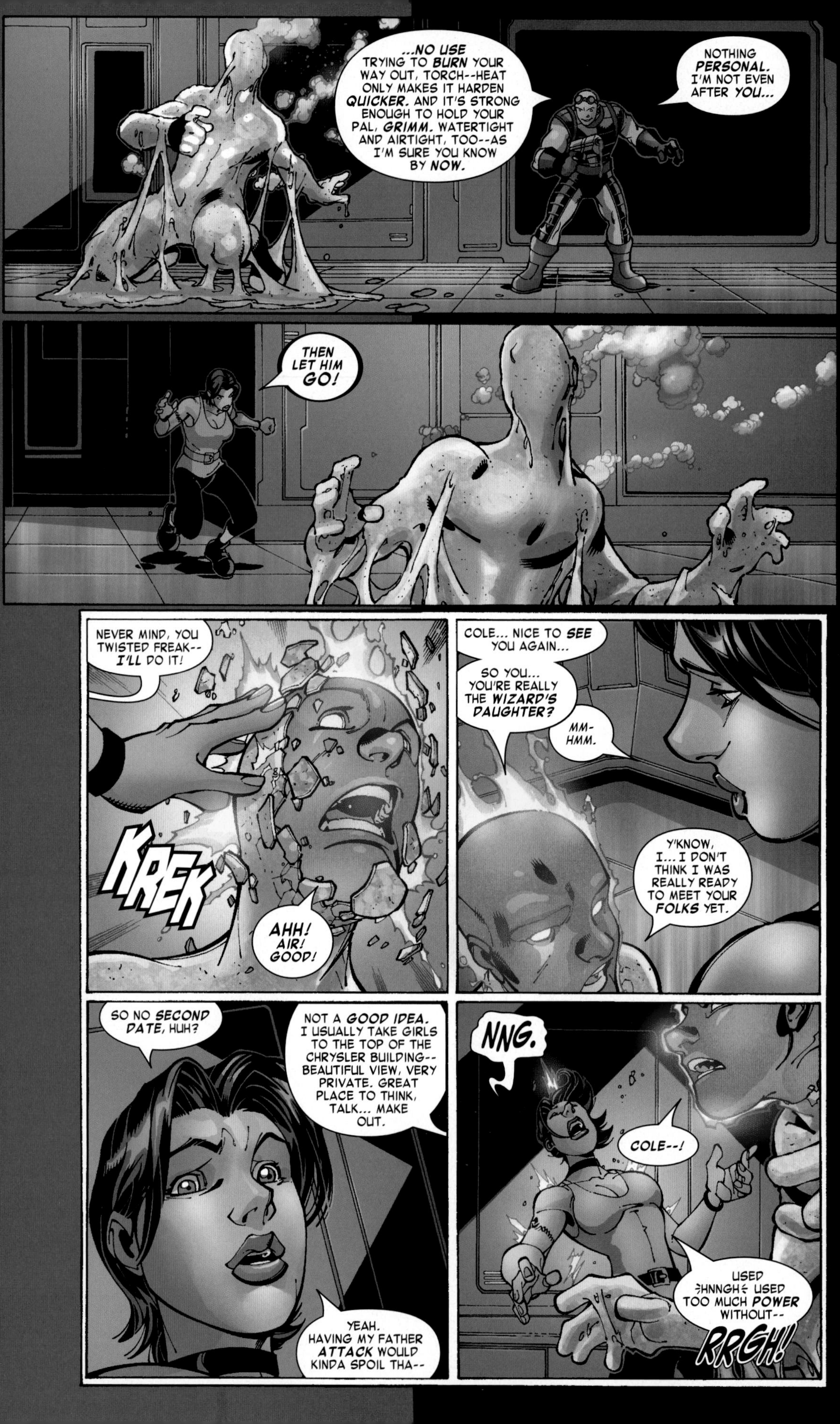
...NO USE TRYING TO BURN YOUR WAY OUT, TORCH--HEAT ONLY MAKES IT HARDEN QUICKER. AND IT'S STRONG ENOUGH TO HOLD YOUR PAL, GRIMM. WATERTIGHT AND AIRTIGHT, TOO--AS I'M SURE YOU KNOW BY NOW.
NOTHING PERSONAL. I'M NOT EVEN AFTER YOU...
THEN LET HIM GO!
NEVER MIND, YOU TWISTED FREAK-- I'LL DO IT!
KREK
AHH! AIR! GOOD!
COLE... NICE TO SEE YOU AGAIN...
SO YOU... YOU'RE REALLY THE WIZARD'S DAUGHTER?
MM-HMM.
Y'KNOW, I... I DON'T THINK I WAS REALLY READY TO MEET YOUR FOLKS YET.
SO NO SECOND DATE, HUH?
NOT A GOOD IDEA. I USUALLY TAKE GIRLS TO THE TOP OF THE CHRYSLER BUILDING-- BEAUTIFUL VIEW, VERY PRIVATE. GREAT PLACE TO THINK, TALK... MAKE OUT.
YEAH. HAVING MY FATHER ATTACK WOULD KINDA SPOIL THA--
NNG.
COLE--!
USED HNNGH USED TOO MUCH POWER WITHOUT--
RRGH!

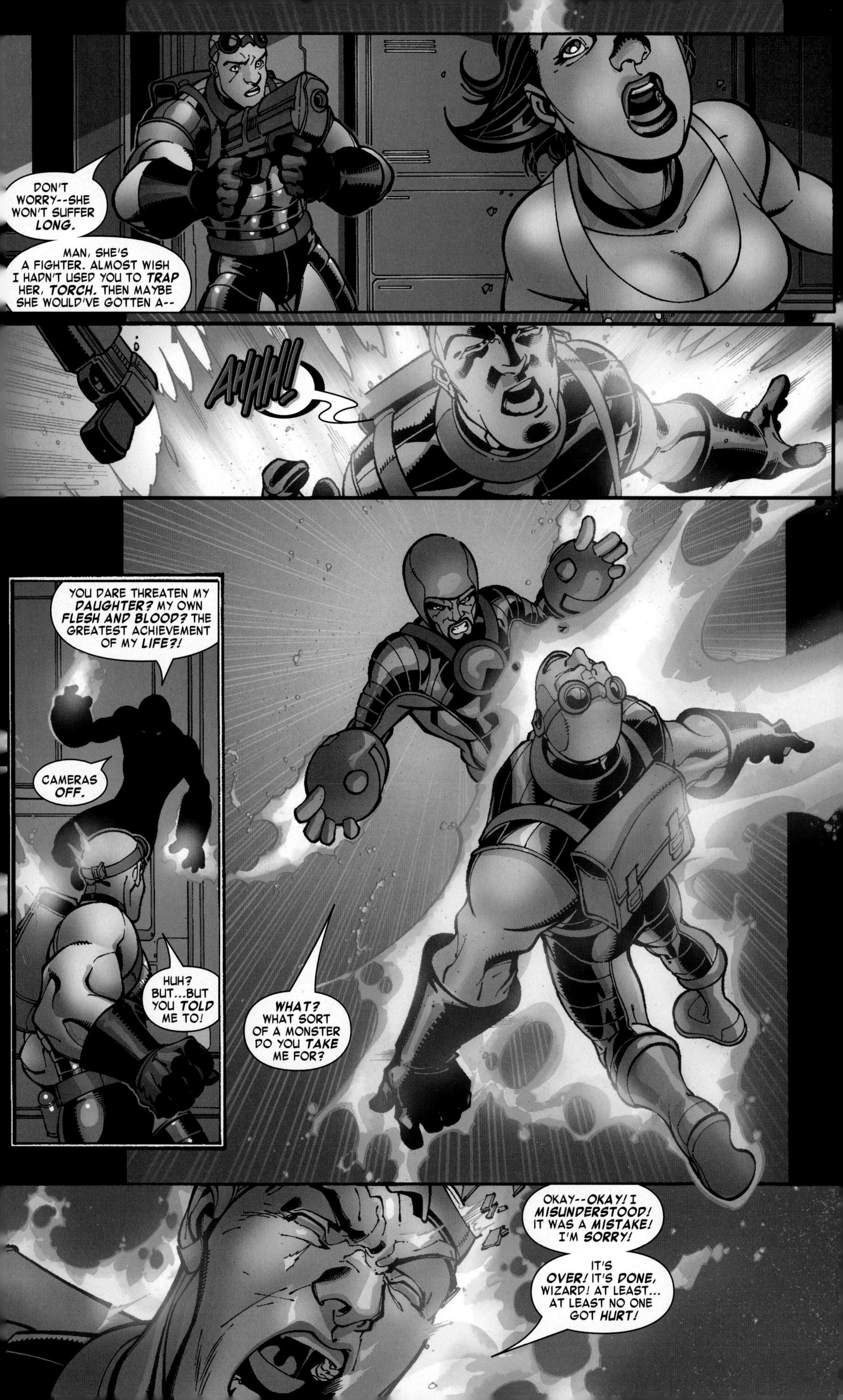
DON'T WORRY--SHE WON'T SUFFER LONG.
MAN, SHE'S A FIGHTER. ALMOST WISH I HADN'T USED YOU TO TRAP HER, TORCH. THEN MAYBE SHE WOULD'VE GOTTEN A--
AHHH!
YOU DARE THREATEN MY DAUGHTER? MY OWN FLESH AND BLOOD? THE GREATEST ACHIEVEMENT OF MY LIFE?!
CAMERAS OFF.
HUH? BUT...BUT YOU TOLD ME TO!
WHAT? WHAT SORT OF A MONSTER DO YOU TAKE ME FOR?
OKAY--OKAY! I MISUNDERSTOOD! IT WAS A MISTAKE! I'M SORRY!
IT'S OVER! IT'S DONE, WIZARD! AT LEAST... AT LEAST NO ONE GOT HURT!

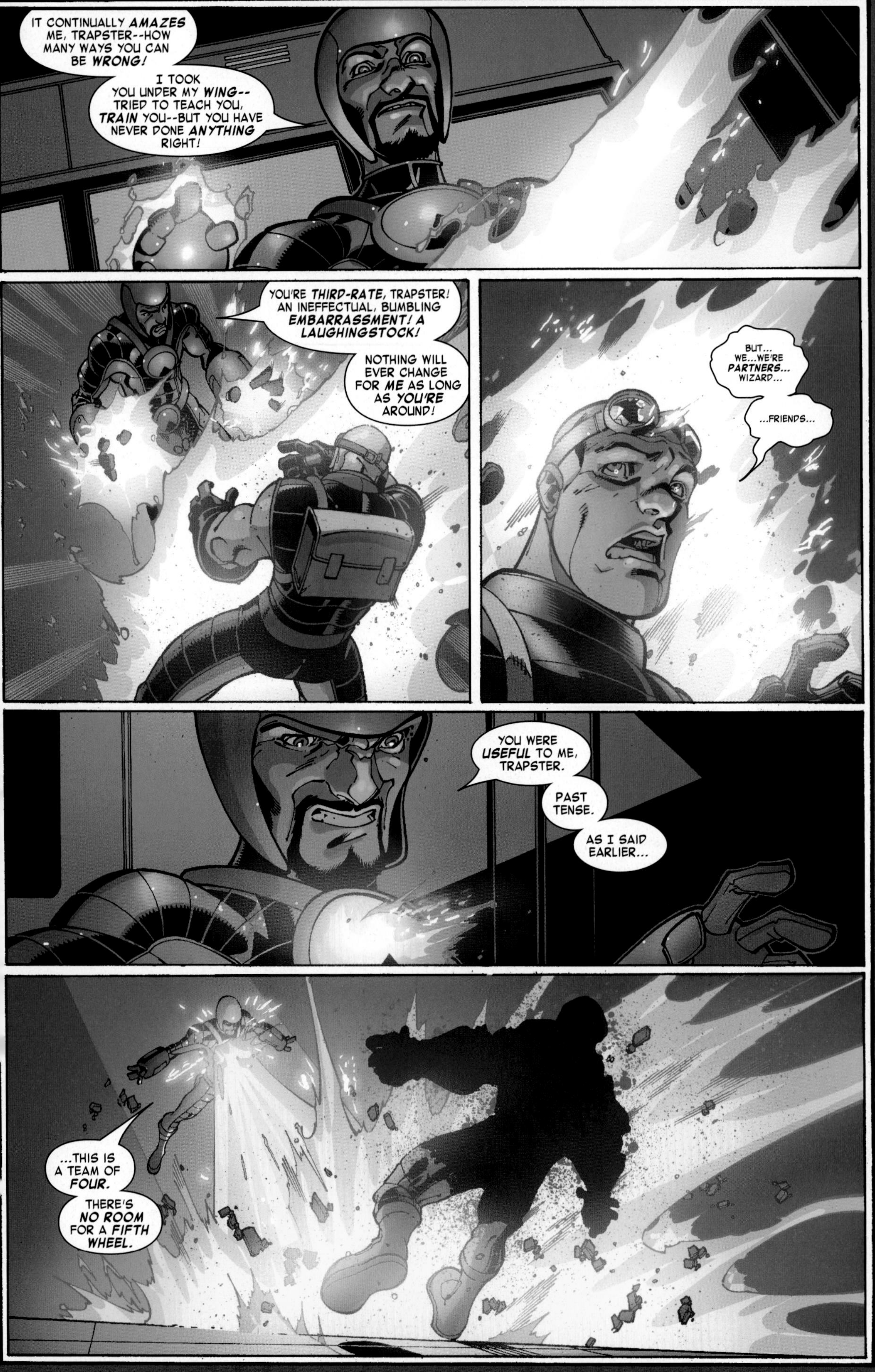
IT CONTINUALLY AMAZES ME, TRAPSTER--HOW MANY WAYS YOU CAN BE WRONG!
I TOOK YOU UNDER MY WING--TRIED TO TEACH YOU, TRAIN YOU--BUT YOU HAVE NEVER DONE ANYTHING RIGHT!
YOU'RE THIRD-RATE, TRAPSTER! AN INEFFECTUAL, BUMBLING EMBARRASSMENT! A LAUGHINGSTOCK!
NOTHING WILL EVER CHANGE FOR ME AS LONG AS YOU'RE AROUND!
BUT... WE...WE'RE PARTNERS... WIZARD...
...FRIENDS...
YOU WERE USEFUL TO ME, TRAPSTER.
PAST TENSE.
AS I SAID EARLIER...
...THIS IS A TEAM OF FOUR.
THERE'S NO ROOM FOR A FIFTH WHEEL.

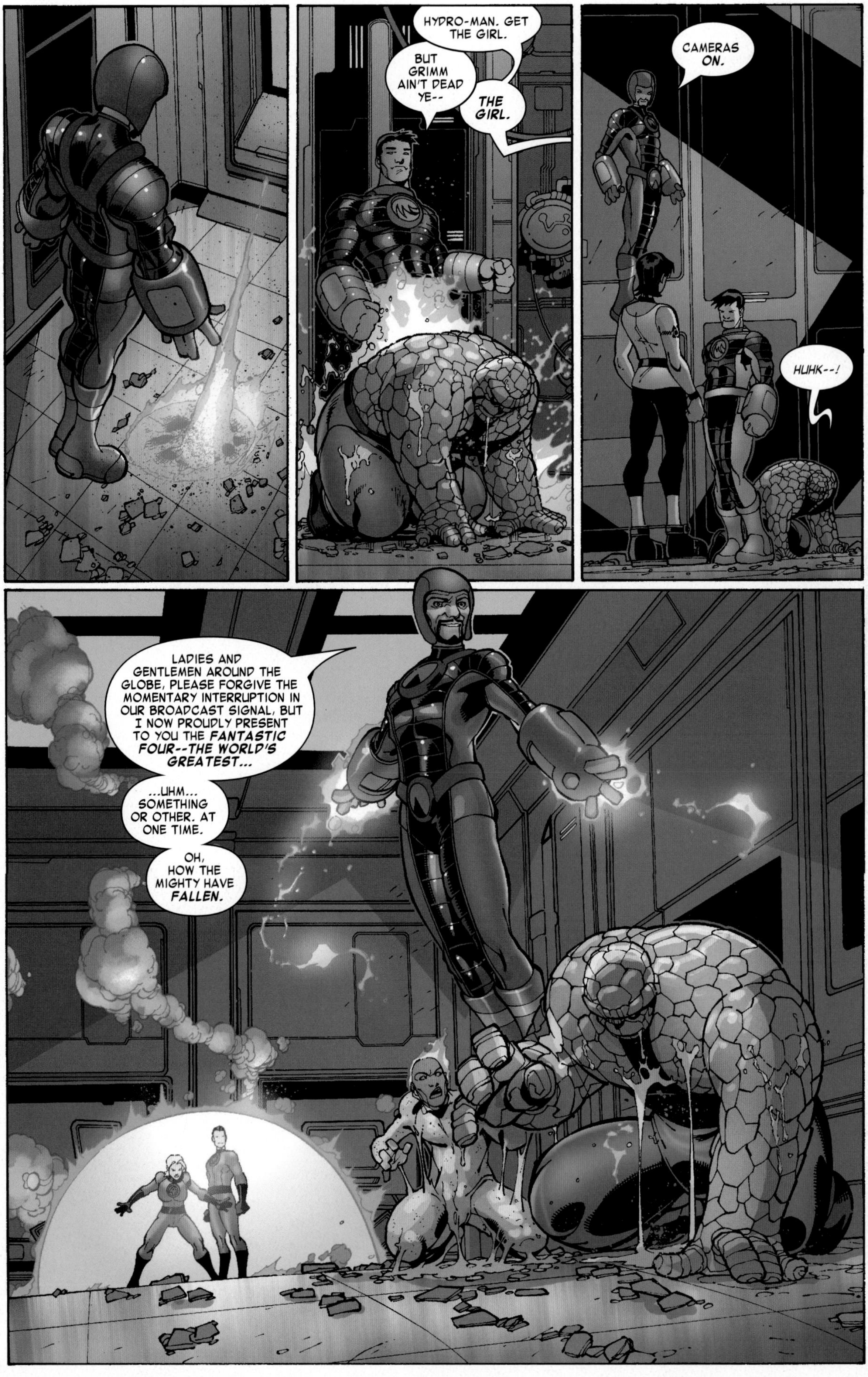

HYDRO-MAN. GET THE GIRL.
BUT GRIMM AIN'T DEAD YE--
THE GIRL.
CAMERAS ON.
HUHK--!
LADIES AND GENTLEMEN AROUND THE GLOBE, PLEASE FORGIVE THE MOMENTARY INTERRUPTION IN OUR BROADCAST SIGNAL, BUT I NOW PROUDLY PRESENT TO YOU THE FANTASTIC FOUR--THE WORLD'S GREATEST...
...UHM... SOMETHING OR OTHER. AT ONE TIME.
OH, HOW THE MIGHTY HAVE FALLEN.

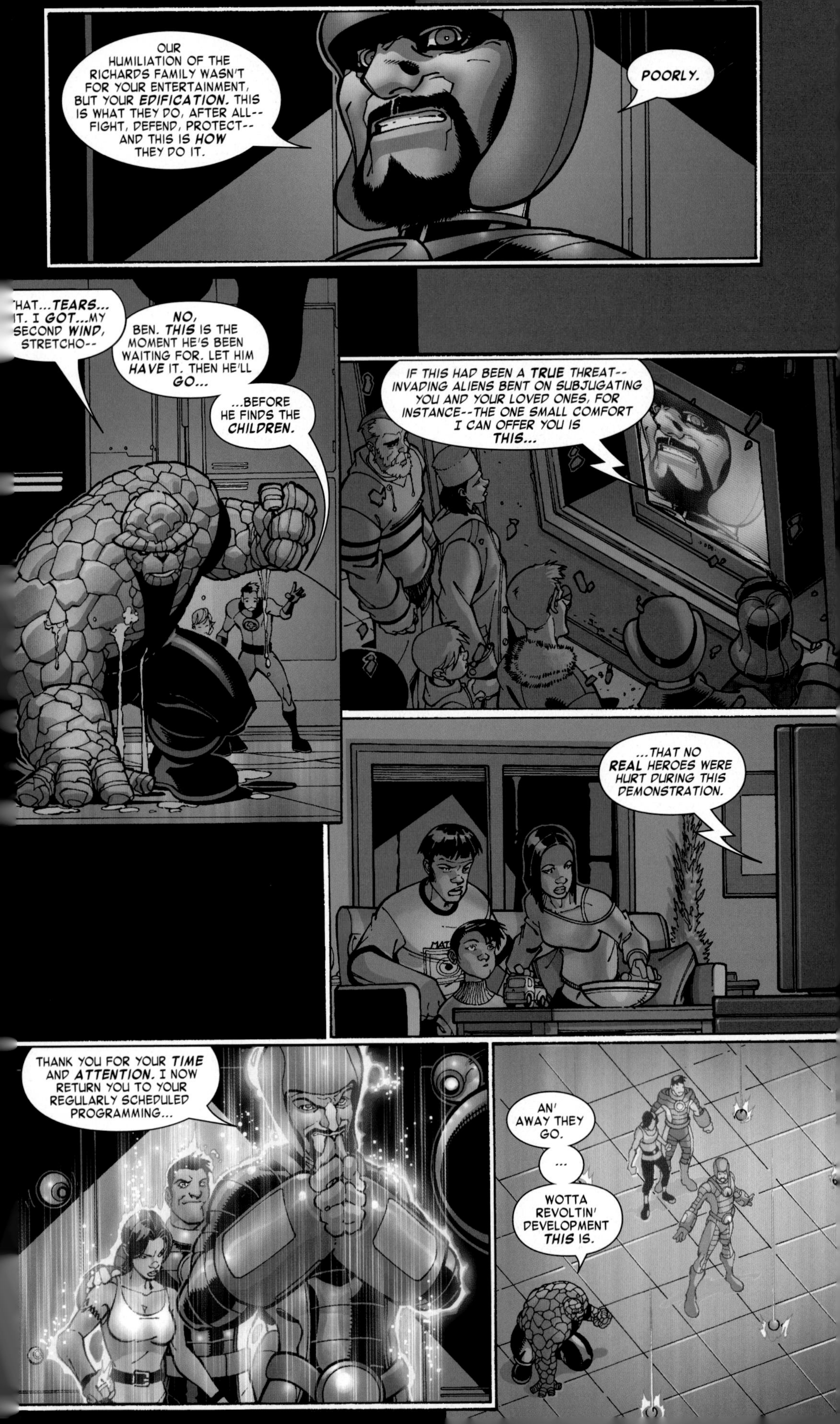
OUR HUMILIATION OF THE RICHARDS FAMILY WASN'T FOR YOUR ENTERTAINMENT, BUT YOUR EDIFICATION. THIS IS WHAT THEY DO, AFTER ALL-- FIGHT, DEFEND, PROTECT-- AND THIS IS HOW THEY DO IT.
POORLY.
THAT...TEARS... IT. I GOT...MY SECOND WIND, STRETCHO--
NO, BEN. THIS IS THE MOMENT HE'S BEEN WAITING FOR. LET HIM HAVE IT. THEN HE'LL GO...
...BEFORE HE FINDS THE CHILDREN.
IF THIS HAD BEEN A TRUE THREAT-- INVADING ALIENS BENT ON SUBJUGATING YOU AND YOUR LOVED ONES, FOR INSTANCE--THE ONE SMALL COMFORT I CAN OFFER YOU IS THIS...
...THAT NO REAL HEROES WERE HURT DURING THIS DEMONSTRATION.
THANK YOU FOR YOUR TIME AND ATTENTION. I NOW RETURN YOU TO YOUR REGULARLY SCHEDULED PROGRAMMING...
AN' AWAY THEY GO.
...
WOTTA REVOLTIN' DEVELOPMENT THIS IS.

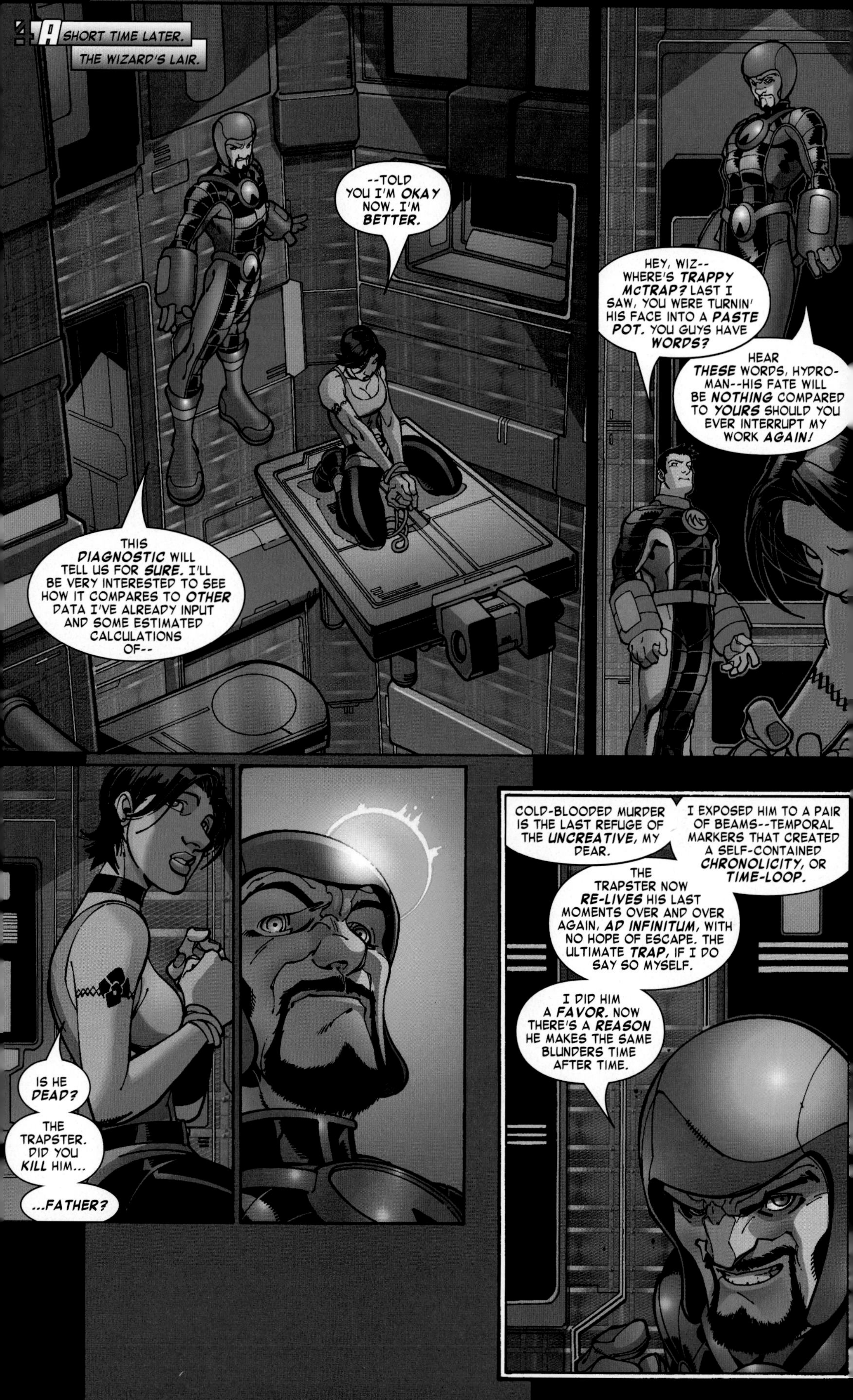
4 A
A SHORT TIME LATER.
THE WIZARD'S LAIR.
--TOLD YOU I'M OKAY NOW. I'M BETTER.
THIS DIAGNOSTIC WILL TELL US FOR SURE. I'LL BE VERY INTERESTED TO SEE HOW IT COMPARES TO OTHER DATA I'VE ALREADY INPUT AND SOME ESTIMATED CALCULATIONS OF--
HEY, WIZ-- WHERE'S TRAPPY McTRAP? LAST I SAW, YOU WERE TURNIN' HIS FACE INTO A PASTE POT. YOU GUYS HAVE WORDS?
HEAR THESE WORDS, HYDRO-MAN--HIS FATE WILL BE NOTHING COMPARED TO YOURS SHOULD YOU EVER INTERRUPT MY WORK AGAIN!
IS HE DEAD?
THE TRAPSTER. DID YOU KILL HIM...
...FATHER?
COLD-BLOODED MURDER IS THE LAST REFUGE OF THE UNCREATIVE, MY DEAR.
I EXPOSED HIM TO A PAIR OF BEAMS--TEMPORAL MARKERS THAT CREATED A SELF-CONTAINED CHRONOLICITY, OR TIME-LOOP.
THE TRAPSTER NOW RE-LIVES HIS LAST MOMENTS OVER AND OVER AGAIN, AD INFINITUM, WITH NO HOPE OF ESCAPE. THE ULTIMATE TRAP, IF I DO SAY SO MYSELF.
I DID HIM A FAVOR. NOW THERE'S A REASON HE MAKES THE SAME BLUNDERS TIME AFTER TIME.

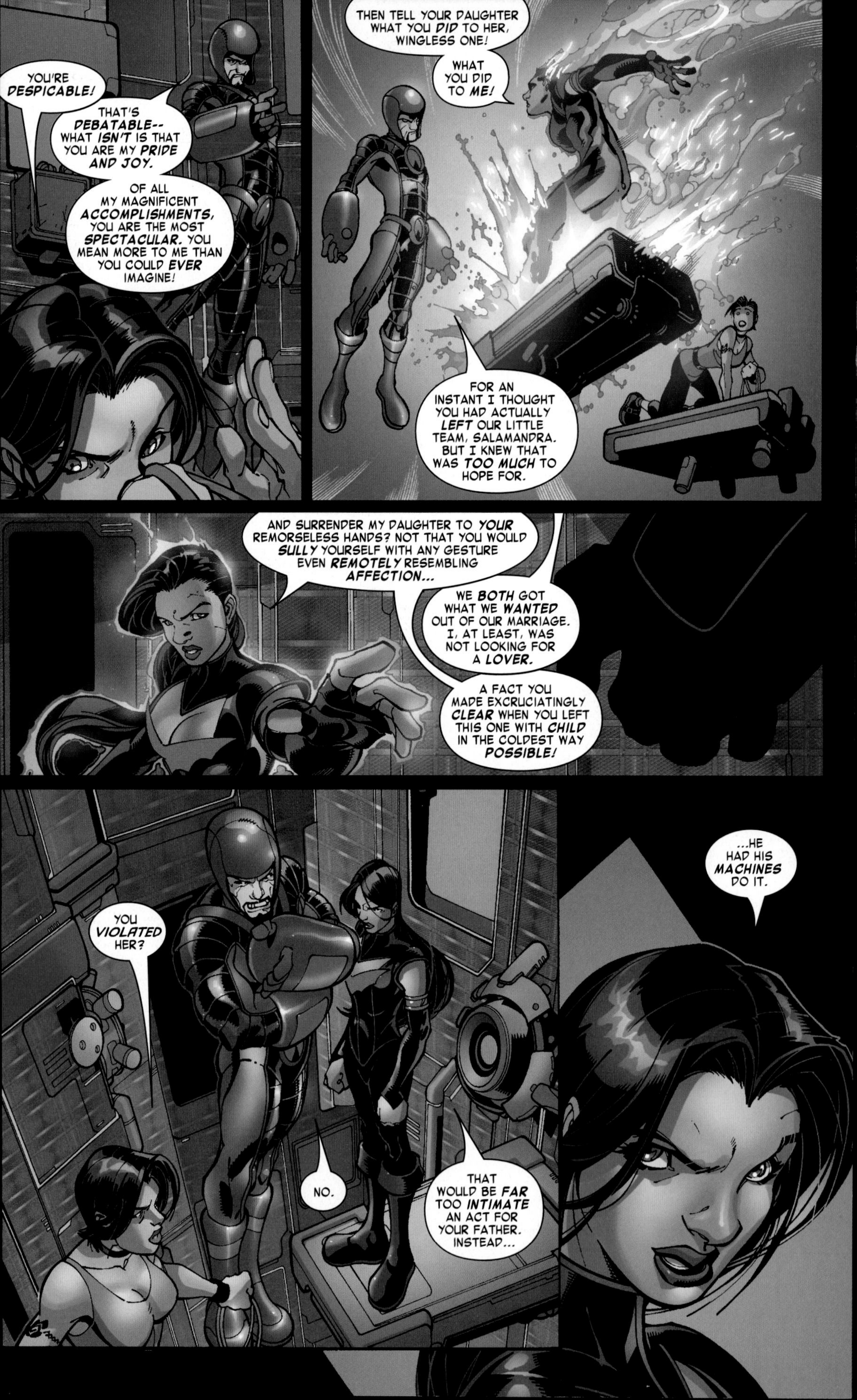
YOU'RE DESPICABLE!
THAT'S DEBATABLE-- WHAT ISN'T IS THAT YOU ARE MY PRIDE AND JOY.
OF ALL MY MAGNIFICENT ACCOMPLISHMENTS, YOU ARE THE MOST SPECTACULAR. YOU MEAN MORE TO ME THAN YOU COULD EVER IMAGINE!
THEN TELL YOUR DAUGHTER WHAT YOU DID TO HER, WINGLESS ONE!
WHAT YOU DID TO ME!
FOR AN INSTANT I THOUGHT YOU HAD ACTUALLY LEFT OUR LITTLE TEAM, SALAMANDRA. BUT I KNEW THAT WAS TOO MUCH TO HOPE FOR.
AND SURRENDER MY DAUGHTER TO YOUR REMORSELESS HANDS? NOT THAT YOU WOULD SULLY YOURSELF WITH ANY GESTURE EVEN REMOTELY RESEMBLING AFFECTION...
WE BOTH GOT WHAT WE WANTED OUT OF OUR MARRIAGE. I, AT LEAST, WAS NOT LOOKING FOR A LOVER.
A FACT YOU MADE EXCRUCIATINGLY CLEAR WHEN YOU LEFT THIS ONE WITH CHILD IN THE COLDEST WAY POSSIBLE!
YOU VIOLATED HER?
NO.
THAT WOULD BE FAR TOO INTIMATE AN ACT FOR YOUR FATHER. INSTEAD...
...HE HAD HIS MACHINES DO IT.

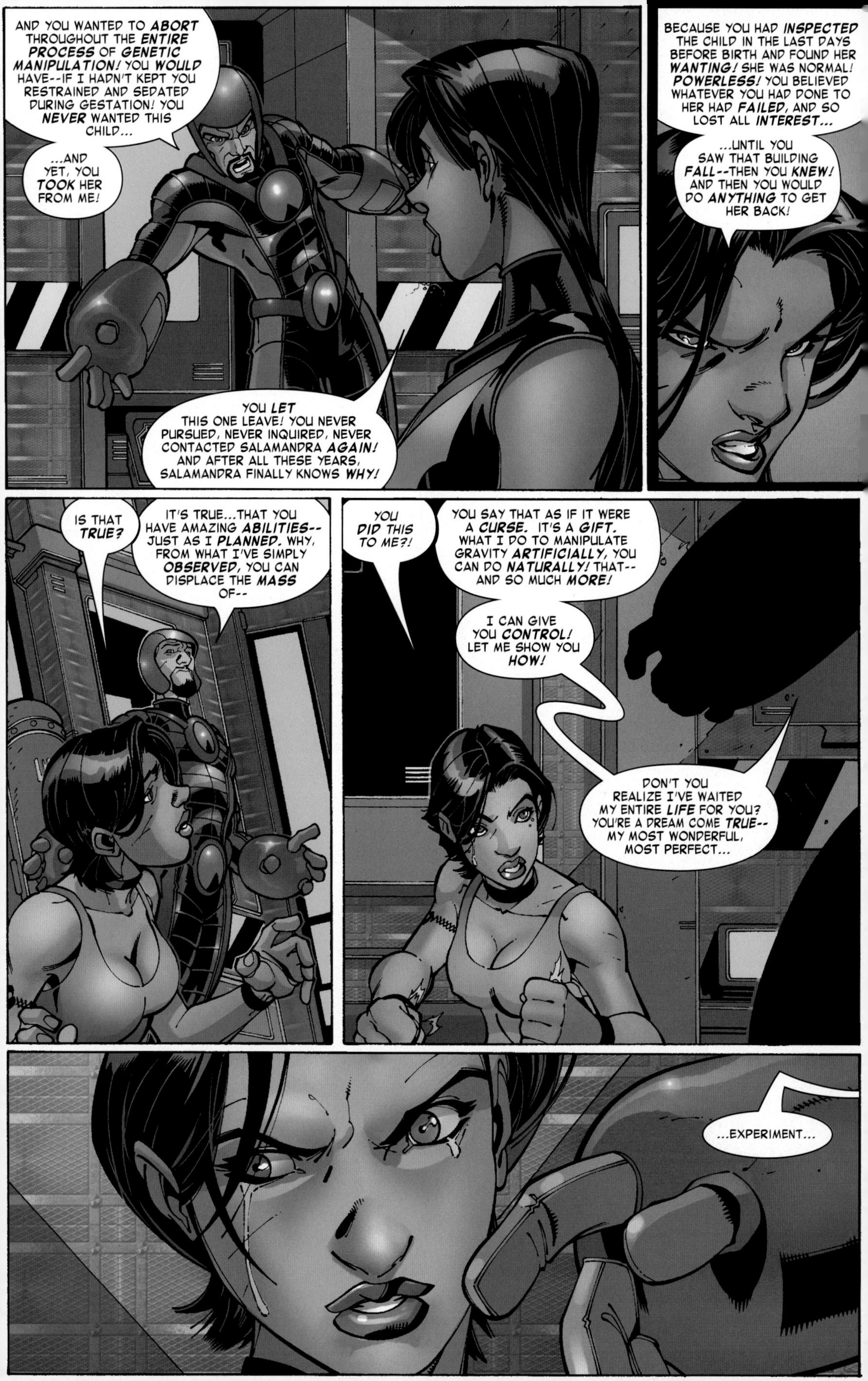
AND YOU WANTED TO ABORT THROUGHOUT THE ENTIRE PROCESS OF GENETIC MANIPULATION! YOU WOULD HAVE--IF I HADN'T KEPT YOU RESTRAINED AND SEDATED DURING GESTATION! YOU NEVER WANTED THIS CHILD...
...AND YET, YOU TOOK HER FROM ME!
YOU LET THIS ONE LEAVE! YOU NEVER PURSUED, NEVER INQUIRED, NEVER CONTACTED SALAMANDRA AGAIN! AND AFTER ALL THESE YEARS, SALAMANDRA FINALLY KNOWS WHY!
BECAUSE YOU HAD INSPECTED THE CHILD IN THE LAST DAYS BEFORE BIRTH AND FOUND HER WANTING! SHE WAS NORMAL! POWERLESS! YOU BELIEVED WHATEVER YOU HAD DONE TO HER HAD FAILED, AND SO LOST ALL INTEREST...
...UNTIL YOU SAW THAT BUILDING FALL--THEN YOU KNEW! AND THEN YOU WOULD DO ANYTHING TO GET HER BACK!
IS THAT TRUE?
IT'S TRUE...THAT YOU HAVE AMAZING ABILITIES--JUST AS I PLANNED. WHY, FROM WHAT I'VE SIMPLY OBSERVED, YOU CAN DISPLACE THE MASS OF--
YOU DID THIS TO ME?!
YOU SAY THAT AS IF IT WERE A CURSE. IT'S A GIFT. WHAT I DO TO MANIPULATE GRAVITY ARTIFICIALLY, YOU CAN DO NATURALLY! THAT--AND SO MUCH MORE!
I CAN GIVE YOU CONTROL! LET ME SHOW YOU HOW!
DON'T YOU REALIZE I'VE WAITED MY ENTIRE LIFE FOR YOU? YOU'RE A DREAM COME TRUE--MY MOST WONDERFUL, MOST PERFECT...
...EXPERIMENT...

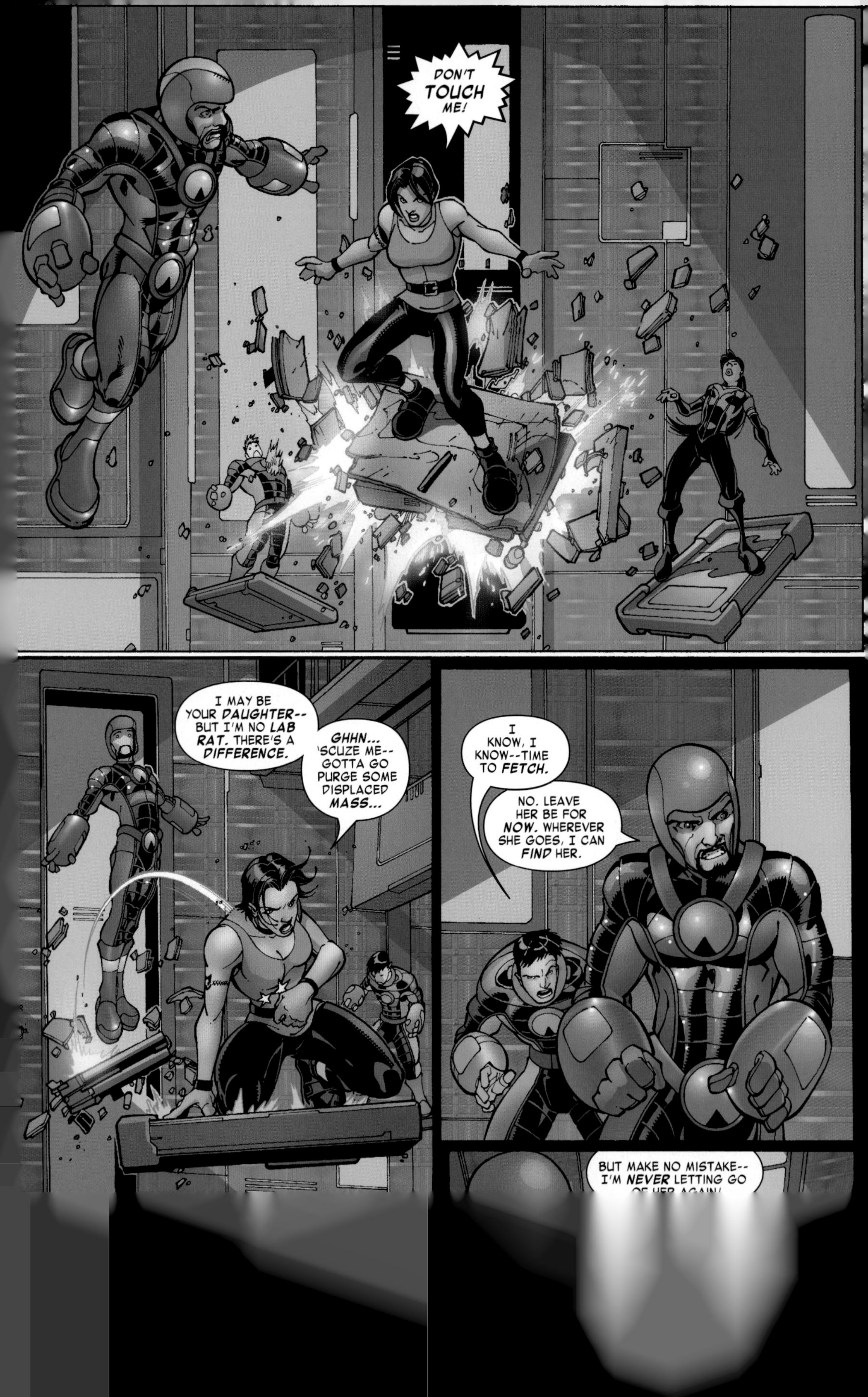
DON'T TOUCH ME!
I MAY BE YOUR DAUGHTER-- BUT I'M NO LAB RAT. THERE'S A DIFFERENCE.
GHHN... 'SCUZE ME-- GOTTA GO PURGE SOME DISPLACED MASS...
I KNOW, I KNOW--TIME TO FETCH.
NO. LEAVE HER BE FOR NOW. WHEREVER SHE GOES, I CAN FIND HER.
BUT MAKE NO MISTAKE-- I'M NEVER LETTING GO

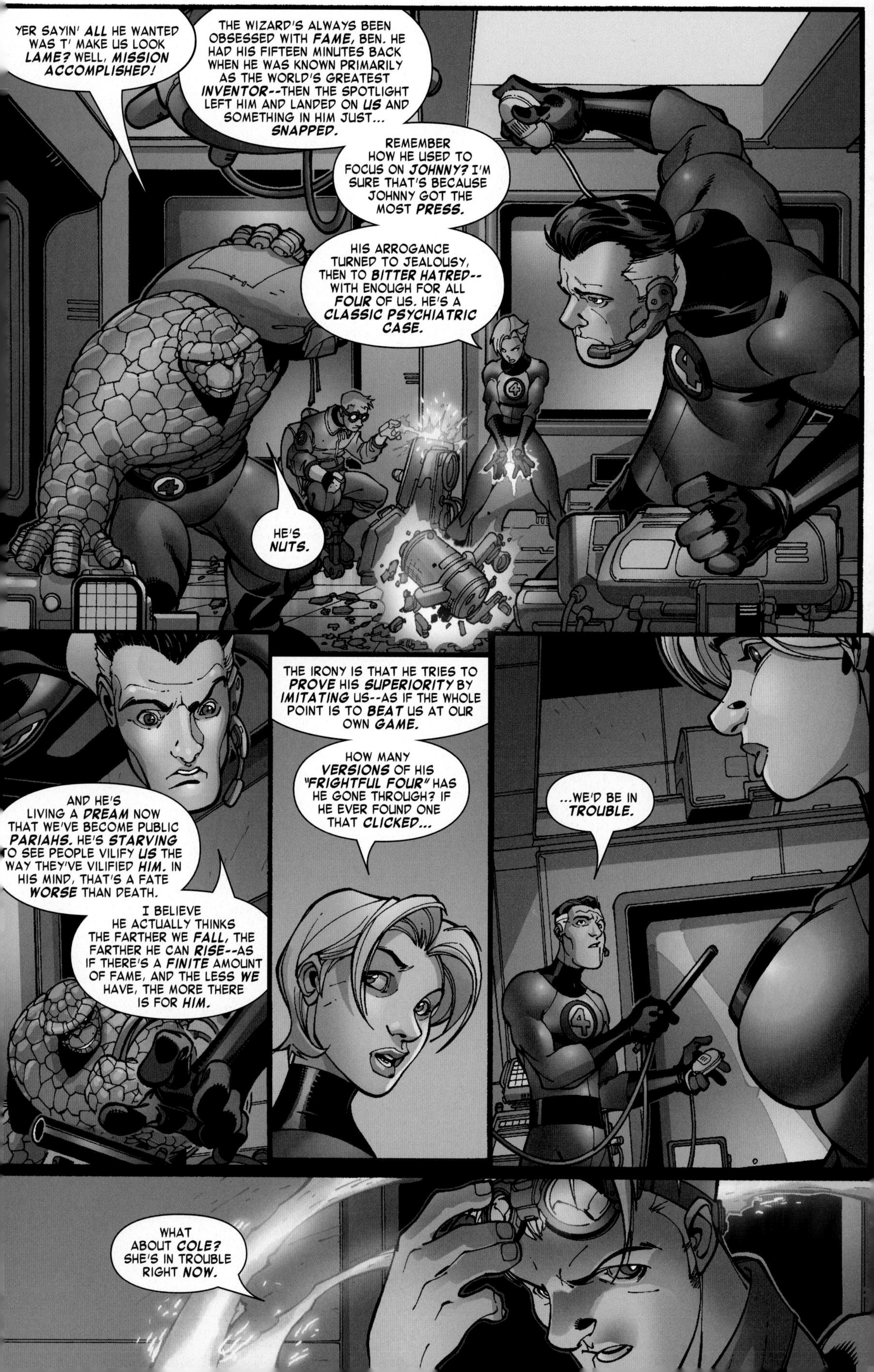

YER SAYIN' ALL HE WANTED WAS T' MAKE US LOOK LAME? WELL, MISSION ACCOMPLISHED!
THE WIZARD'S ALWAYS BEEN OBSESSED WITH FAME, BEN. HE HAD HIS FIFTEEN MINUTES BACK WHEN HE WAS KNOWN PRIMARILY AS THE WORLD'S GREATEST INVENTOR--THEN THE SPOTLIGHT LEFT HIM AND LANDED ON US AND SOMETHING IN HIM JUST... SNAPPED.
REMEMBER HOW HE USED TO FOCUS ON JOHNNY? I'M SURE THAT'S BECAUSE JOHNNY GOT THE MOST PRESS.
HIS ARROGANCE TURNED TO JEALOUSY, THEN TO BITTER HATRED-- WITH ENOUGH FOR ALL FOUR OF US. HE'S A CLASSIC PSYCHIATRIC CASE.
HE'S NUTS.
AND HE'S LIVING A DREAM NOW THAT WE'VE BECOME PUBLIC PARIAHS. HE'S STARVING TO SEE PEOPLE VILIFY US THE WAY THEY'VE VILIFIED HIM. IN HIS MIND, THAT'S A FATE WORSE THAN DEATH.
I BELIEVE HE ACTUALLY THINKS THE FARTHER WE FALL, THE FARTHER HE CAN RISE--AS IF THERE'S A FINITE AMOUNT OF FAME, AND THE LESS WE HAVE, THE MORE THERE IS FOR HIM.
THE IRONY IS THAT HE TRIES TO PROVE HIS SUPERIORITY BY IMITATING US--AS IF THE WHOLE POINT IS TO BEAT US AT OUR OWN GAME.
HOW MANY VERSIONS OF HIS "FRIGHTFUL FOUR" HAS HE GONE THROUGH? IF HE EVER FOUND ONE THAT CLICKED...
...WE'D BE IN TROUBLE.
WHAT ABOUT COLE? SHE'S IN TROUBLE RIGHT NOW.

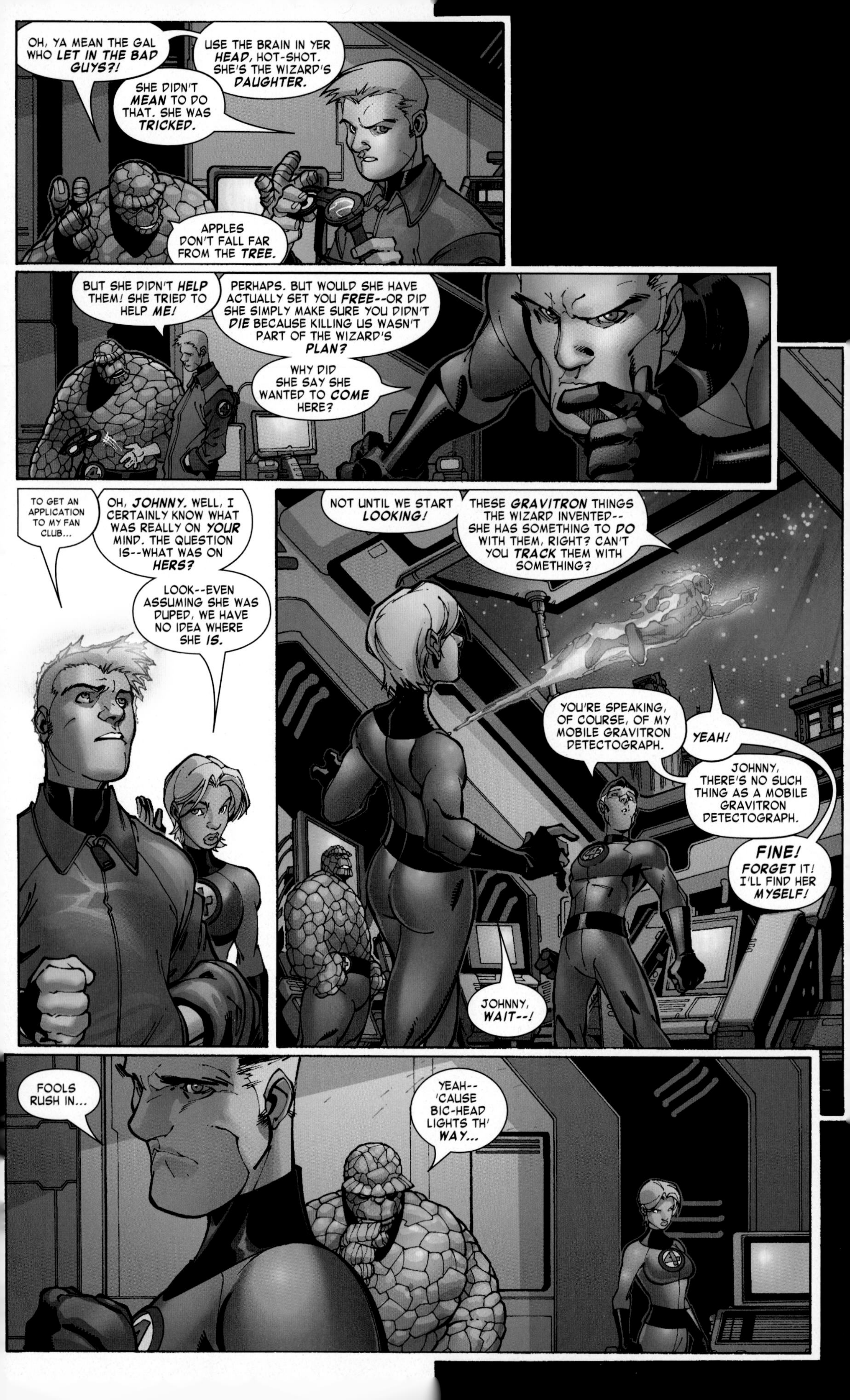

OH, YA MEAN THE GAL WHO LET IN THE BAD GUYS?!
USE THE BRAIN IN YER HEAD, HOT-SHOT. SHE'S THE WIZARD'S DAUGHTER.
SHE DIDN'T MEAN TO DO THAT. SHE WAS TRICKED.
APPLES DON'T FALL FAR FROM THE TREE.
BUT SHE DIDN'T HELP THEM! SHE TRIED TO HELP ME!
PERHAPS. BUT WOULD SHE HAVE ACTUALLY SET YOU FREE--OR DID SHE SIMPLY MAKE SURE YOU DIDN'T DIE BECAUSE KILLING US WASN'T PART OF THE WIZARD'S PLAN?
WHY DID SHE SAY SHE WANTED TO COME HERE?
TO GET AN APPLICATION TO MY FAN CLUB...
OH, JOHNNY. WELL, I CERTAINLY KNOW WHAT WAS REALLY ON YOUR MIND. THE QUESTION IS--WHAT WAS ON HERS?
LOOK--EVEN ASSUMING SHE WAS DUPED, WE HAVE NO IDEA WHERE SHE IS.
NOT UNTIL WE START LOOKING!
THESE GRAVITRON THINGS THE WIZARD INVENTED--SHE HAS SOMETHING TO DO WITH THEM, RIGHT? CAN'T YOU TRACK THEM WITH SOMETHING?
YOU'RE SPEAKING, OF COURSE, OF MY MOBILE GRAVITRON DETECTOGRAPH.
YEAH!
JOHNNY, THERE'S NO SUCH THING AS A MOBILE GRAVITRON DETECTOGRAPH.
FINE! FORGET IT! I'LL FIND HER MYSELF!
JOHNNY, WAIT--!
FOOLS RUSH IN...
YEAH--'CAUSE BIG-HEAD LIGHTS TH' WAY...

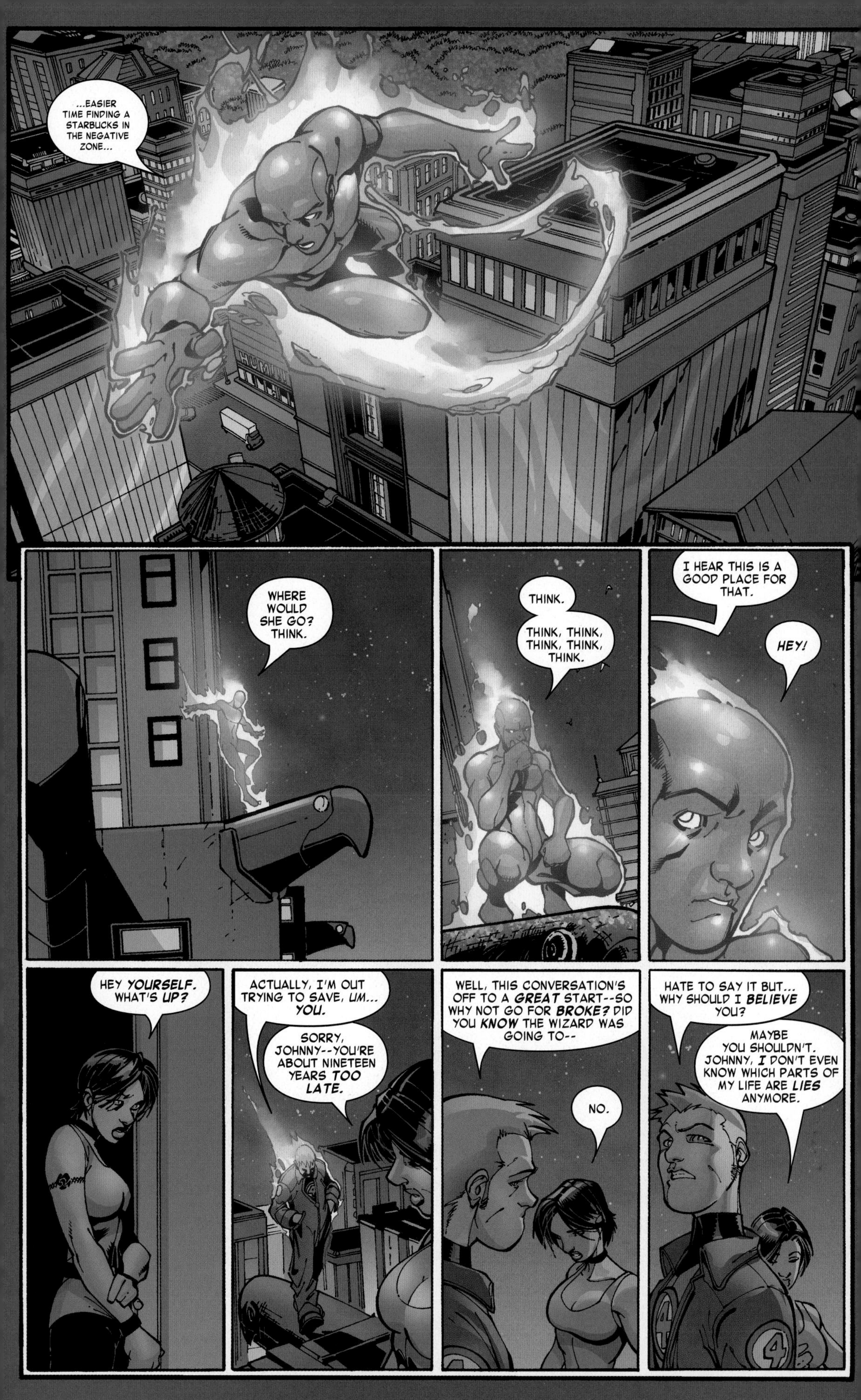

...EASIER TIME FINDING A STARBUCKS IN THE NEGATIVE ZONE...
WHERE WOULD SHE GO? THINK.
THINK.
THINK, THINK, THINK, THINK, THINK.
I HEAR THIS IS A GOOD PLACE FOR THAT.
HEY!
HEY YOURSELF. WHAT'S UP?
ACTUALLY, I'M OUT TRYING TO SAVE, UM... YOU.
SORRY, JOHNNY--YOU'RE ABOUT NINETEEN YEARS TOO LATE.
WELL, THIS CONVERSATION'S OFF TO A GREAT START--SO WHY NOT GO FOR BROKE? DID YOU KNOW THE WIZARD WAS GOING TO--
NO.
HATE TO SAY IT BUT... WHY SHOULD I BELIEVE YOU?
MAYBE YOU SHOULDN'T. JOHNNY, I DON'T EVEN KNOW WHICH PARTS OF MY LIFE ARE LIES ANYMORE.

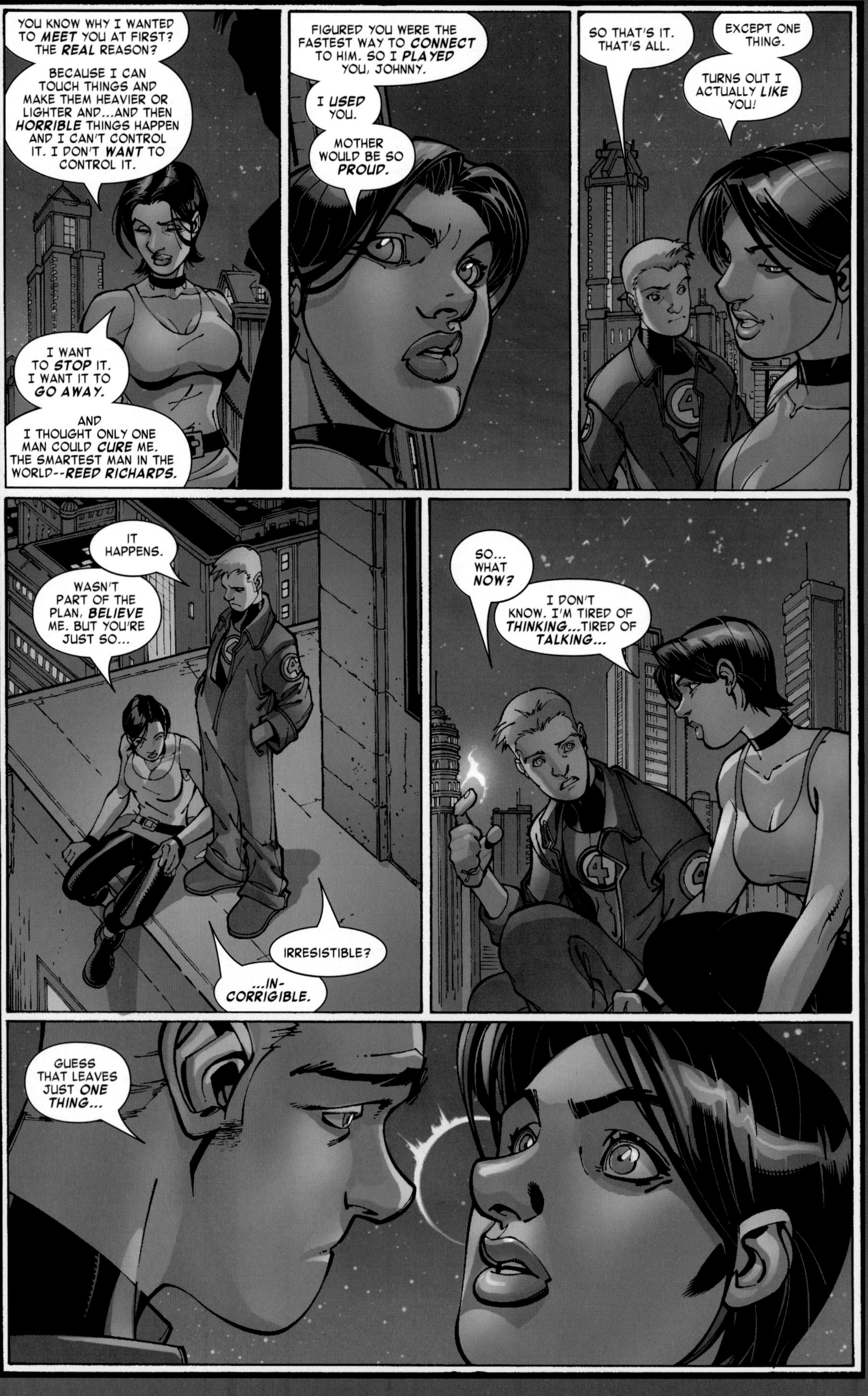

YOU KNOW WHY I WANTED TO MEET YOU AT FIRST? THE REAL REASON?
BECAUSE I CAN TOUCH THINGS AND MAKE THEM HEAVIER OR LIGHTER AND...AND THEN HORRIBLE THINGS HAPPEN AND I CAN'T CONTROL IT. I DON'T WANT TO CONTROL IT.
I WANT TO STOP IT. I WANT IT TO GO AWAY.
AND I THOUGHT ONLY ONE MAN COULD CURE ME. THE SMARTEST MAN IN THE WORLD--REED RICHARDS.
FIGURED YOU WERE THE FASTEST WAY TO CONNECT TO HIM. SO I PLAYED YOU, JOHNNY.
I USED YOU.
MOTHER WOULD BE SO PROUD.
SO THAT'S IT. THAT'S ALL.
EXCEPT ONE THING.
TURNS OUT I ACTUALLY LIKE YOU!
IT HAPPENS.
WASN'T PART OF THE PLAN, BELIEVE ME. BUT YOU'RE JUST SO...
IRRESISTIBLE?
...IN-CORRIGIBLE.
SO... WHAT NOW?
I DON'T KNOW. I'M TIRED OF THINKING...TIRED OF TALKING...
GUESS THAT LEAVES JUST ONE THING...

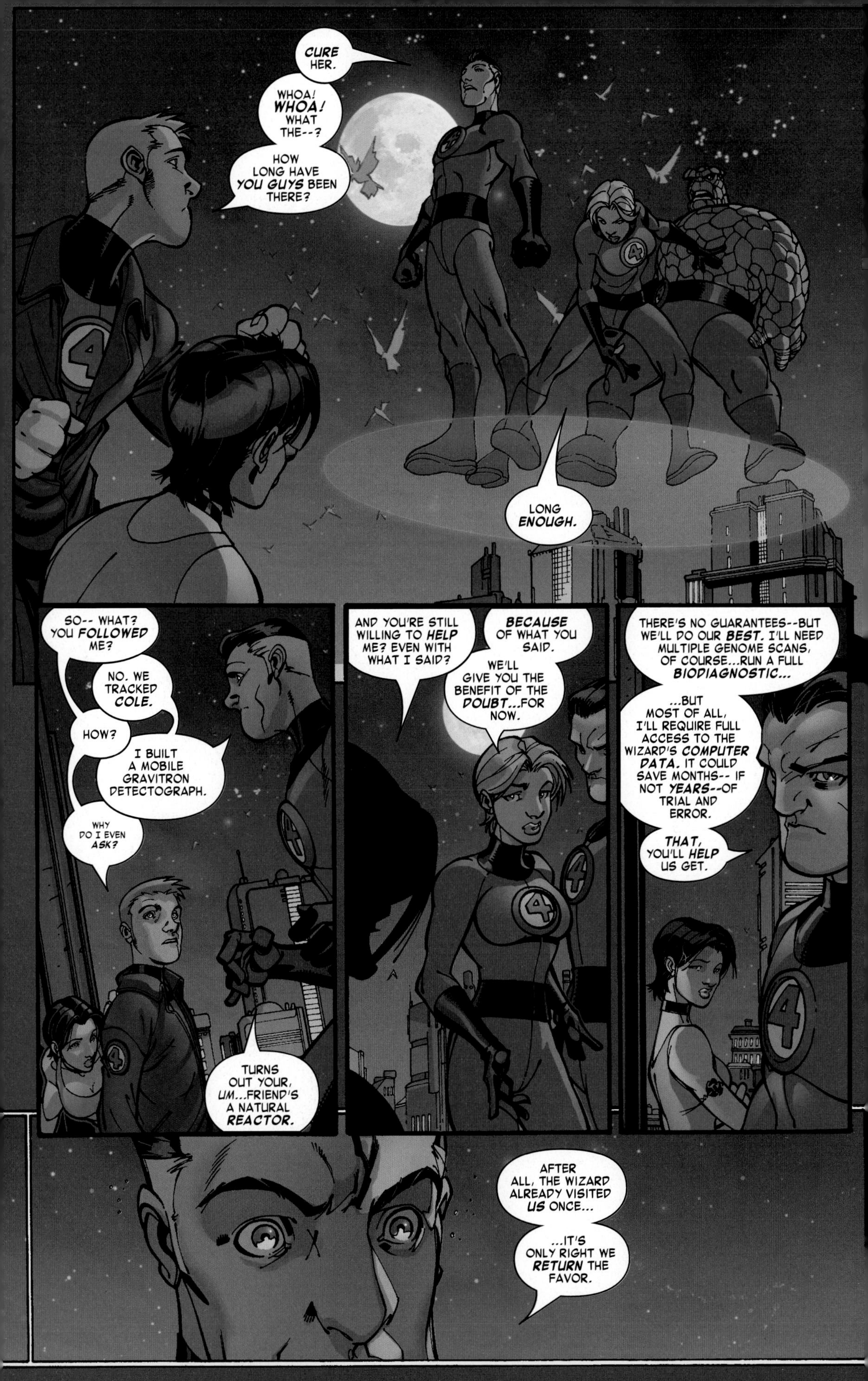
CURE HER.
WHOA! WHOA! WHAT THE--?
HOW LONG HAVE YOU GUYS BEEN THERE?
LONG ENOUGH.
SO-- WHAT? YOU FOLLOWED ME?
NO. WE TRACKED COLE.
HOW?
I BUILT A MOBILE GRAVITRON DETECTOGRAPH.
WHY DO I EVEN ASK?
TURNS OUT YOUR, UM...FRIEND'S A NATURAL REACTOR.
AND YOU'RE STILL WILLING TO HELP ME? EVEN WITH WHAT I SAID?
BECAUSE OF WHAT YOU SAID.
WE'LL GIVE YOU THE BENEFIT OF THE DOUBT...FOR NOW.
THERE'S NO GUARANTEES--BUT WE'LL DO OUR BEST. I'LL NEED MULTIPLE GENOME SCANS, OF COURSE...RUN A FULL BIODIAGNOSTIC...
...BUT MOST OF ALL, I'LL REQUIRE FULL ACCESS TO THE WIZARD'S COMPUTER DATA. IT COULD SAVE MONTHS-- IF NOT YEARS--OF TRIAL AND ERROR.
THAT, YOU'LL HELP US GET.
AFTER ALL, THE WIZARD ALREADY VISITED US ONCE...
...IT'S ONLY RIGHT WE RETURN THE FAVOR.

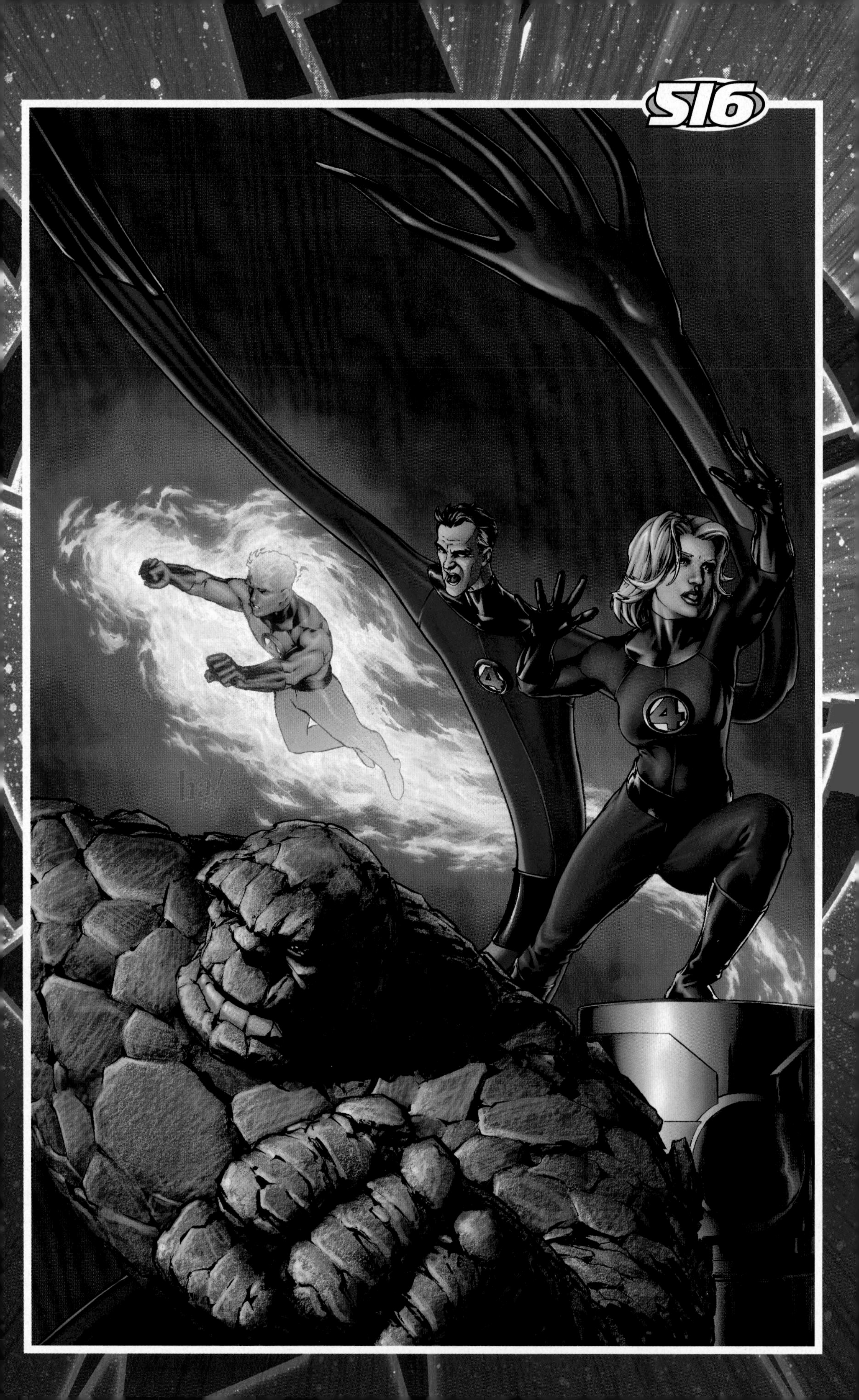
516

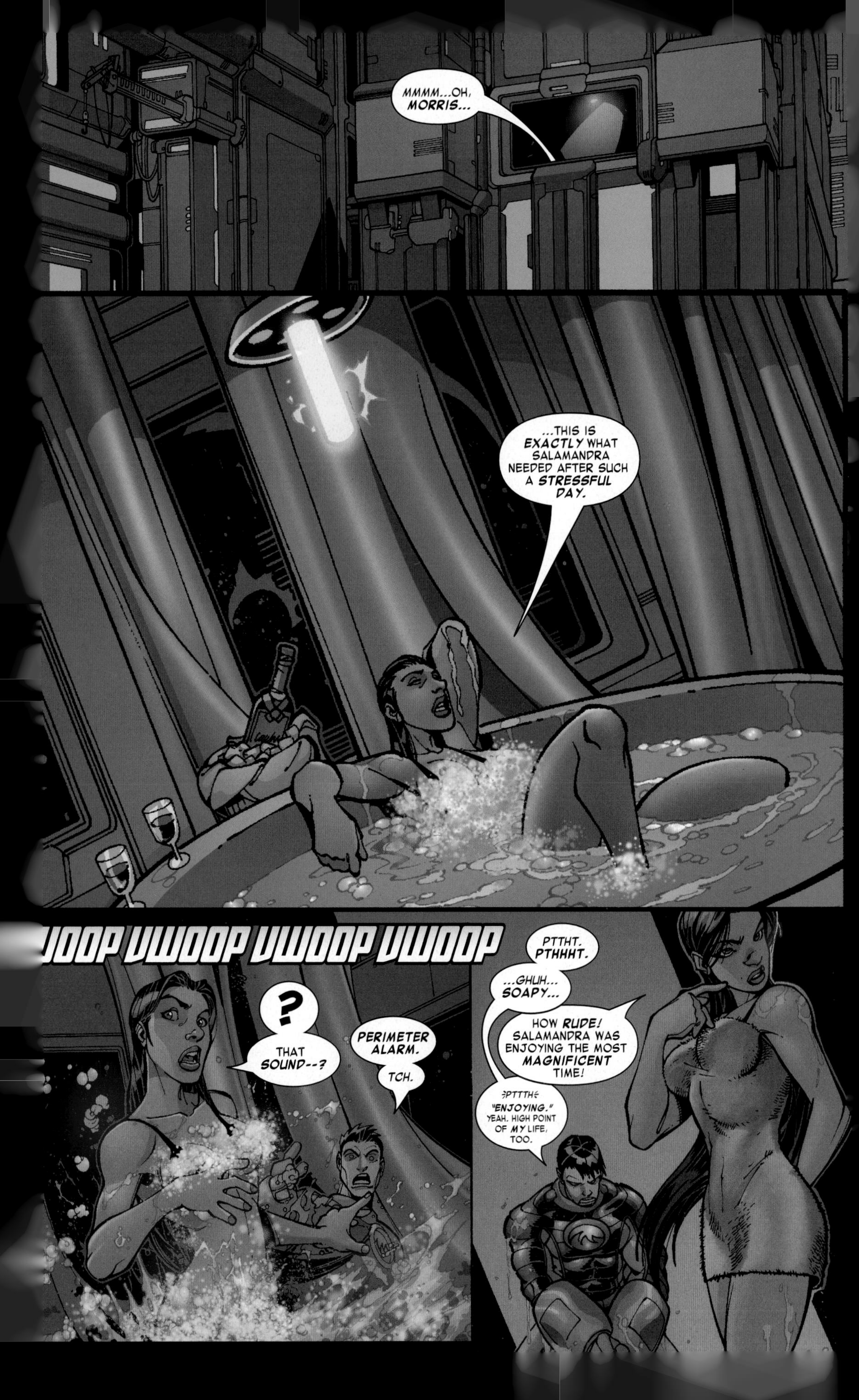
MMMM...OH, MORRIS...
...THIS IS EXACTLY WHAT SALAMANDRA NEEDED AFTER SUCH A STRESSFUL DAY.
VWOOP VWOOP VWOOP VWOOP
?
THAT SOUND--?
PERIMETER ALARM.
TCH.
PTTHT. PTHHHT.
...GHUH... SOAPY...
HOW RUDE! SALAMANDRA WAS ENJOYING THE MOST MAGNIFICENT TIME!
PTTTH
"ENJOYING." YEAH. HIGH POINT OF MY LIFE, TOO.

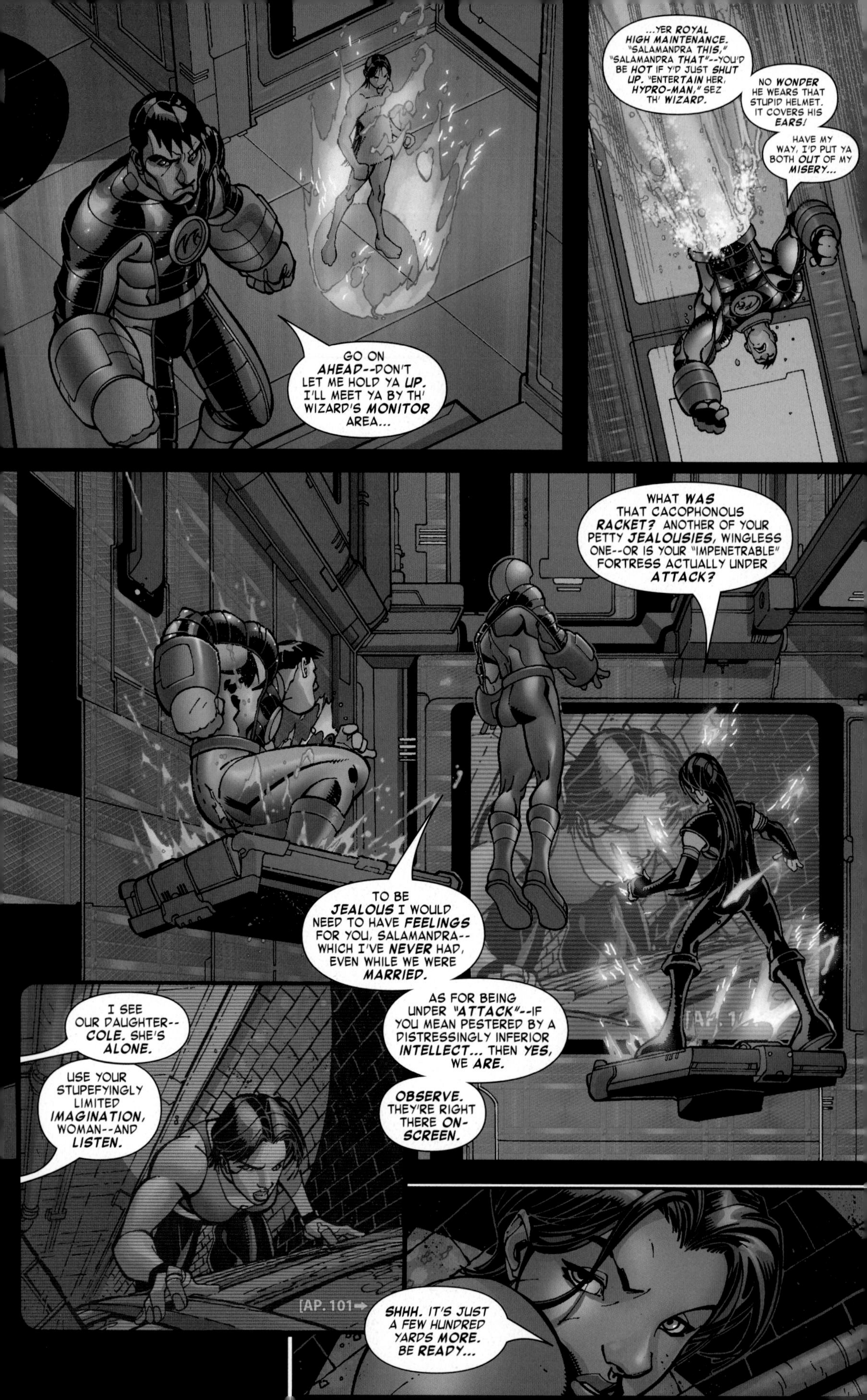
GO ON AHEAD--DON'T LET ME HOLD YA UP. I'LL MEET YA BY TH' WIZARD'S MONITOR AREA...
...YER ROYAL HIGH MAINTENANCE. "SALAMANDRA THIS," "SALAMANDRA THAT"--YOU'D BE HOT IF Y'D JUST SHUT UP. "ENTERTAIN HER, HYDRO-MAN," SEZ TH' WIZARD.
NO WONDER HE WEARS THAT STUPID HELMET. IT COVERS HIS EARS!
HAVE MY WAY, I'D PUT YA BOTH OUT OF MY MISERY...
WHAT WAS THAT CACOPHONOUS RACKET? ANOTHER OF YOUR PETTY JEALOUSIES, WINGLESS ONE--OR IS YOUR "IMPENETRABLE" FORTRESS ACTUALLY UNDER ATTACK?
TO BE JEALOUS I WOULD NEED TO HAVE FEELINGS FOR YOU, SALAMANDRA--WHICH I'VE NEVER HAD, EVEN WHILE WE WERE MARRIED.
AS FOR BEING UNDER "ATTACK"--IF YOU MEAN PESTERED BY A DISTRESSINGLY INFERIOR INTELLECT... THEN YES, WE ARE.
OBSERVE. THEY'RE RIGHT THERE ON-SCREEN.
I SEE OUR DAUGHTER--COLE. SHE'S ALONE.
USE YOUR STUPEFYINGLY LIMITED IMAGINATION, WOMAN--AND LISTEN.
[AP. 101→
SHHH. IT'S JUST A FEW HUNDRED YARDS MORE. BE READY...

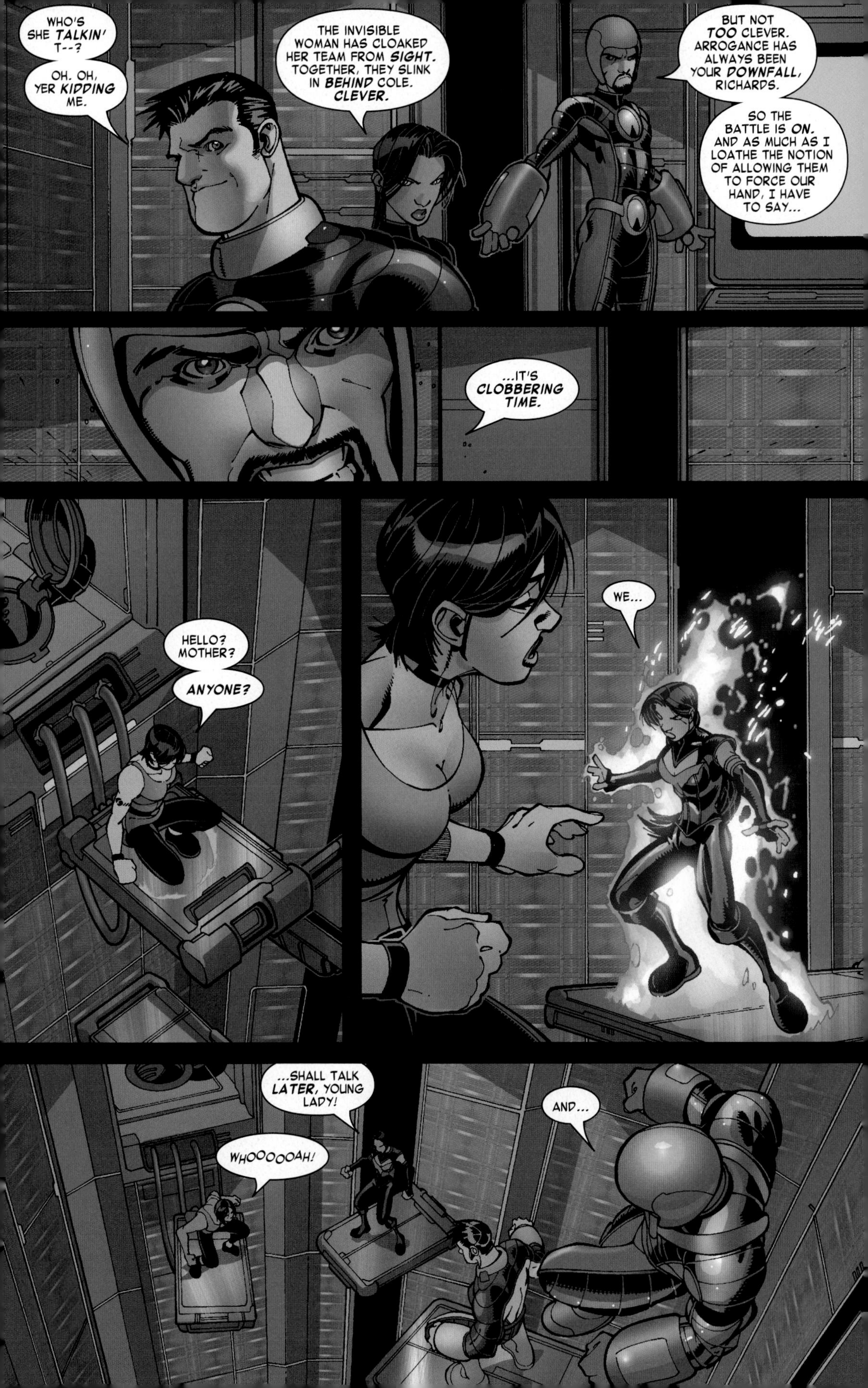
WHO'S SHE TALKIN' T--?
OH. OH, YER KIDDING ME.
THE INVISIBLE WOMAN HAS CLOAKED HER TEAM FROM SIGHT. TOGETHER, THEY SLINK IN BEHIND COLE. CLEVER.
BUT NOT TOO CLEVER. ARROGANCE HAS ALWAYS BEEN YOUR DOWNFALL, RICHARDS.
SO THE BATTLE IS ON. AND AS MUCH AS I LOATHE THE NOTION OF ALLOWING THEM TO FORCE OUR HAND, I HAVE TO SAY...
...IT'S CLOBBERING TIME.
HELLO? MOTHER?
ANYONE?
WE...
...SHALL TALK LATER, YOUNG LADY!
WHOOOOOAH!
AND...

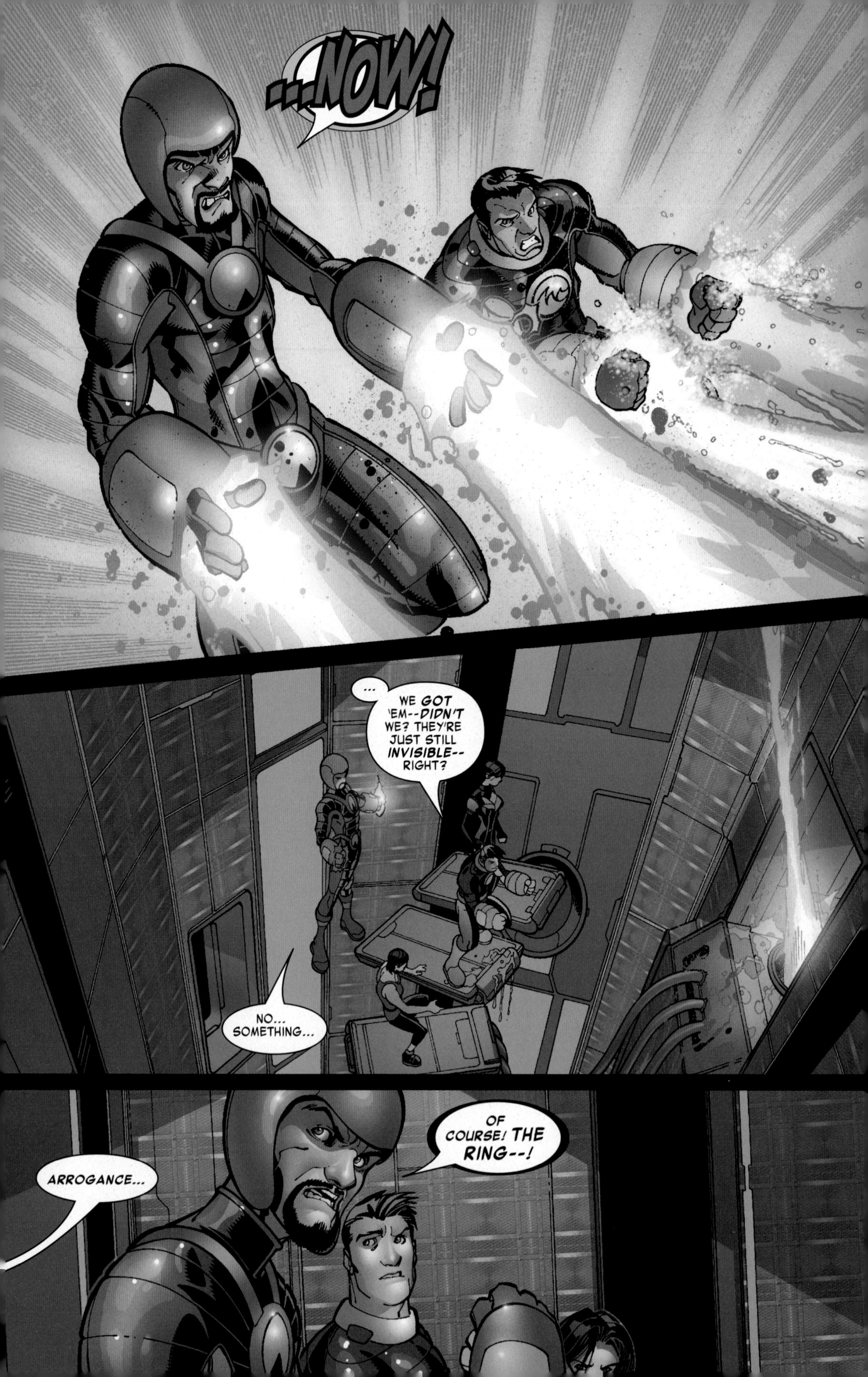

...NOW!
...
WE GOT 'EM--DIDN'T WE? THEY'RE JUST STILL INVISIBLE--RIGHT?
NO... SOMETHING...
ARROGANCE...
OF COURSE! THE RING--!

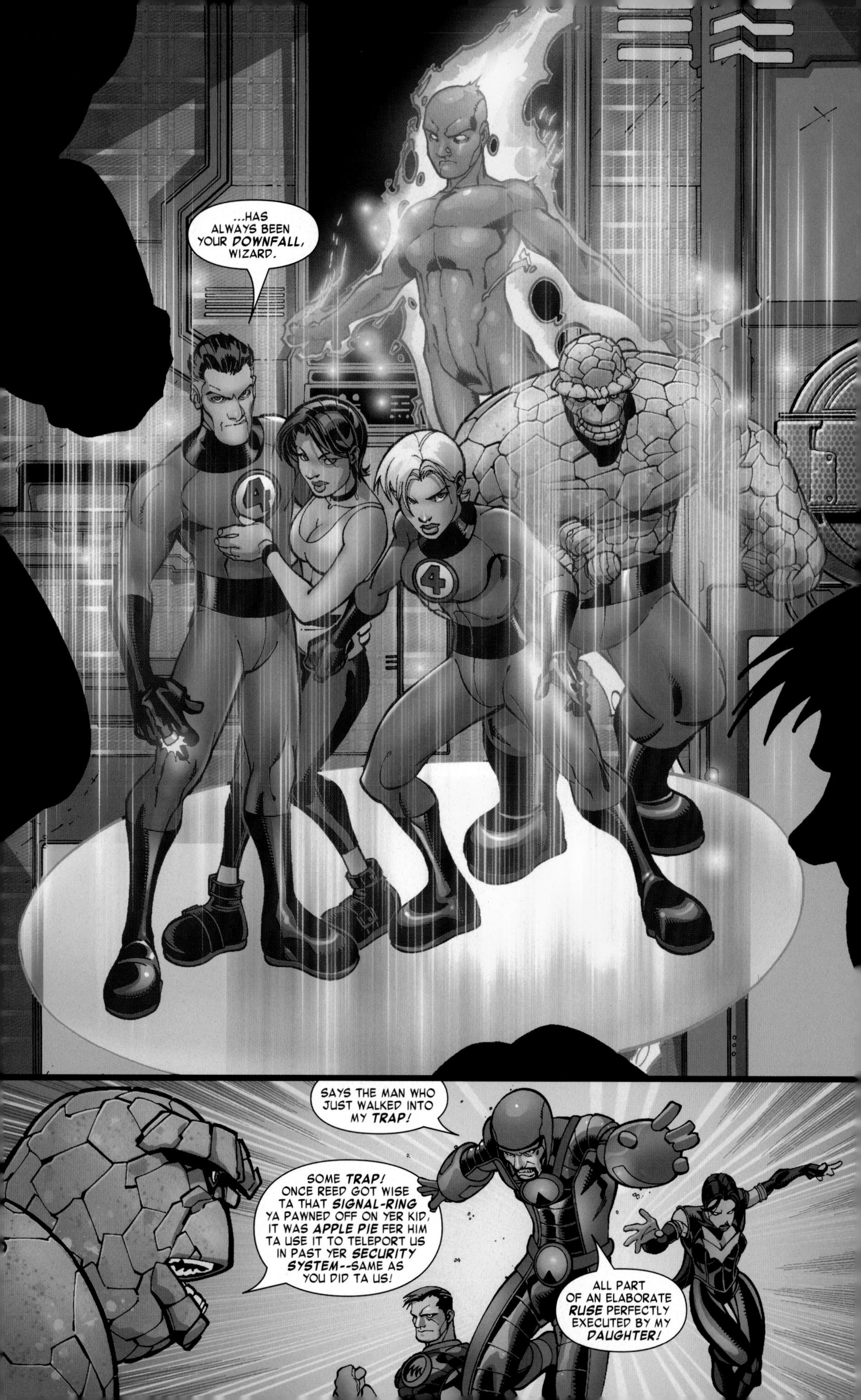
...HAS ALWAYS BEEN YOUR DOWNFALL, WIZARD.
SAYS THE MAN WHO JUST WALKED INTO MY TRAP!
SOME TRAP! ONCE REED GOT WISE TA THAT SIGNAL-RING YA PAWNED OFF ON YER KID, IT WAS APPLE PIE FER HIM TA USE IT TO TELEPORT US IN PAST YER SECURITY SYSTEM--SAME AS YOU DID TA US!
ALL PART OF AN ELABORATE RUSE PERFECTLY EXECUTED BY MY DAUGHTER!

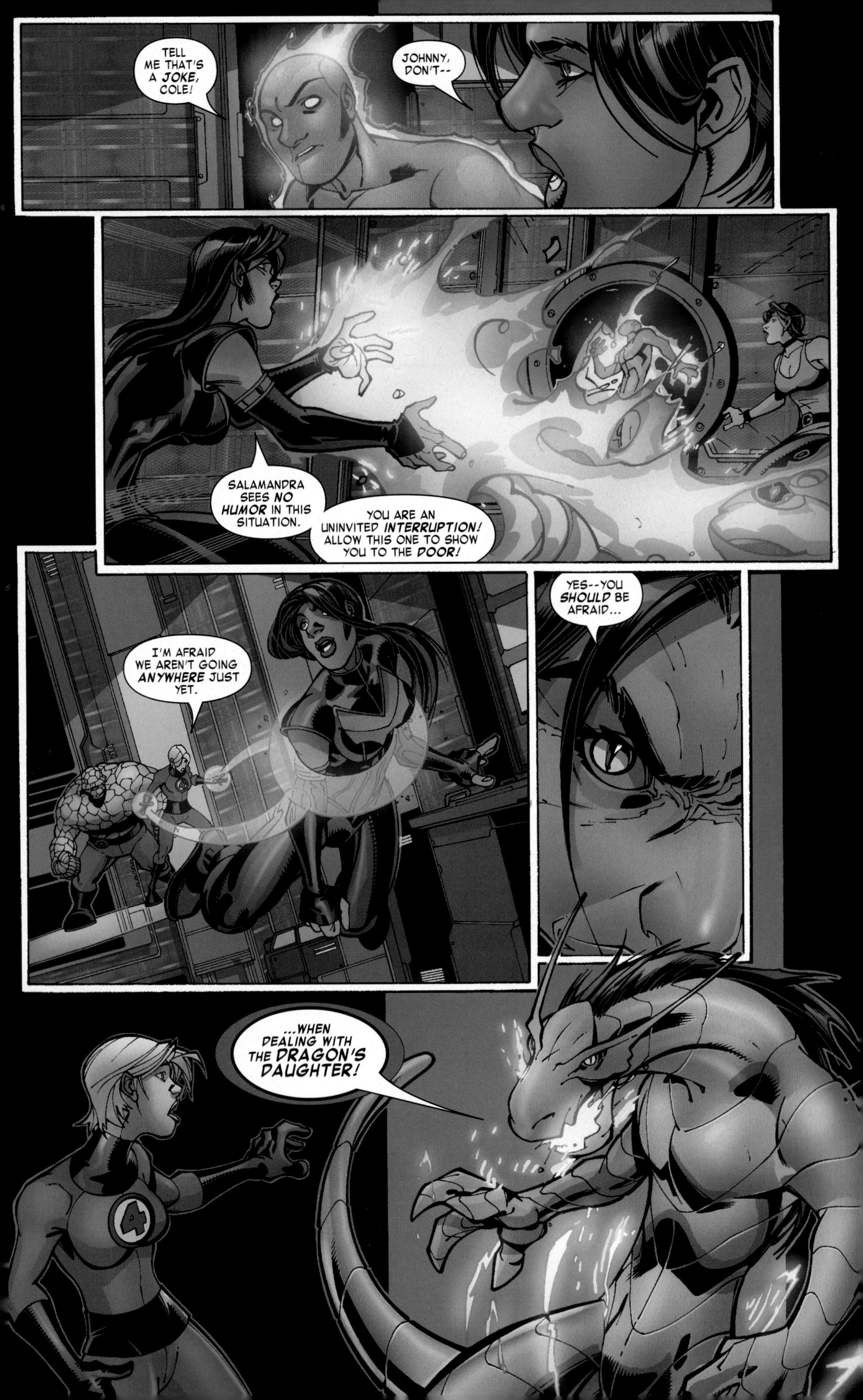
TELL ME THAT'S A JOKE, COLE!
JOHNNY, DON'T--
SALAMANDRA SEES NO HUMOR IN THIS SITUATION.
YOU ARE AN UNINVITED INTERRUPTION! ALLOW THIS ONE TO SHOW YOU TO THE DOOR!
I'M AFRAID WE AREN'T GOING ANYWHERE JUST YET.
YES--YOU SHOULD BE AFRAID...
...WHEN DEALING WITH THE DRAGON'S DAUGHTER!

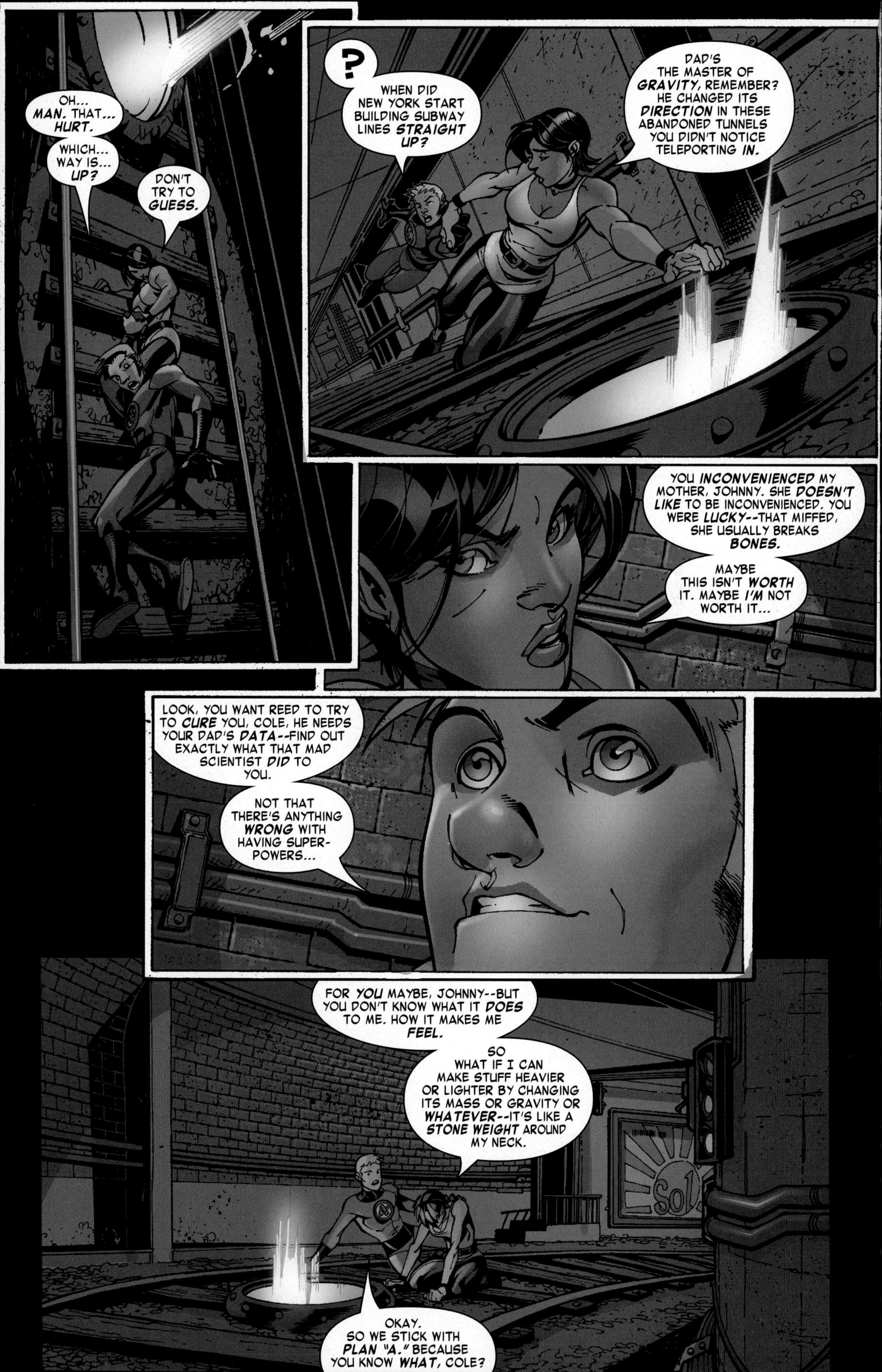

OH... MAN. THAT... HURT.
WHICH... WAY IS... UP?
DON'T TRY TO GUESS.
?
WHEN DID NEW YORK START BUILDING SUBWAY LINES STRAIGHT UP?
DAD'S THE MASTER OF GRAVITY, REMEMBER? HE CHANGED ITS DIRECTION IN THESE ABANDONED TUNNELS YOU DIDN'T NOTICE TELEPORTING IN.
YOU INCONVENIENCED MY MOTHER, JOHNNY. SHE DOESN'T LIKE TO BE INCONVENIENCED. YOU WERE LUCKY--THAT MIFFED, SHE USUALLY BREAKS BONES.
MAYBE THIS ISN'T WORTH IT. MAYBE I'M NOT WORTH IT...
LOOK, YOU WANT REED TO TRY TO CURE YOU, COLE, HE NEEDS YOUR DAD'S DATA--FIND OUT EXACTLY WHAT THAT MAD SCIENTIST DID TO YOU.
NOT THAT THERE'S ANYTHING WRONG WITH HAVING SUPER-POWERS...
FOR YOU MAYBE, JOHNNY--BUT YOU DON'T KNOW WHAT IT DOES TO ME. HOW IT MAKES ME FEEL.
SO WHAT IF I CAN MAKE STUFF HEAVIER OR LIGHTER BY CHANGING ITS MASS OR GRAVITY OR WHATEVER--IT'S LIKE A STONE WEIGHT AROUND MY NECK.
Sol
OKAY. SO WE STICK WITH PLAN "A." BECAUSE YOU KNOW WHAT, COLE?

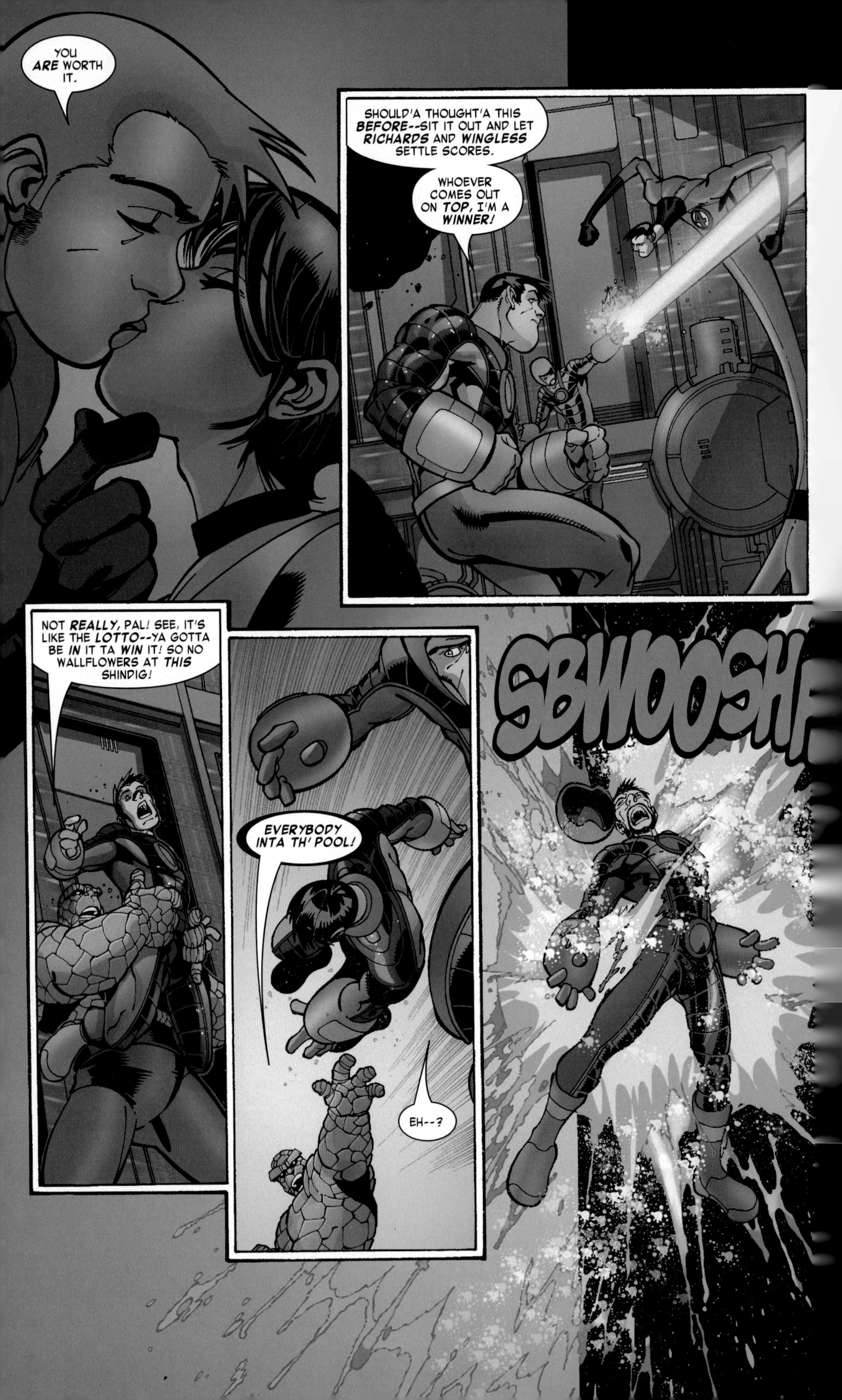

YOU ARE WORTH IT.
SHOULD'A THOUGHT'A THIS BEFORE--SIT IT OUT AND LET RICHARDS AND WINGLESS SETTLE SCORES.
WHOEVER COMES OUT ON TOP, I'M A WINNER!
NOT REALLY, PAL! SEE, IT'S LIKE THE LOTTO--YA GOTTA BE IN IT TA WIN IT! SO NO WALLFLOWERS AT THIS SHINDIG!
EVERYBODY INTA TH' POOL!
EH--?
SBWOOSH

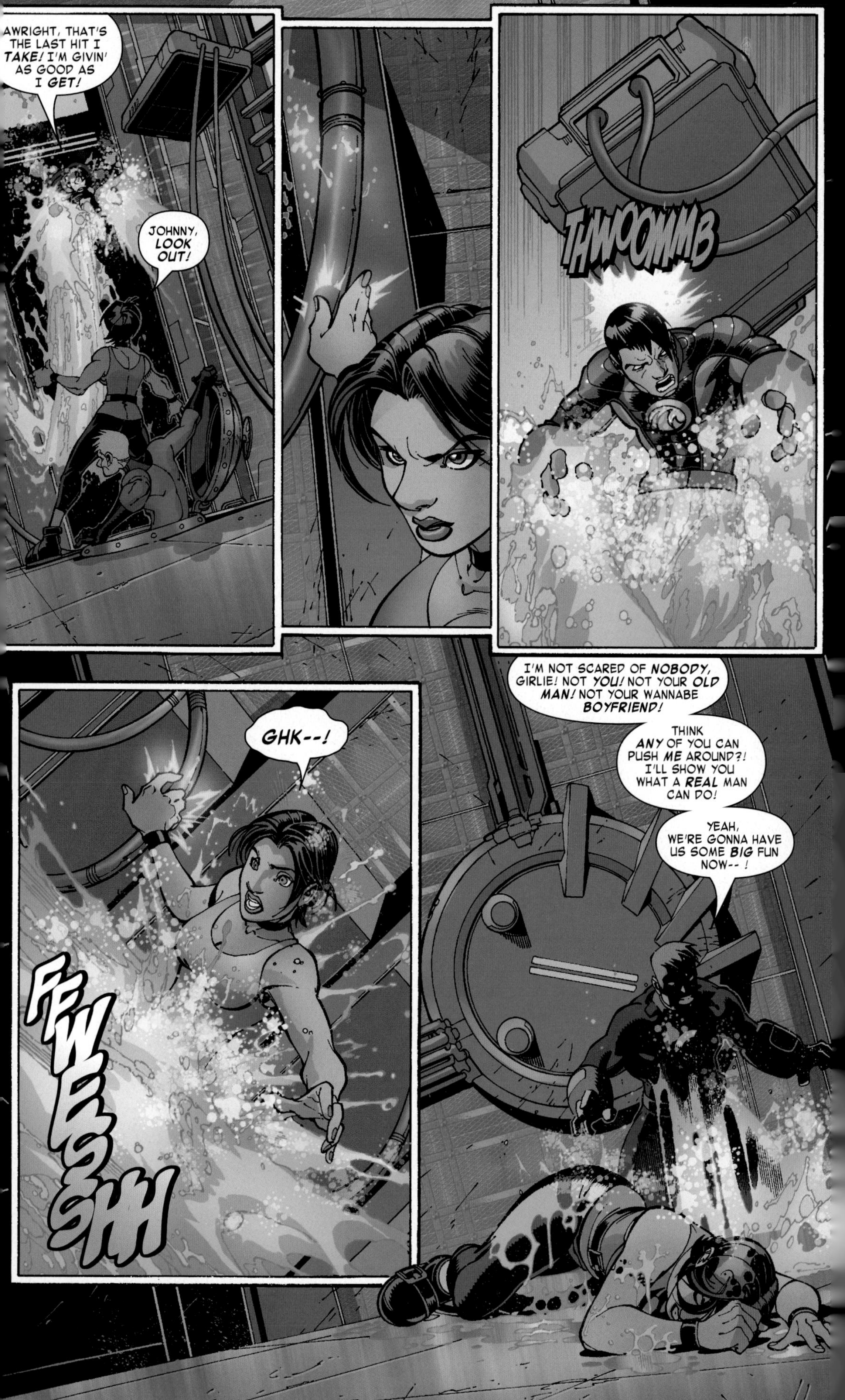

AWRIGHT, THAT'S THE LAST HIT I *TAKE!* I'M GIVIN' AS GOOD AS I *GET!*
JOHNNY, *LOOK OUT!*
THWOOMMB
GHK--!
FFWSSHH
I'M NOT SCARED OF *NOBODY,* GIRLIE! NOT *YOU!* NOT YOUR *OLD MAN!* NOT YOUR WANNABE *BOYFRIEND!*
THINK *ANY* OF YOU CAN PUSH *ME* AROUND?! I'LL SHOW YOU WHAT A *REAL* MAN CAN DO!
YEAH, WE'RE GONNA HAVE US SOME *BIG* FUN NOW-- !

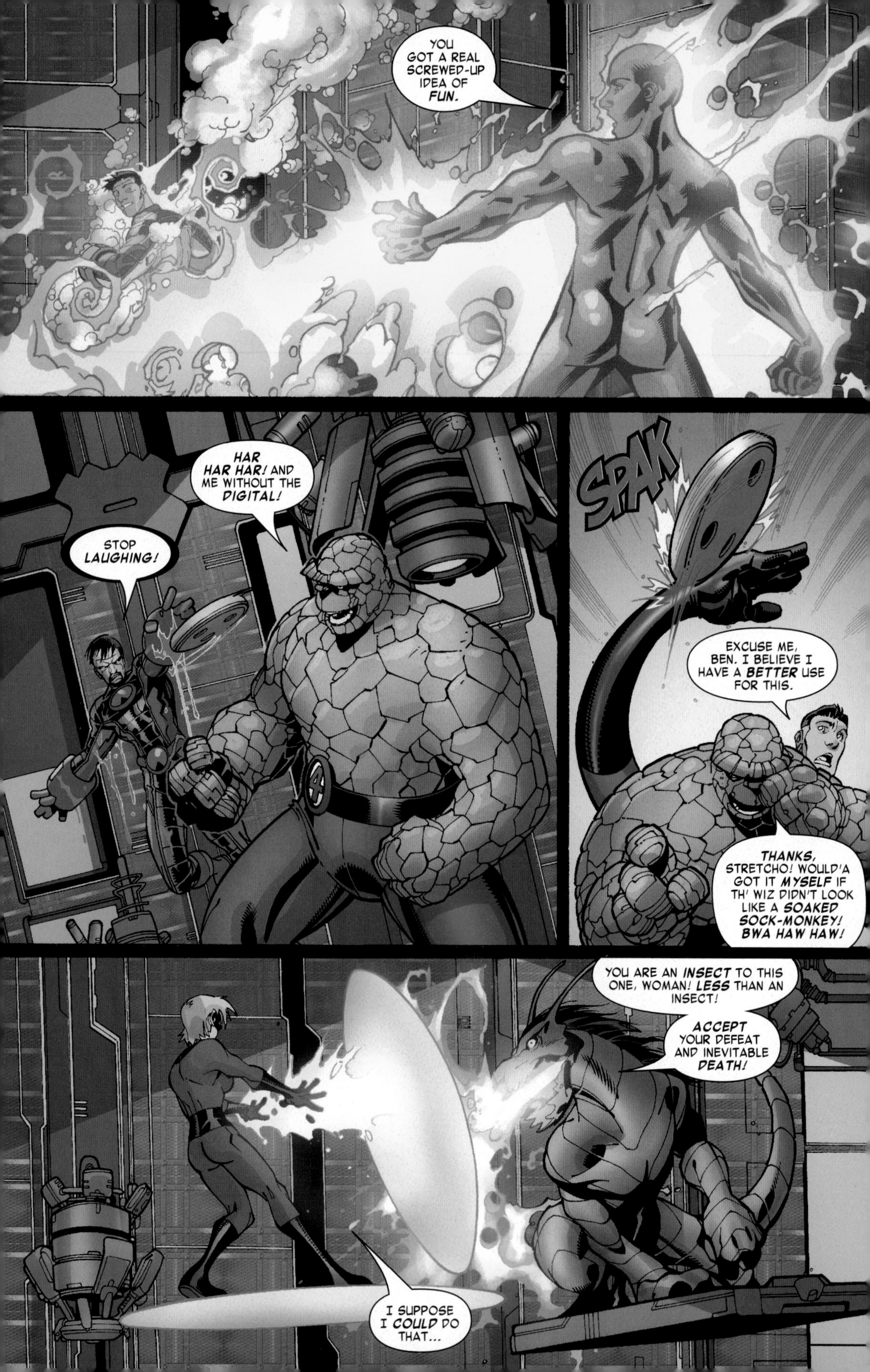
YOU GOT A REAL SCREWED-UP IDEA OF FUN.
HAR HAR HAR! AND ME WITHOUT THE DIGITAL!
STOP LAUGHING!
SPAK
EXCUSE ME, BEN. I BELIEVE I HAVE A BETTER USE FOR THIS.
THANKS, STRETCHO! WOULD'A GOT IT MYSELF IF TH' WIZ DIDN'T LOOK LIKE A SOAKED SOCK-MONKEY! BWA HAW HAW!
YOU ARE AN INSECT TO THIS ONE, WOMAN! LESS THAN AN INSECT!
ACCEPT YOUR DEFEAT AND INEVITABLE DEATH!
I SUPPOSE I COULD DO THAT...

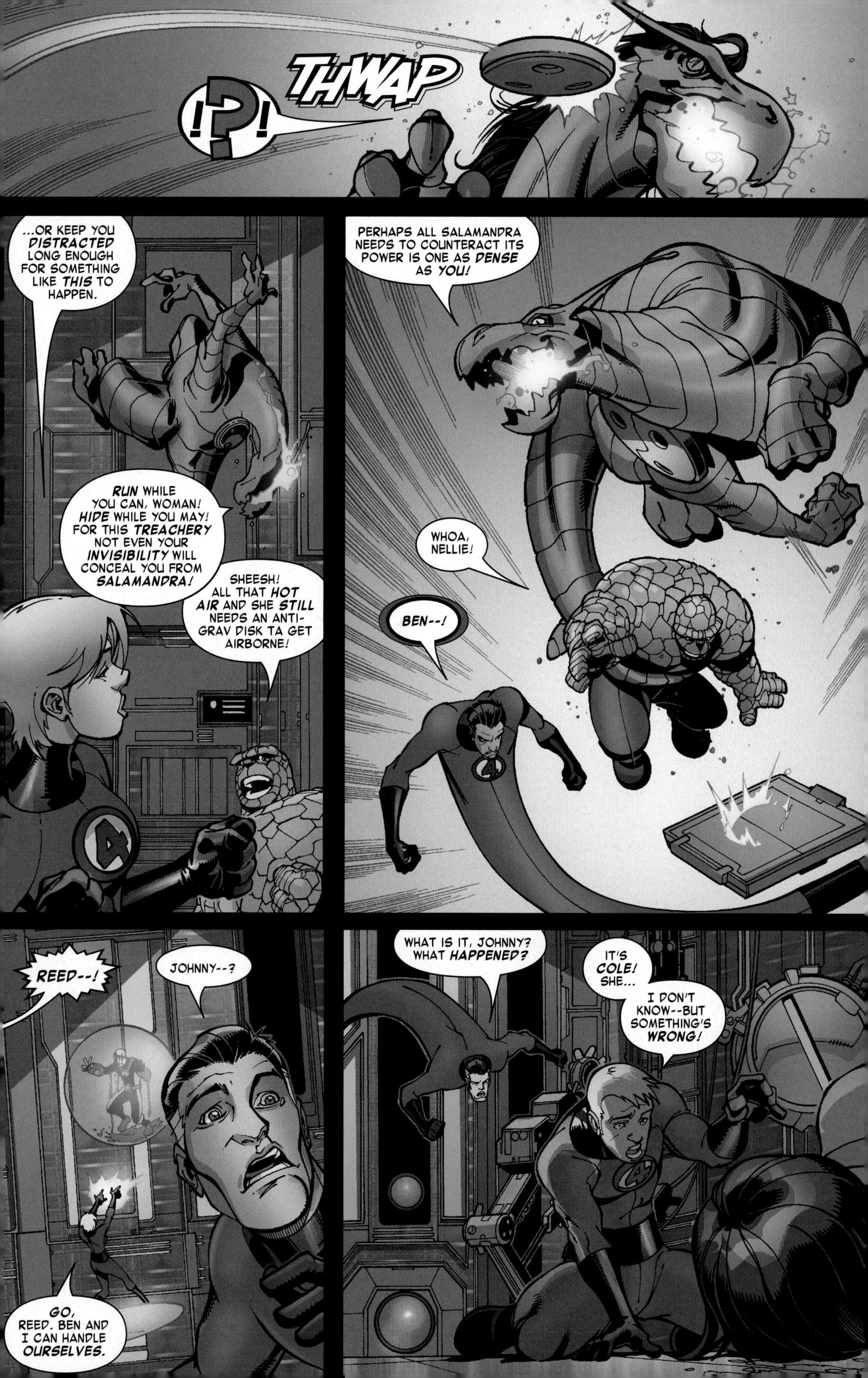
!?!
THWAP
...OR KEEP YOU DISTRACTED LONG ENOUGH FOR SOMETHING LIKE THIS TO HAPPEN.
RUN WHILE YOU CAN, WOMAN! HIDE WHILE YOU MAY! FOR THIS TREACHERY NOT EVEN YOUR INVISIBILITY WILL CONCEAL YOU FROM SALAMANDRA!
SHEESH! ALL THAT HOT AIR AND SHE STILL NEEDS AN ANTI-GRAV DISK TA GET AIRBORNE!
PERHAPS ALL SALAMANDRA NEEDS TO COUNTERACT ITS POWER IS ONE AS DENSE AS YOU!
WHOA, NELLIE!
BEN--!
REED--!
JOHNNY--?
GO, REED. BEN AND I CAN HANDLE OURSELVES.
WHAT IS IT, JOHNNY? WHAT HAPPENED?
IT'S COLE! SHE...
I DON'T KNOW--BUT SOMETHING'S WRONG!

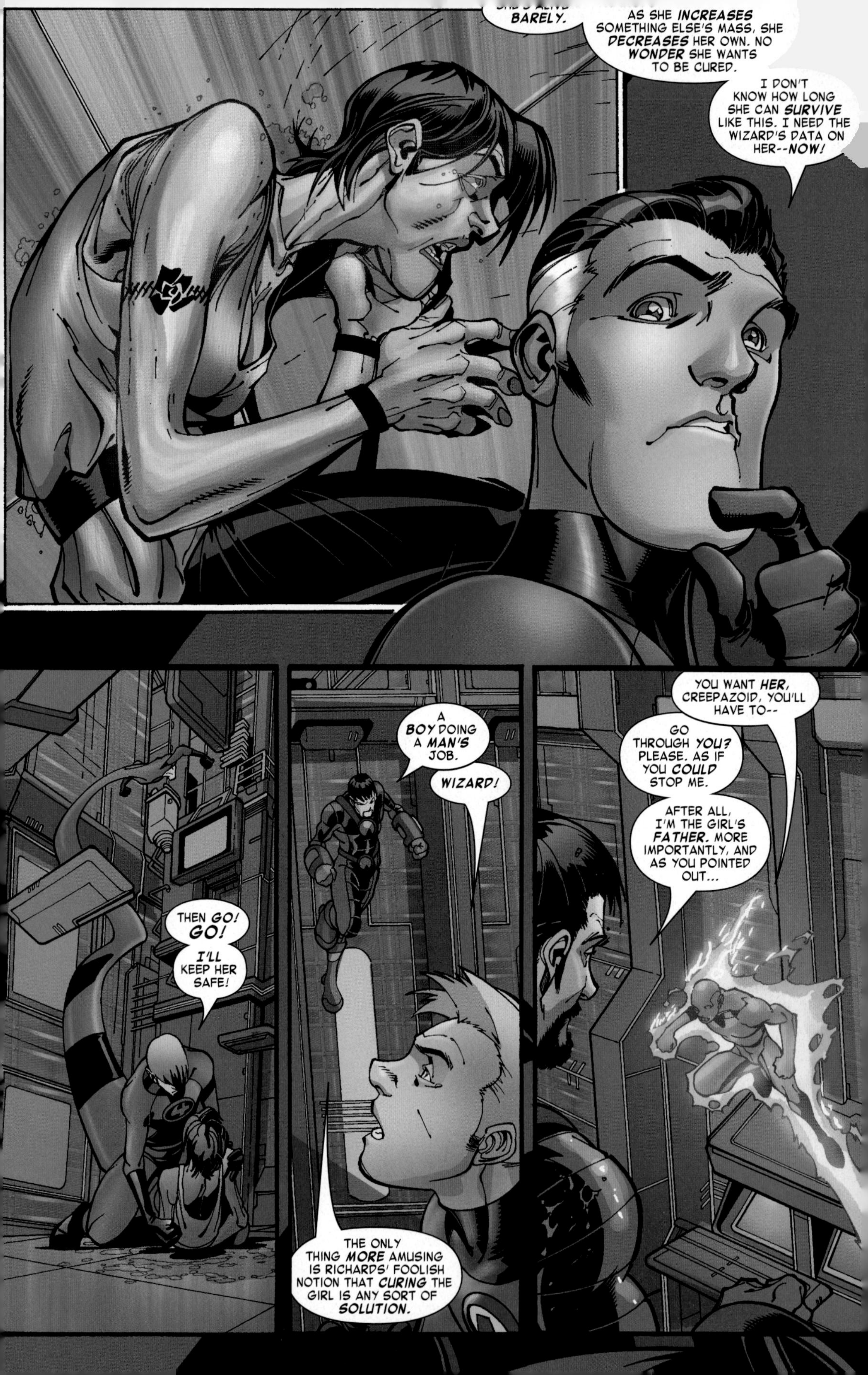

BARELY.
AS SHE INCREASES SOMETHING ELSE'S MASS, SHE DECREASES HER OWN. NO WONDER SHE WANTS TO BE CURED.
I DON'T KNOW HOW LONG SHE CAN SURVIVE LIKE THIS. I NEED THE WIZARD'S DATA ON HER--NOW!
THEN GO! GO!
I'LL KEEP HER SAFE!
A BOY DOING A MAN'S JOB.
WIZARD!
THE ONLY THING MORE AMUSING IS RICHARDS' FOOLISH NOTION THAT CURING THE GIRL IS ANY SORT OF SOLUTION.
YOU WANT HER, CREEPAZOID, YOU'LL HAVE TO--
GO THROUGH YOU? PLEASE. AS IF YOU COULD STOP ME.
AFTER ALL, I'M THE GIRL'S FATHER. MORE IMPORTANTLY, AND AS YOU POINTED OUT...

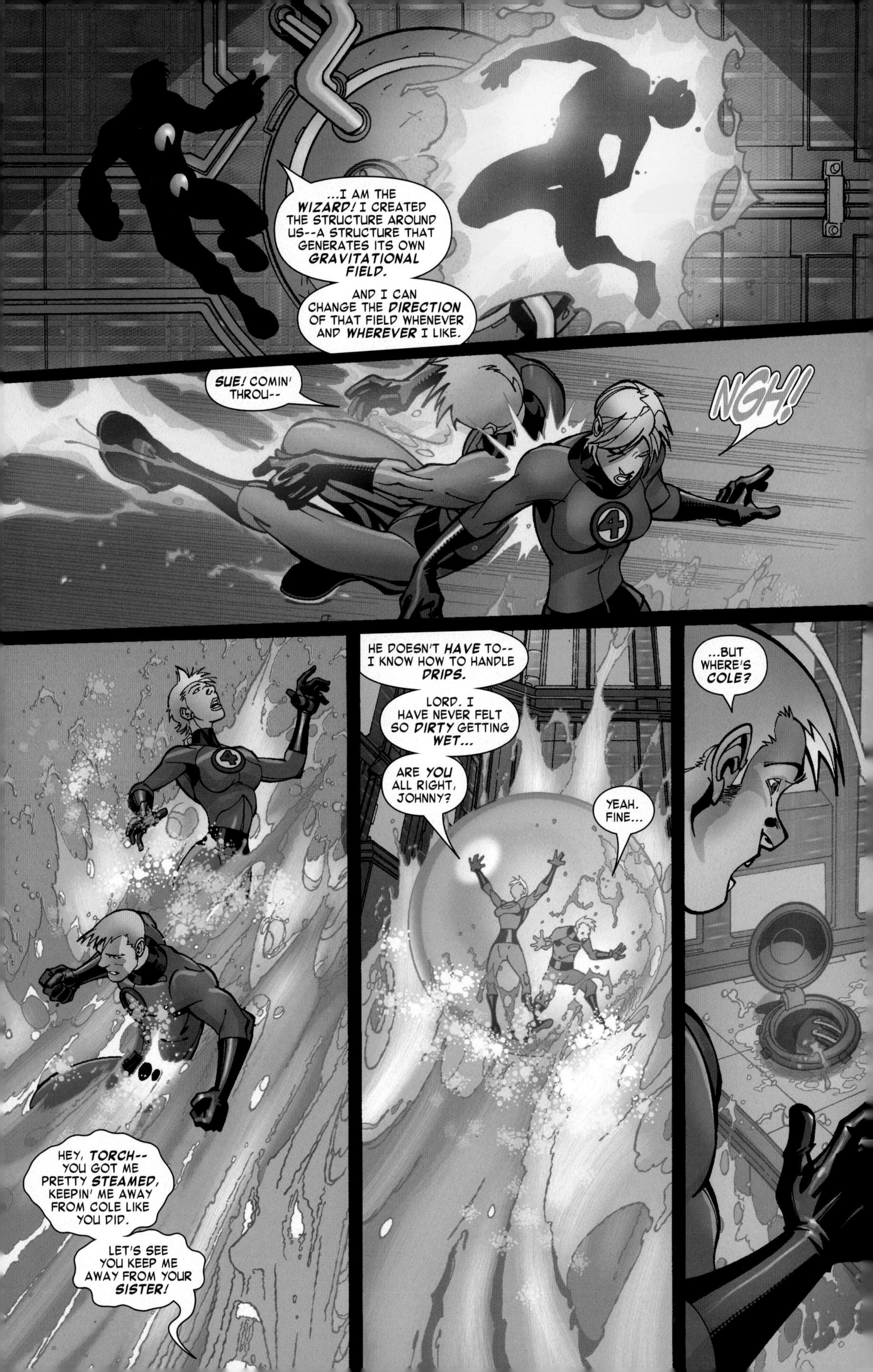
...I AM THE WIZARD! I CREATED THE STRUCTURE AROUND US--A STRUCTURE THAT GENERATES ITS OWN GRAVITATIONAL FIELD.
AND I CAN CHANGE THE DIRECTION OF THAT FIELD WHENEVER AND WHEREVER I LIKE.
SUE! COMIN' THROU--
NGH!
HEY, TORCH--YOU GOT ME PRETTY STEAMED, KEEPIN' ME AWAY FROM COLE LIKE YOU DID.
LET'S SEE YOU KEEP ME AWAY FROM YOUR SISTER!
HE DOESN'T HAVE TO--I KNOW HOW TO HANDLE DRIPS.
LORD. I HAVE NEVER FELT SO DIRTY GETTING WET...
ARE YOU ALL RIGHT, JOHNNY?
YEAH. FINE...
...BUT WHERE'S COLE?

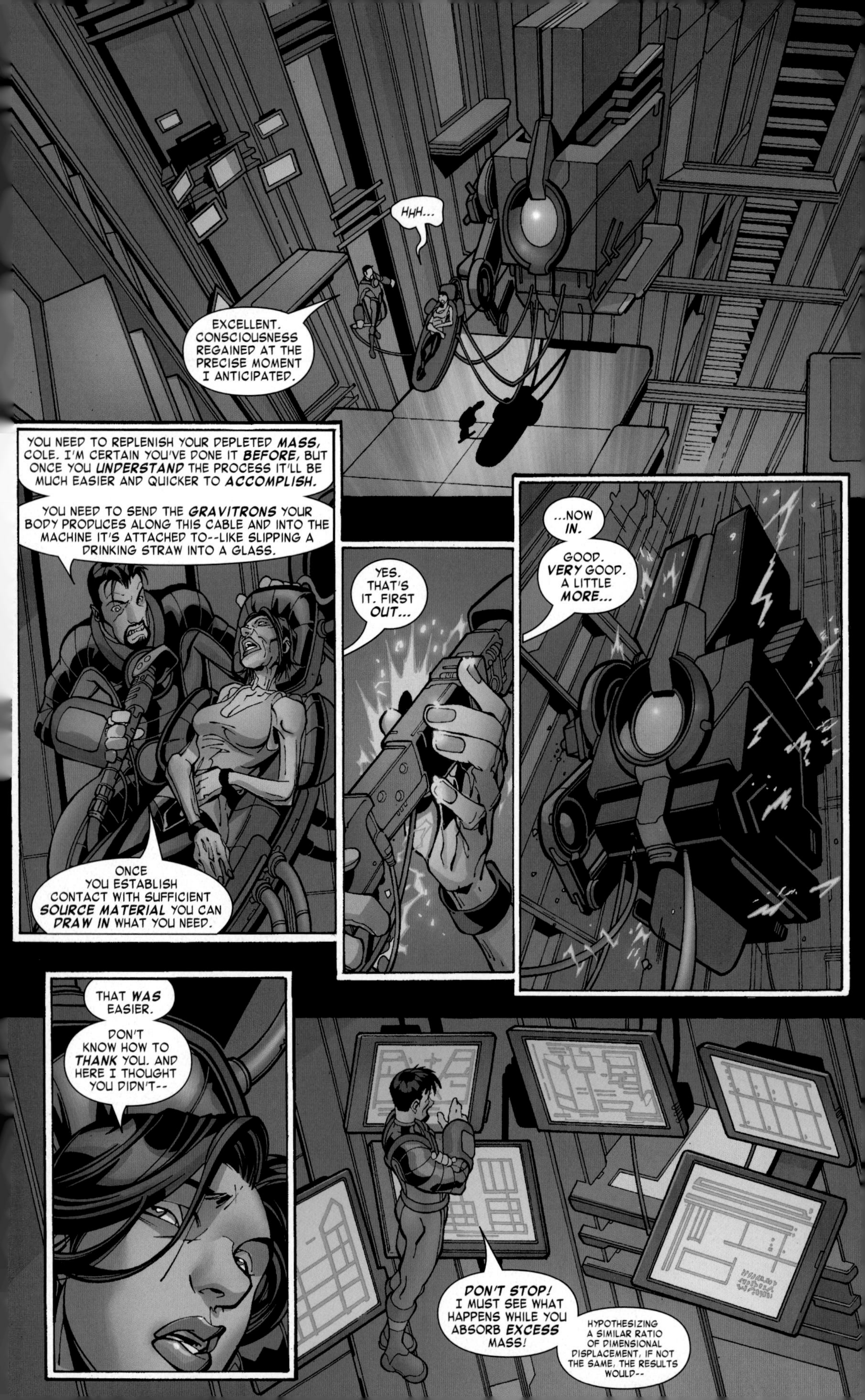
HHH...
EXCELLENT. CONSCIOUSNESS REGAINED AT THE PRECISE MOMENT I ANTICIPATED.
YOU NEED TO REPLENISH YOUR DEPLETED MASS, COLE. I'M CERTAIN YOU'VE DONE IT BEFORE, BUT ONCE YOU UNDERSTAND THE PROCESS IT'LL BE MUCH EASIER AND QUICKER TO ACCOMPLISH.
YOU NEED TO SEND THE GRAVITRONS YOUR BODY PRODUCES ALONG THIS CABLE AND INTO THE MACHINE IT'S ATTACHED TO--LIKE SLIPPING A DRINKING STRAW INTO A GLASS.
ONCE YOU ESTABLISH CONTACT WITH SUFFICIENT SOURCE MATERIAL YOU CAN DRAW IN WHAT YOU NEED.
YES. THAT'S IT. FIRST OUT...
...NOW IN.
GOOD. VERY GOOD. A LITTLE MORE...
THAT WAS EASIER.
DON'T KNOW HOW TO THANK YOU. AND HERE I THOUGHT YOU DIDN'T--
DON'T STOP! I MUST SEE WHAT HAPPENS WHILE YOU ABSORB EXCESS MASS!
HYPOTHESIZING A SIMILAR RATIO OF DIMENSIONAL DISPLACEMENT, IF NOT THE SAME, THE RESULTS WOULD--

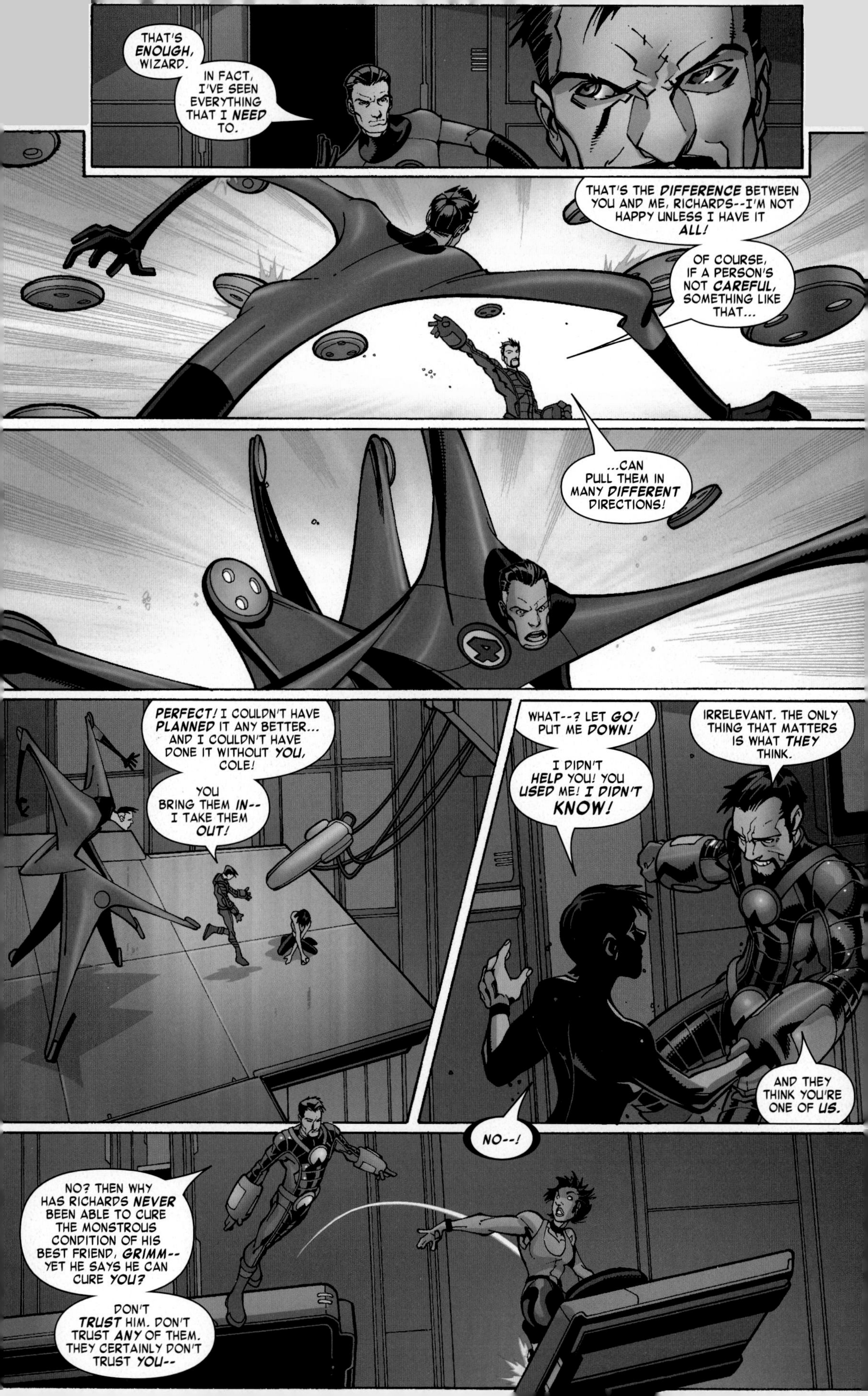
THAT'S *ENOUGH,* WIZARD.
IN FACT, I'VE SEEN EVERYTHING THAT I *NEED* TO.
THAT'S THE *DIFFERENCE* BETWEEN YOU AND ME, RICHARDS--I'M NOT HAPPY UNLESS I HAVE IT *ALL!*
OF COURSE, IF A PERSON'S NOT *CAREFUL,* SOMETHING LIKE THAT...
...CAN PULL THEM IN MANY *DIFFERENT* DIRECTIONS!
PERFECT! I COULDN'T HAVE *PLANNED* IT ANY BETTER... AND I COULDN'T HAVE DONE IT WITHOUT *YOU,* COLE!
YOU BRING THEM *IN--* I TAKE THEM *OUT!*
WHAT--? LET *GO!* PUT ME *DOWN!*
I DIDN'T *HELP* YOU! YOU *USED* ME! *I DIDN'T KNOW!*
IRRELEVANT. THE ONLY THING THAT MATTERS IS WHAT *THEY* THINK.
AND THEY THINK YOU'RE ONE OF *US.*
NO--!
NO? THEN WHY HAS RICHARDS *NEVER* BEEN ABLE TO CURE THE MONSTROUS CONDITION OF HIS BEST FRIEND, *GRIMM--* YET HE SAYS HE CAN CURE *YOU?*
DON'T *TRUST* HIM. DON'T TRUST *ANY* OF THEM. THEY CERTAINLY DON'T TRUST *YOU--*

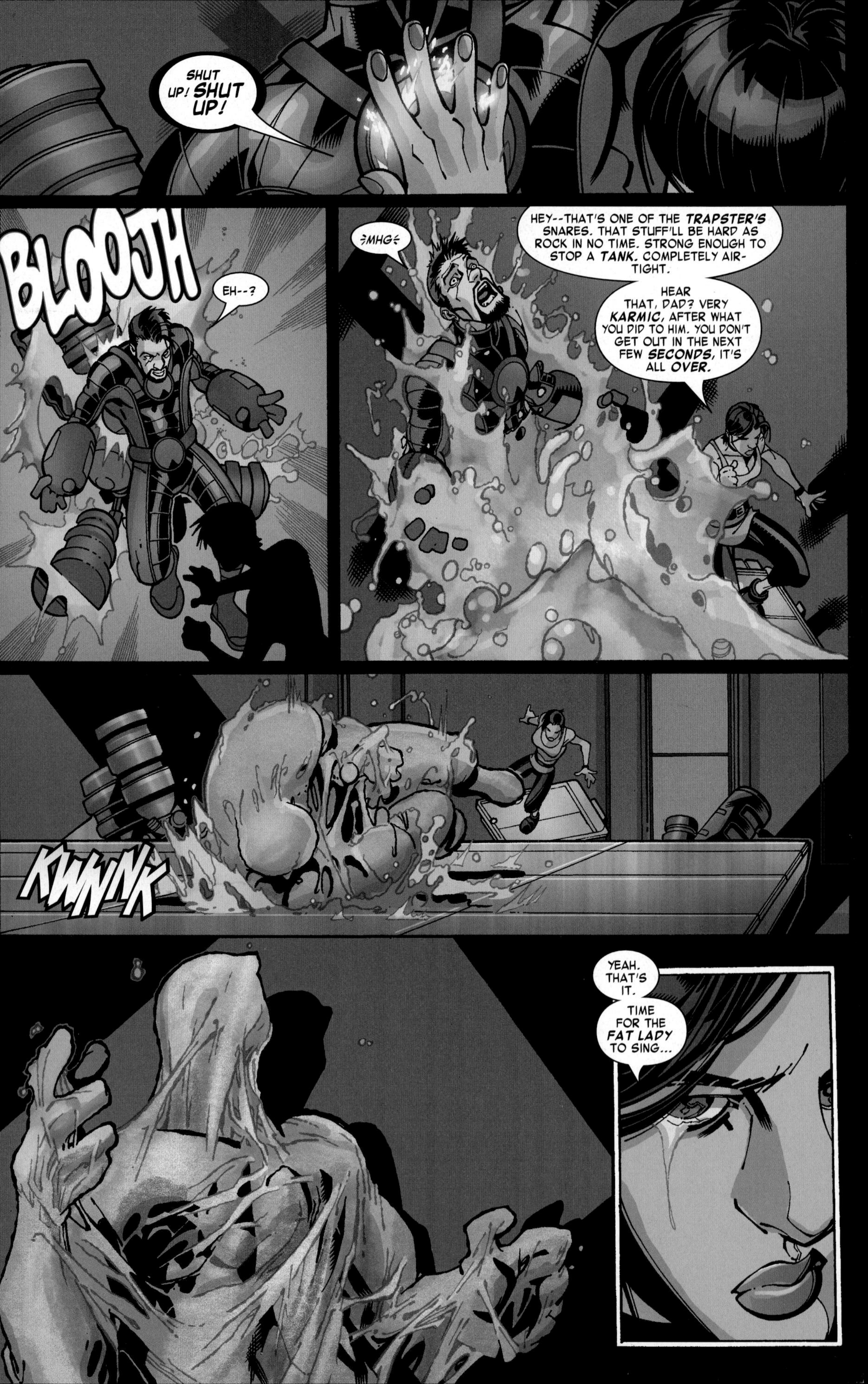
SHUT UP! SHUT UP!
BLOOJH
EH--?
≤MHG≤
HEY--THAT'S ONE OF THE TRAPSTER'S SNARES. THAT STUFF'LL BE HARD AS ROCK IN NO TIME. STRONG ENOUGH TO STOP A TANK. COMPLETELY AIR-TIGHT.
HEAR THAT, DAD? VERY KARMIC, AFTER WHAT YOU DID TO HIM. YOU DON'T GET OUT IN THE NEXT FEW SECONDS, IT'S ALL OVER.
KWINK
YEAH. THAT'S IT.
TIME FOR THE FAT LADY TO SING...

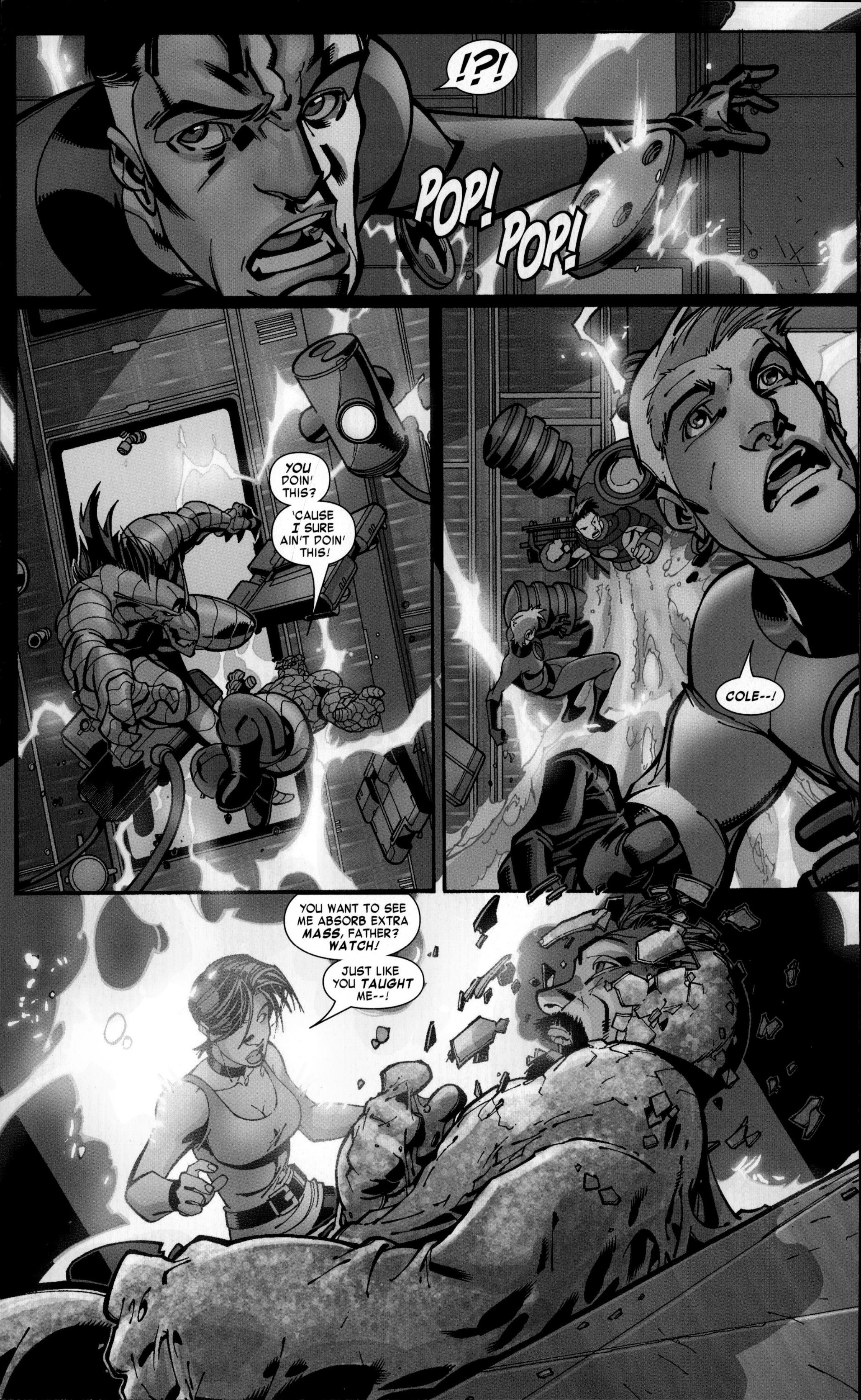
!?!
POP! POP!
YOU DOIN' THIS?
'CAUSE I SURE AIN'T DOIN' THIS!
COLE--!
YOU WANT TO SEE ME ABSORB EXTRA MASS, FATHER? WATCH!
JUST LIKE YOU TAUGHT ME--!
76

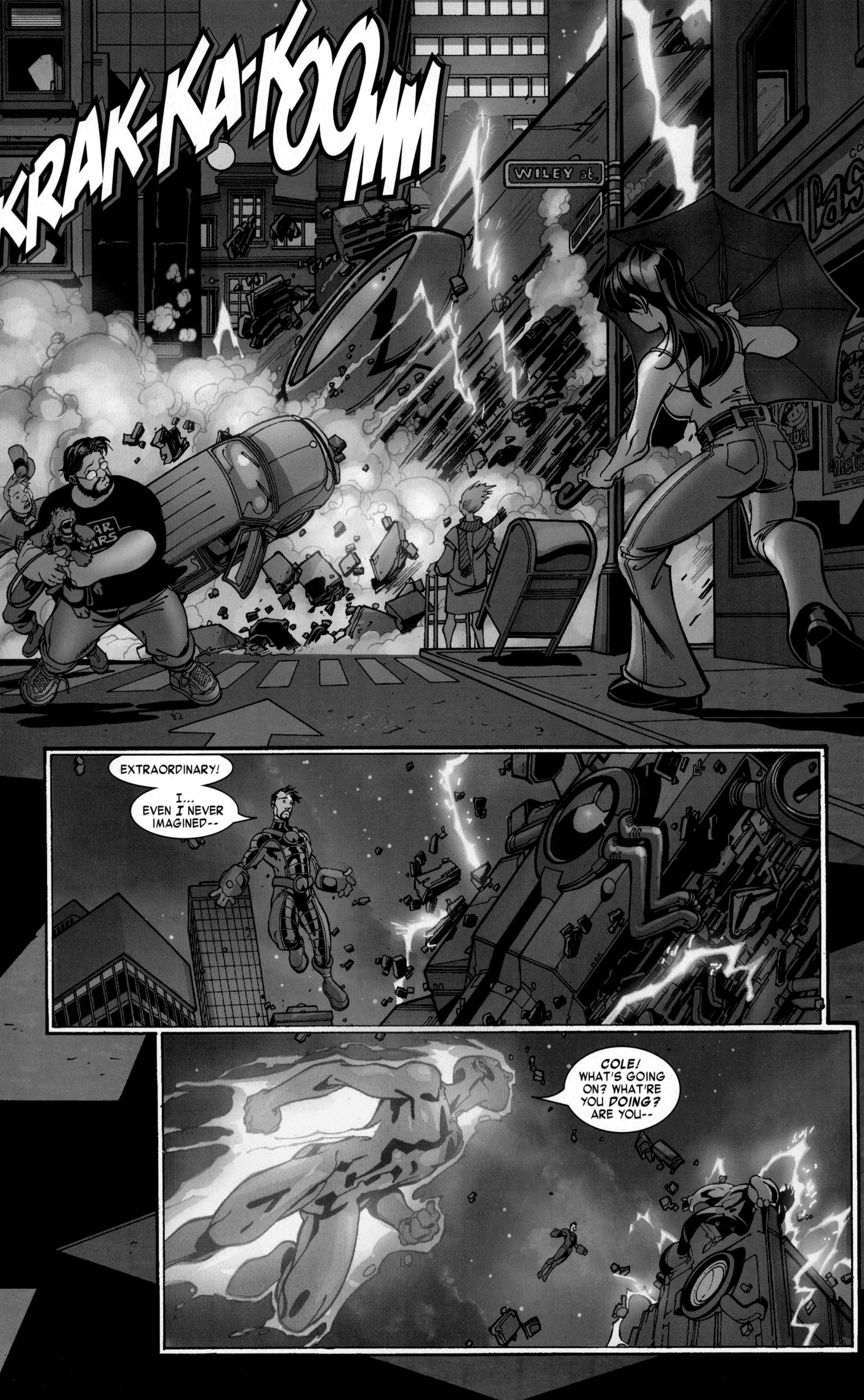
KRAK-KA-KOOMM
WILEY st.
EXTRAORDINARY!
I... EVEN I NEVER IMAGINED--
COLE! WHAT'S GOING ON? WHAT'RE YOU DOING? ARE YOU--

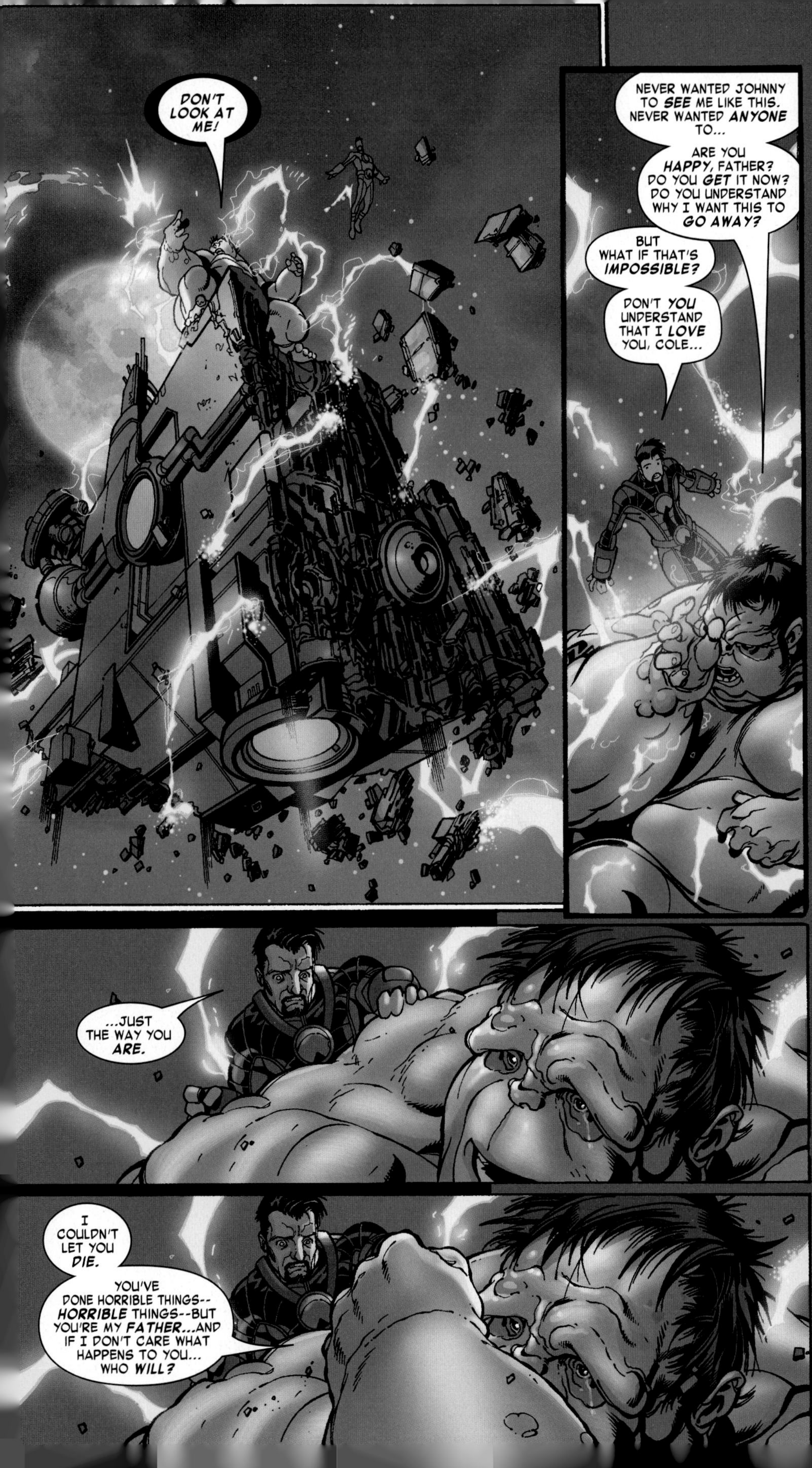
DON'T LOOK AT ME!
NEVER WANTED JOHNNY TO SEE ME LIKE THIS. NEVER WANTED ANYONE TO...
ARE YOU HAPPY, FATHER? DO YOU GET IT NOW? DO YOU UNDERSTAND WHY I WANT THIS TO GO AWAY?
BUT WHAT IF THAT'S IMPOSSIBLE?
DON'T YOU UNDERSTAND THAT I LOVE YOU, COLE...
...JUST THE WAY YOU ARE.
I COULDN'T LET YOU DIE.
YOU'VE DONE HORRIBLE THINGS--HORRIBLE THINGS--BUT YOU'RE MY FATHER...AND IF I DON'T CARE WHAT HAPPENS TO YOU... WHO WILL?

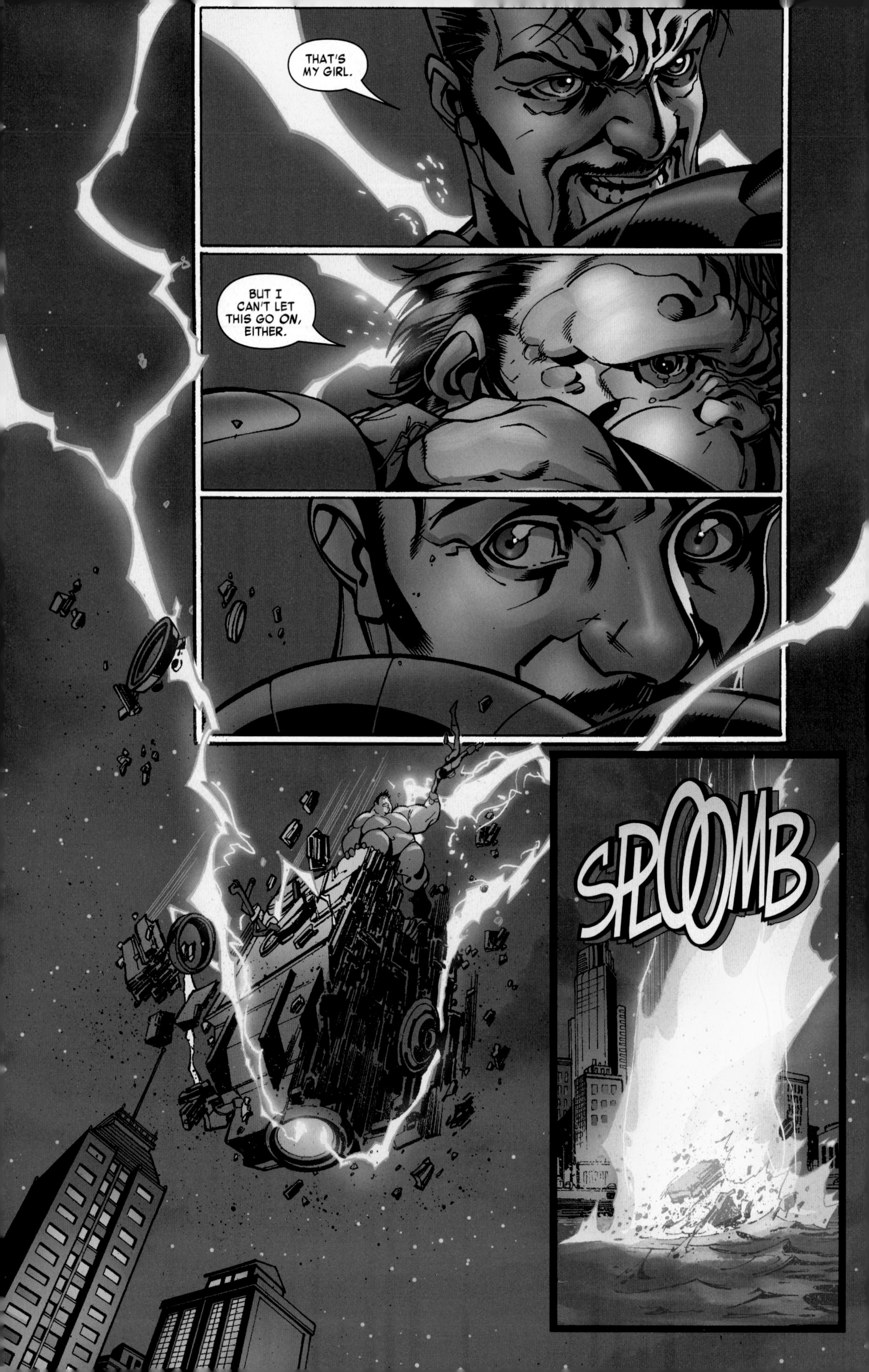
THAT'S MY GIRL.
BUT I CAN'T LET THIS GO ON, EITHER.
SPLOOMB

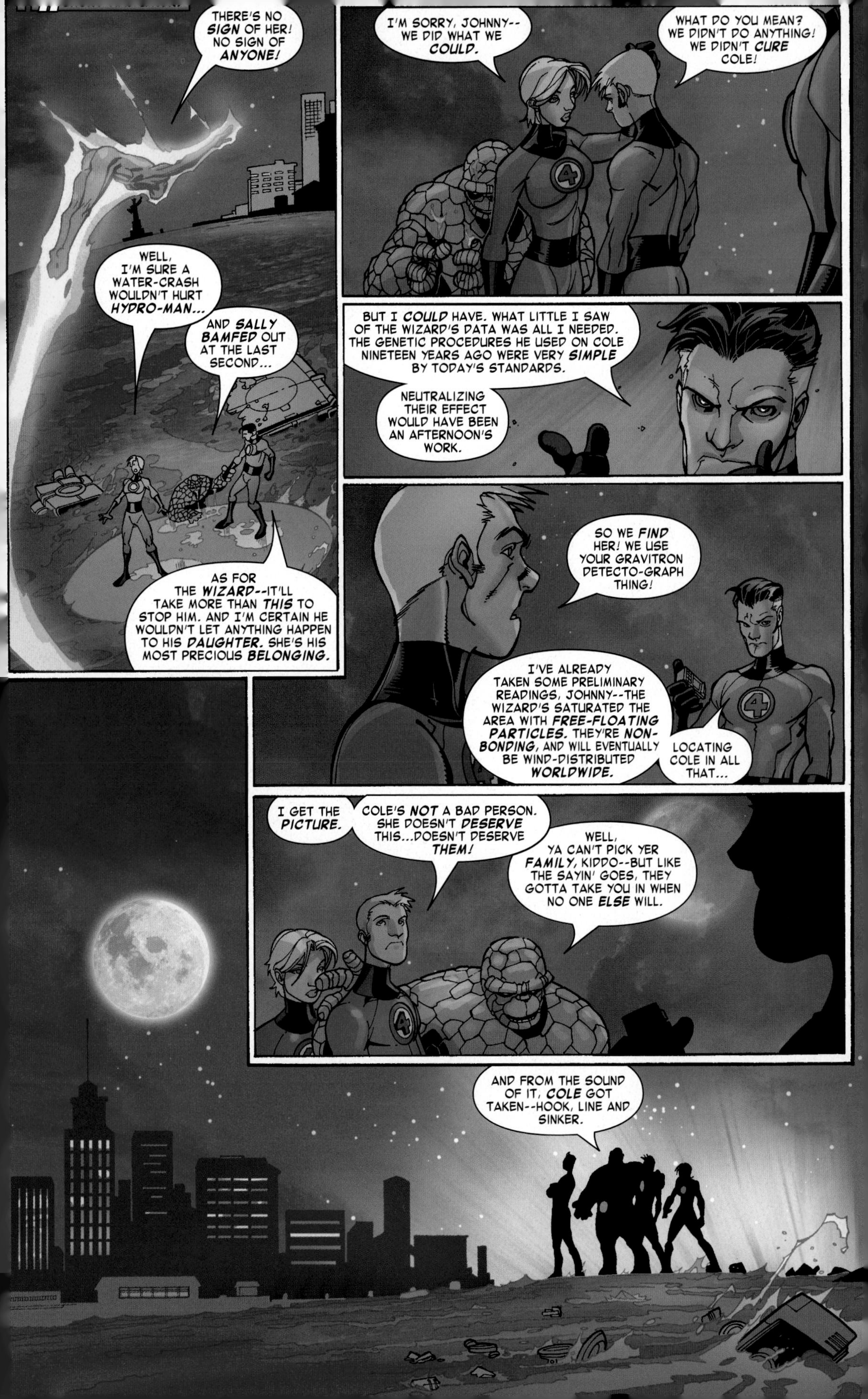
THERE'S NO SIGN OF HER! NO SIGN OF ANYONE!
WELL, I'M SURE A WATER-CRASH WOULDN'T HURT HYDRO-MAN...
AND SALLY BAMFED OUT AT THE LAST SECOND...
AS FOR THE WIZARD--IT'LL TAKE MORE THAN THIS TO STOP HIM. AND I'M CERTAIN HE WOULDN'T LET ANYTHING HAPPEN TO HIS DAUGHTER. SHE'S HIS MOST PRECIOUS BELONGING.
I'M SORRY, JOHNNY--WE DID WHAT WE COULD.
WHAT DO YOU MEAN? WE DIDN'T DO ANYTHING! WE DIDN'T CURE COLE!
BUT I COULD HAVE. WHAT LITTLE I SAW OF THE WIZARD'S DATA WAS ALL I NEEDED. THE GENETIC PROCEDURES HE USED ON COLE NINETEEN YEARS AGO WERE VERY SIMPLE BY TODAY'S STANDARDS.
NEUTRALIZING THEIR EFFECT WOULD HAVE BEEN AN AFTERNOON'S WORK.
SO WE FIND HER! WE USE YOUR GRAVITRON DETECTO-GRAPH THING!
I'VE ALREADY TAKEN SOME PRELIMINARY READINGS, JOHNNY--THE WIZARD'S SATURATED THE AREA WITH FREE-FLOATING PARTICLES. THEY'RE NON-BONDING, AND WILL EVENTUALLY BE WIND-DISTRIBUTED WORLDWIDE.
LOCATING COLE IN ALL THAT...
I GET THE PICTURE.
COLE'S NOT A BAD PERSON. SHE DOESN'T DESERVE THIS...DOESN'T DESERVE THEM!
WELL, YA CAN'T PICK YER FAMILY, KIDDO--BUT LIKE THE SAYIN' GOES, THEY GOTTA TAKE YOU IN WHEN NO ONE ELSE WILL.
AND FROM THE SOUND OF IT, COLE GOT TAKEN--HOOK, LINE AND SINKER.

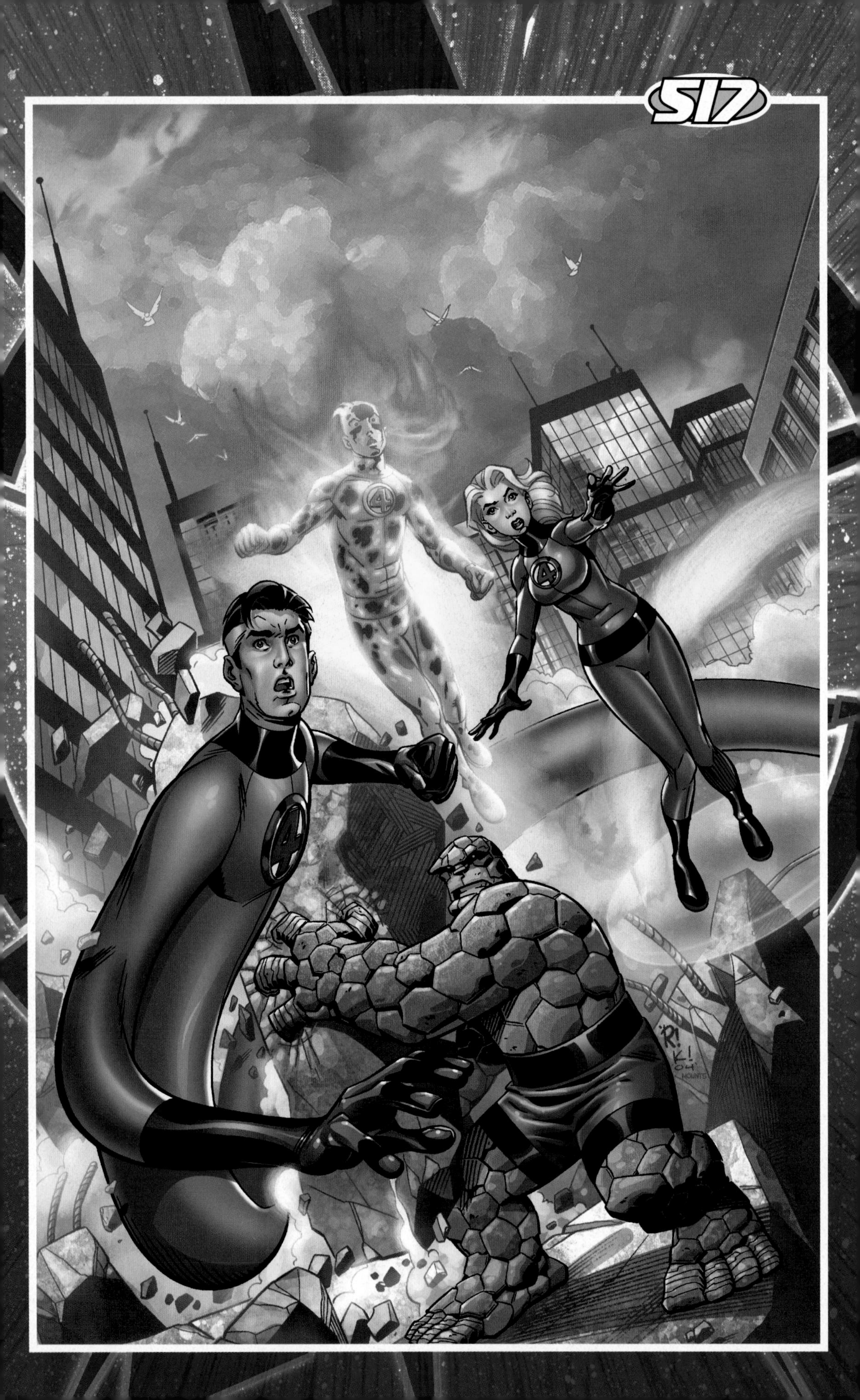
517

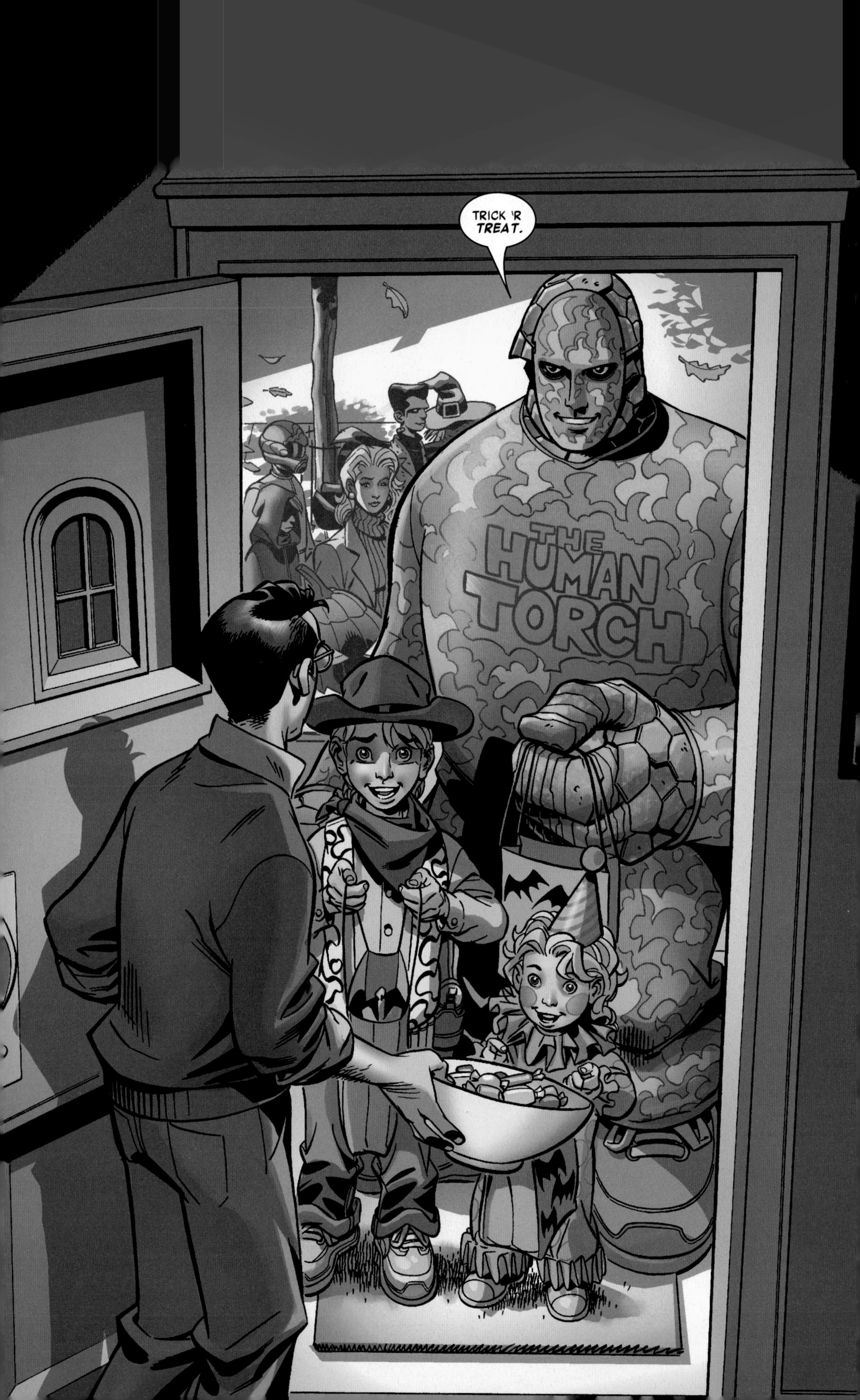
TRICK 'R TREAT.
THE HUMAN TORCH

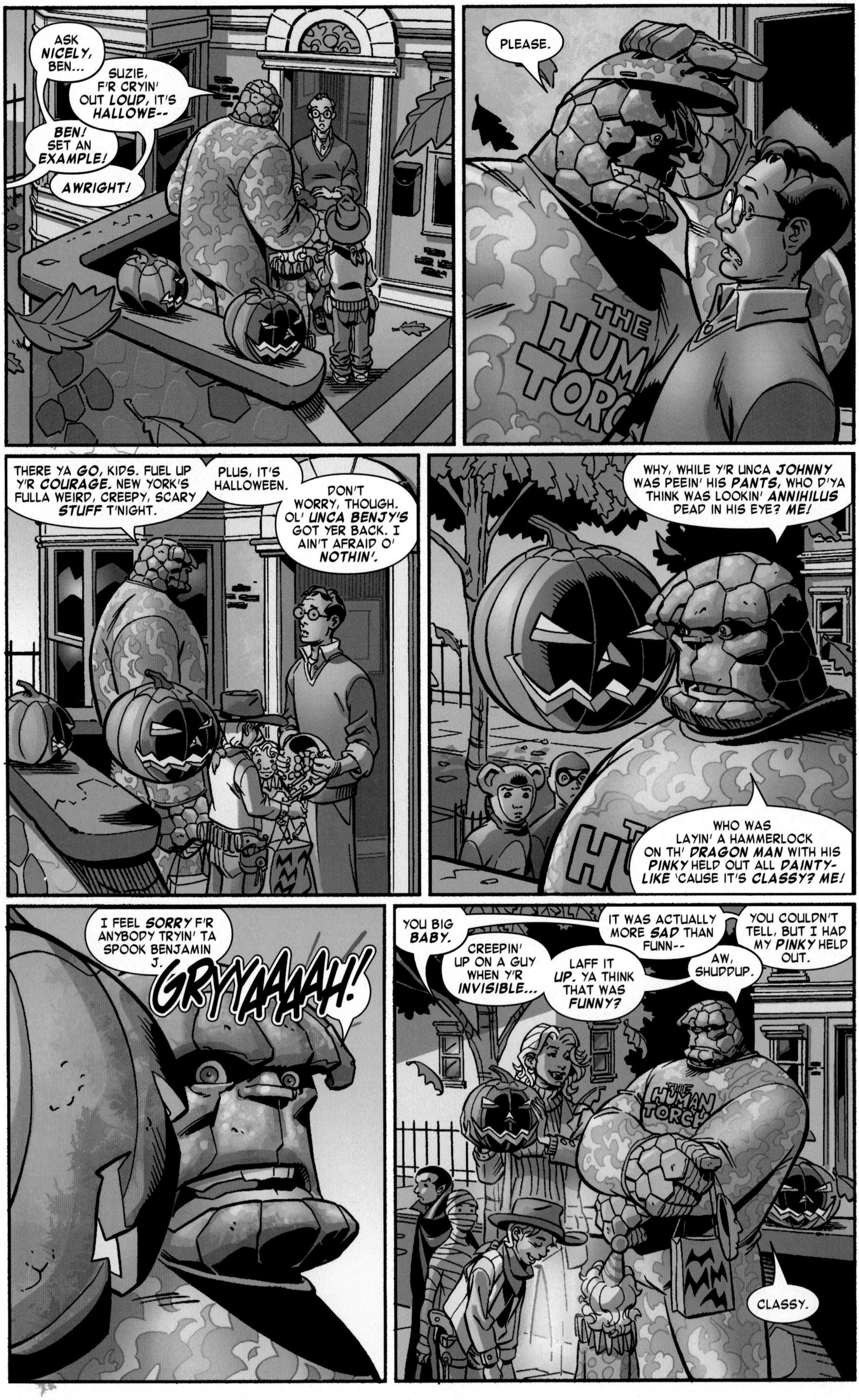
ASK NICELY, BEN...
SUZIE, F'R CRYIN' OUT LOUD, IT'S HALLOWE--
BEN! SET AN EXAMPLE!
AWRIGHT!
PLEASE.
THERE YA GO, KIDS. FUEL UP Y'R COURAGE. NEW YORK'S FULLA WEIRD, CREEPY, SCARY STUFF T'NIGHT.
PLUS, IT'S HALLOWEEN.
DON'T WORRY, THOUGH. OL' UNCA BENJY'S GOT YER BACK. I AIN'T AFRAID O' NOTHIN'.
WHY, WHILE Y'R UNCA JOHNNY WAS PEEIN' HIS PANTS, WHO D'YA THINK WAS LOOKIN' ANNIHILUS DEAD IN HIS EYE? ME!
WHO WAS LAYIN' A HAMMERLOCK ON TH' DRAGON MAN WITH HIS PINKY HELD OUT ALL DAINTY-LIKE 'CAUSE IT'S CLASSY? ME!
I FEEL SORRY F'R ANYBODY TRYIN' TA SPOOK BENJAMIN J.
GRYYAAAAH!
YOU BIG BABY.
CREEPIN' UP ON A GUY WHEN Y'R INVISIBLE...
LAFF IT UP. YA THINK THAT WAS FUNNY?
IT WAS ACTUALLY MORE SAD THAN FUNN--
AW, SHUDDUP.
YOU COULDN'T TELL, BUT I HAD MY PINKY HELD OUT.
CLASSY.

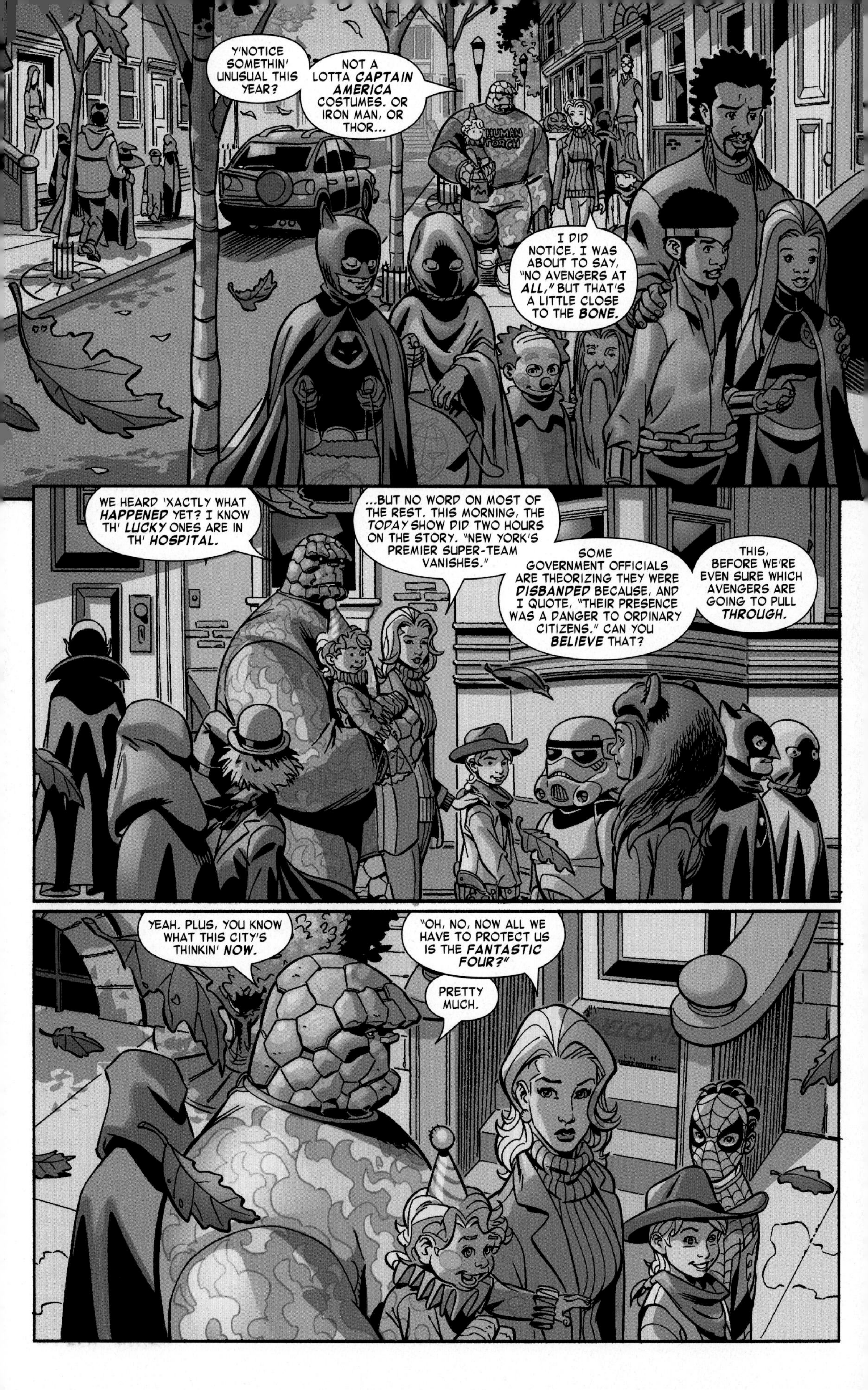

Y'NOTICE SOMETHIN' UNUSUAL THIS YEAR?
NOT A LOTTA CAPTAIN AMERICA COSTUMES. OR IRON MAN, OR THOR...
HUMAN TORCH
I DID NOTICE. I WAS ABOUT TO SAY, "NO AVENGERS AT ALL," BUT THAT'S A LITTLE CLOSE TO THE BONE.
WE HEARD 'XACTLY WHAT HAPPENED YET? I KNOW TH' LUCKY ONES ARE IN TH' HOSPITAL.
...BUT NO WORD ON MOST OF THE REST. THIS MORNING, THE TODAY SHOW DID TWO HOURS ON THE STORY. "NEW YORK'S PREMIER SUPER-TEAM VANISHES."
SOME GOVERNMENT OFFICIALS ARE THEORIZING THEY WERE DISBANDED BECAUSE, AND I QUOTE, "THEIR PRESENCE WAS A DANGER TO ORDINARY CITIZENS." CAN YOU BELIEVE THAT?
THIS, BEFORE WE'RE EVEN SURE WHICH AVENGERS ARE GOING TO PULL THROUGH.
YEAH. PLUS, YOU KNOW WHAT THIS CITY'S THINKIN' NOW.
"OH, NO, NOW ALL WE HAVE TO PROTECT US IS THE FANTASTIC FOUR?"
PRETTY MUCH.

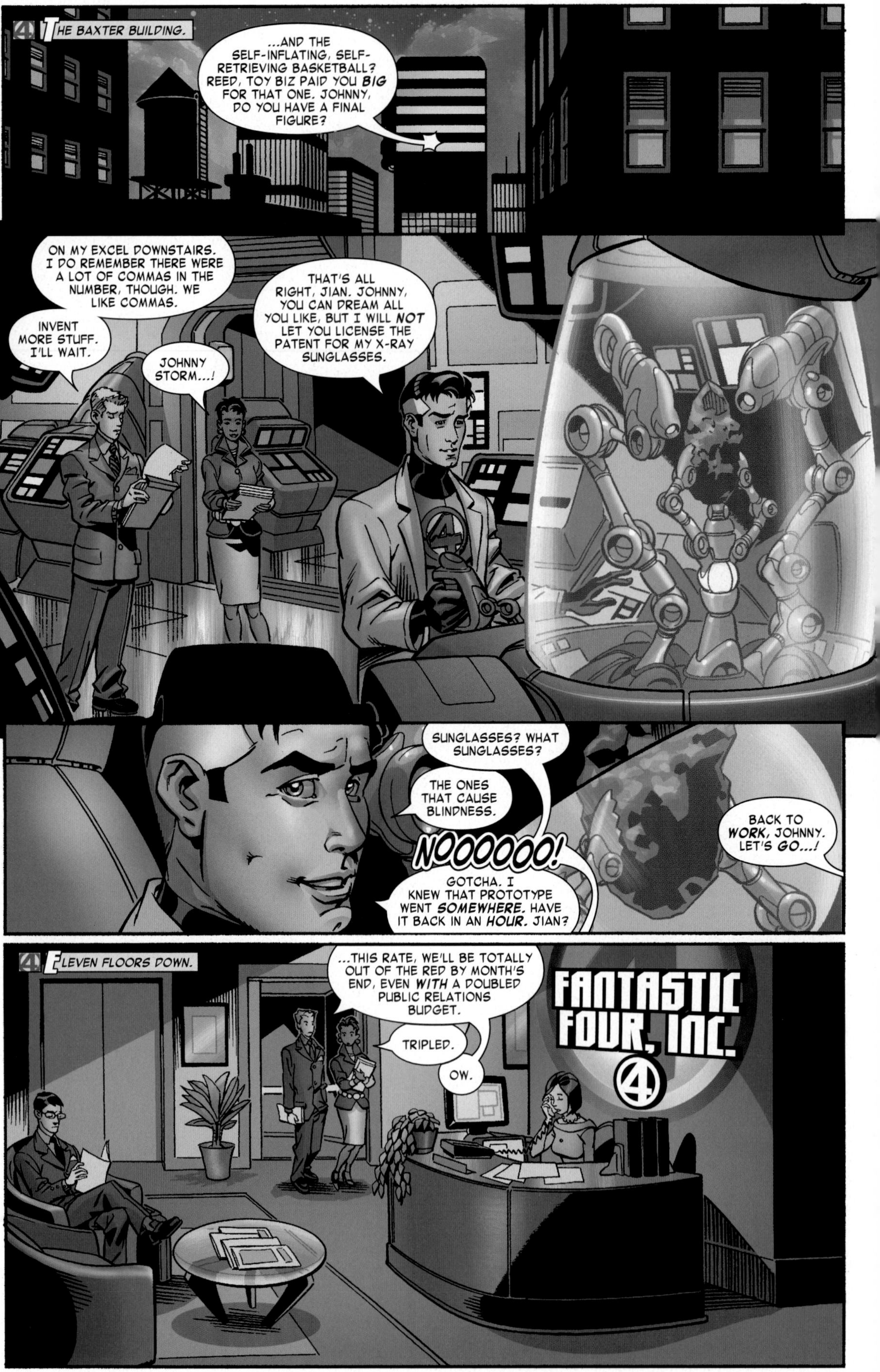
THE BAXTER BUILDING.
...AND THE SELF-INFLATING, SELF-RETRIEVING BASKETBALL? REED, TOY BIZ PAID YOU BIG FOR THAT ONE. JOHNNY, DO YOU HAVE A FINAL FIGURE?
ON MY EXCEL DOWNSTAIRS. I DO REMEMBER THERE WERE A LOT OF COMMAS IN THE NUMBER, THOUGH. WE LIKE COMMAS.
INVENT MORE STUFF. I'LL WAIT.
JOHNNY STORM...!
THAT'S ALL RIGHT, JIAN. JOHNNY, YOU CAN DREAM ALL YOU LIKE, BUT I WILL NOT LET YOU LICENSE THE PATENT FOR MY X-RAY SUNGLASSES.
SUNGLASSES? WHAT SUNGLASSES?
THE ONES THAT CAUSE BLINDNESS.
NOOOOOO!
GOTCHA. I KNEW THAT PROTOTYPE WENT SOMEWHERE. HAVE IT BACK IN AN HOUR. JIAN?
BACK TO WORK, JOHNNY. LET'S GO...!
ELEVEN FLOORS DOWN.
...THIS RATE, WE'LL BE TOTALLY OUT OF THE RED BY MONTH'S END, EVEN WITH A DOUBLED PUBLIC RELATIONS BUDGET.
TRIPLED.
OW.
FANTASTIC FOUR, INC.

JIAN, YOU'VE REALLY BEEN GREAT THESE LAST FEW MONTHS. AS CO-FINANCIAL MANAGER OF THIS ORGANIZATION, I HEREBY AUTHORIZE A *RAISE* FOR YOU.

JOHNNY, WE CAN'T AFFORD ME *NOW*. BUT I'LL TAKE THE COMPLIMENT.

WELL, WE OWE YOU *SOMETHING*. YOU MUST'VE HAD SECOND THOUGHTS ABOUT THE FF LATELY SINCE, Y'KNOW, YOU'RE AN *EARTHLING* AND ALL. I APOLOGIZE THAT YOU'RE *STUCK* WITH US.

STUCK HOW?

YOU DON'T HAVE TO SPARE MY FEELINGS. WE'RE NOT THE GREATEST REFERENCE TO PUT ON A *RESUME* THESE DAYS.

I'M NOT LOOKING.

I'D UNDERSTAND IF--

I'M *NOT* LOOKING.

SEE YOU TOMORROW. REMEMBER, I'LL BE A LITTLE LATE.

INTERVIEW?

MOM AT THE AIRPORT. I'M. NOT. LOOKING. G'NIGHT.

HELLO, MR. CIRCULAR FILE.

IT'S *NOT* SPYING IF IT'S IN THE *TRASH CAN.* RIGHT?

HEADHUNTING NY E[M]

PAPER CLIPS

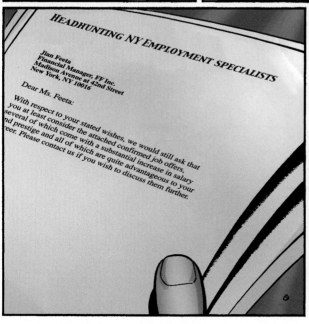

HEADHUNTING NY EMPLOYMENT SPECIALISTS

Jian Feeta
Financial Manager, FF Inc.
Madison Avenue at 42nd Street
New York, NY 10016

Dear Ms. Feeta:

With respect to your stated wishes, we would still ask that you at least consider the attached confirmed job offers, several of which come with a substantial increase in salary and prestige and all of which are quite advantageous to your career. Please contact us if you wish to discuss them further.

SHE'S *NOT* LOOKING.

COOL. AT LEAST *SOME* PEOPLE STILL BELIEVE IN THE FANTASTIC FOUR.

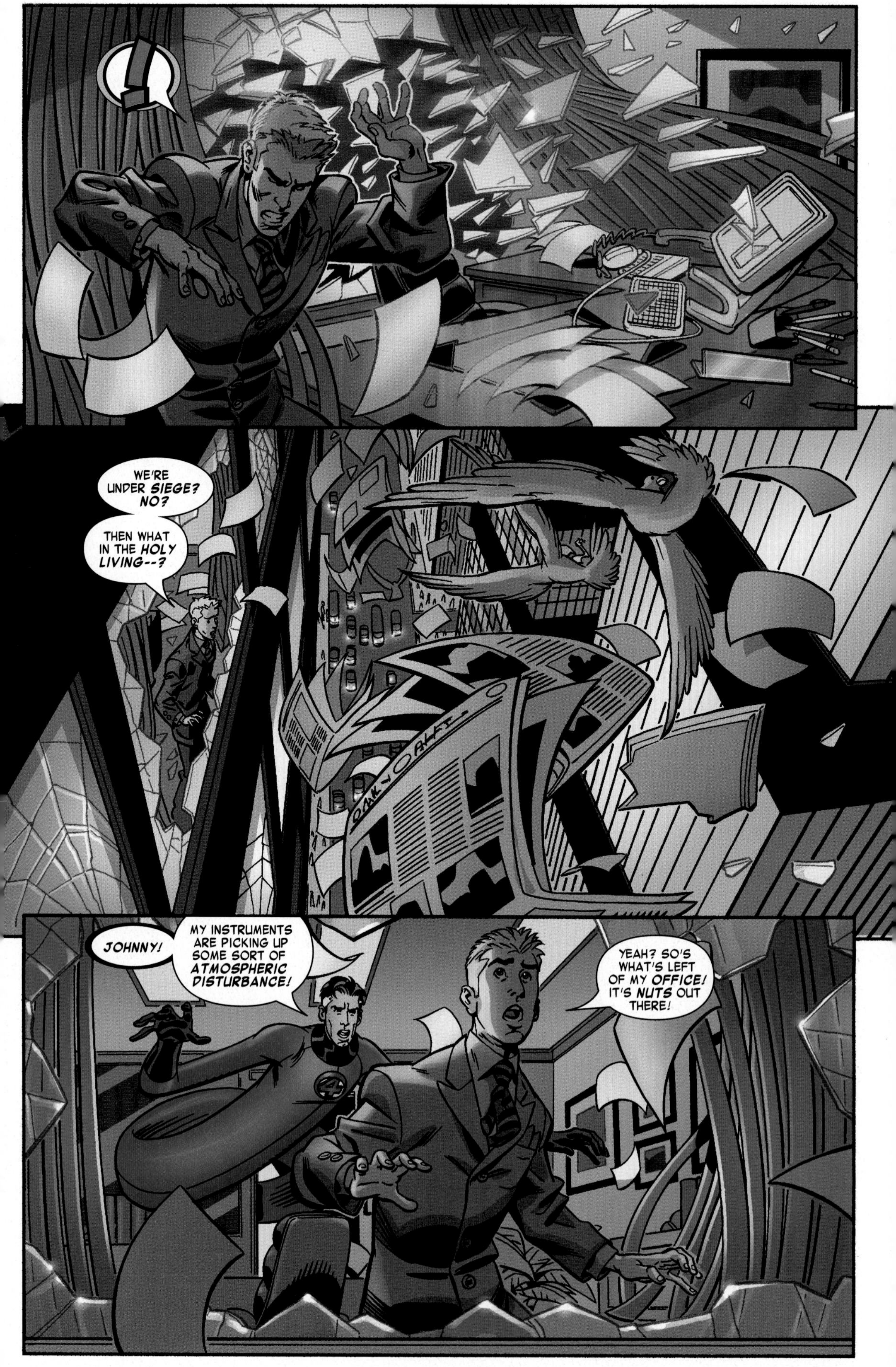
!
WE'RE UNDER SIEGE? NO?
THEN WHAT IN THE HOLY LIVING--?
JOHNNY!
MY INSTRUMENTS ARE PICKING UP SOME SORT OF ATMOSPHERIC DISTURBANCE!
YEAH? SO'S WHAT'S LEFT OF MY OFFICE! IT'S NUTS OUT THERE!

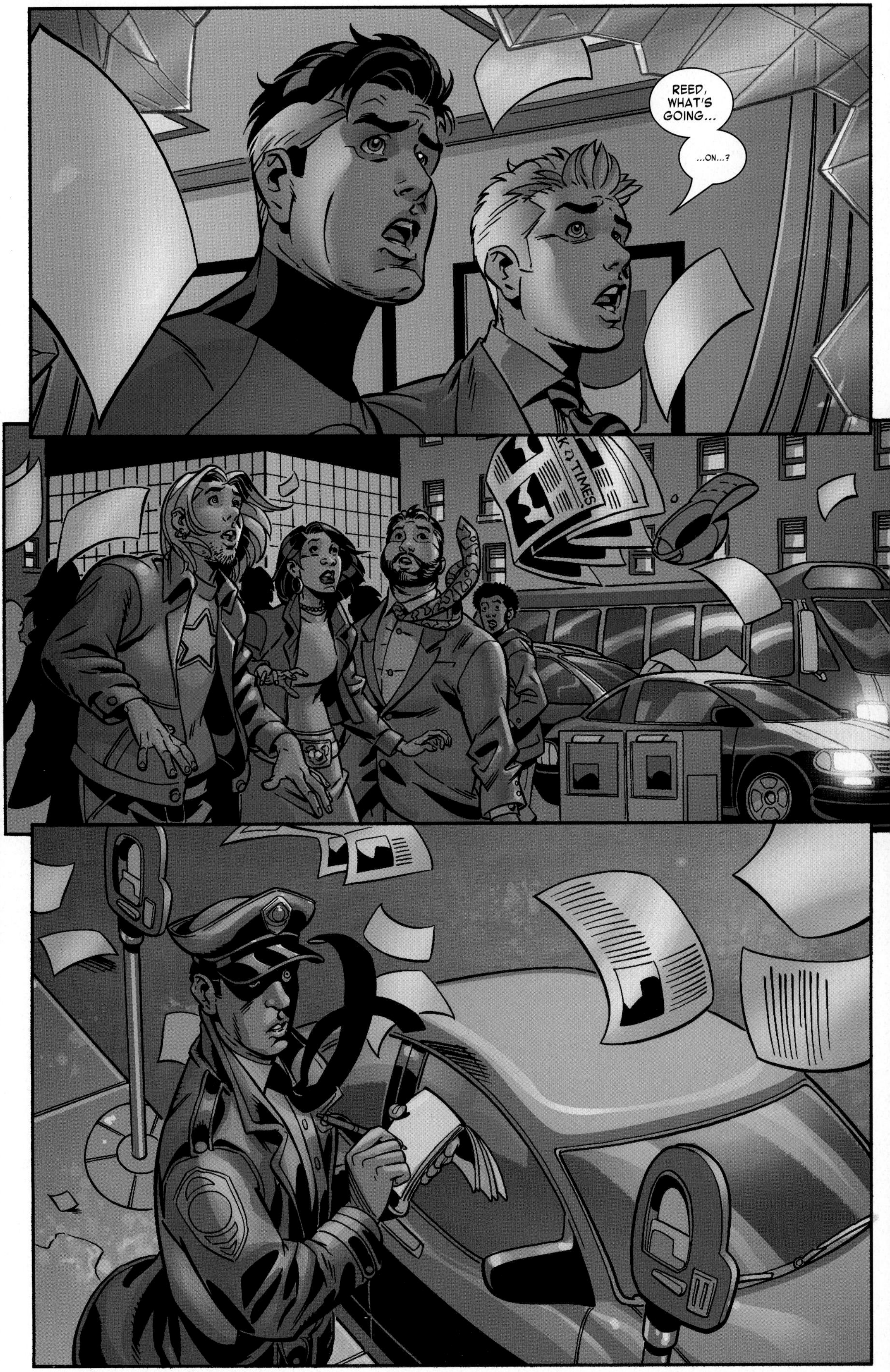
REED, WHAT'S GOING...
...ON...?

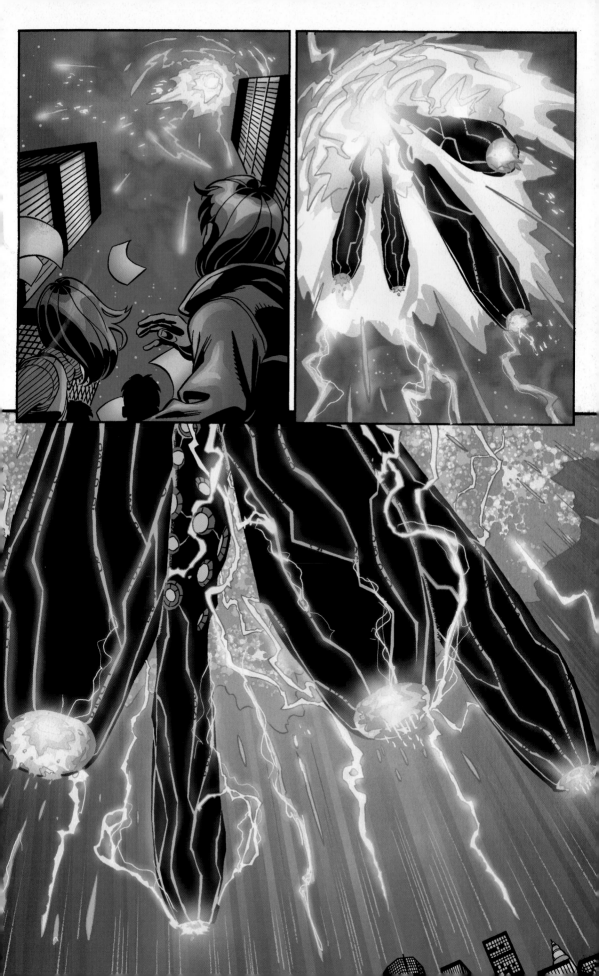

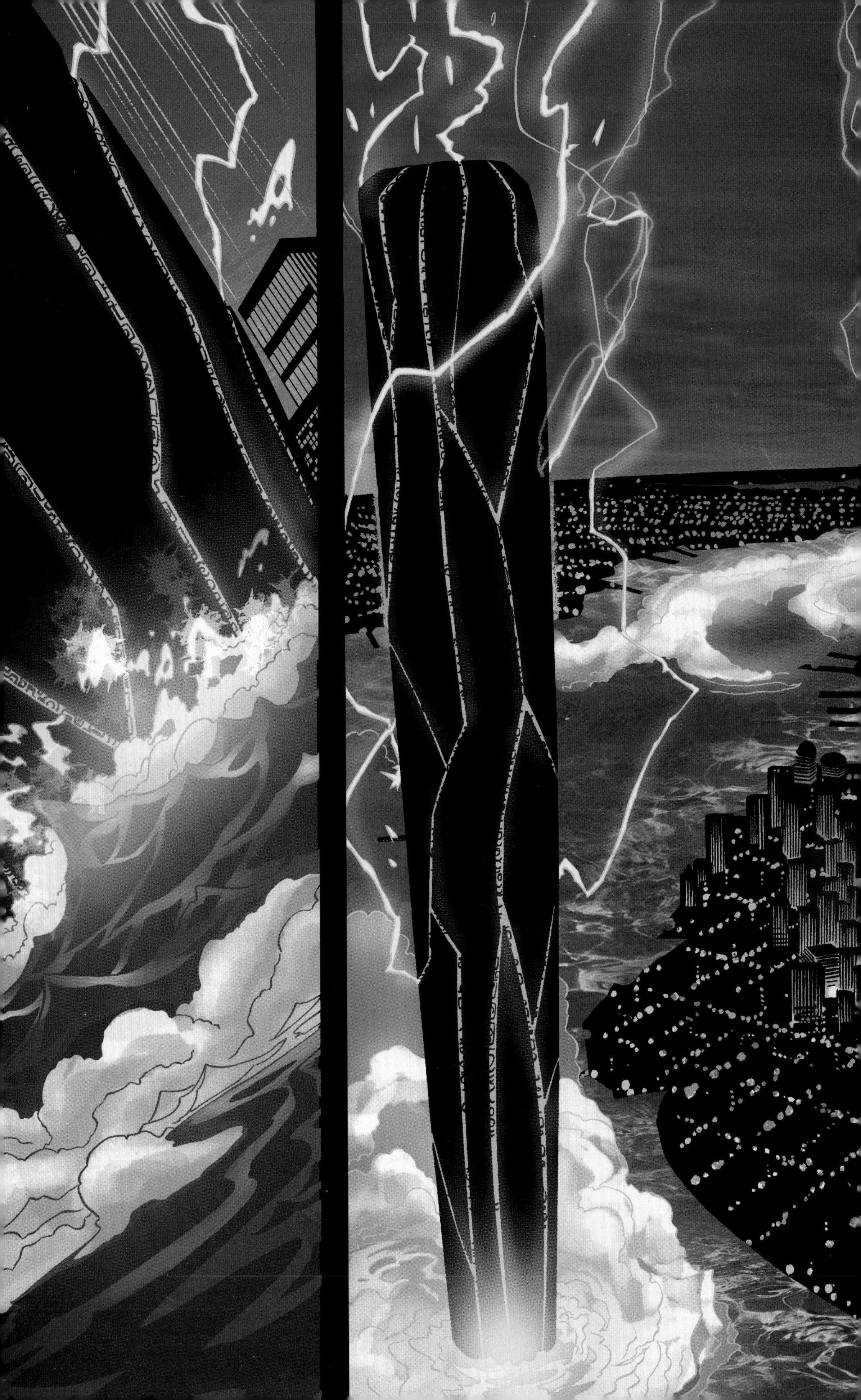

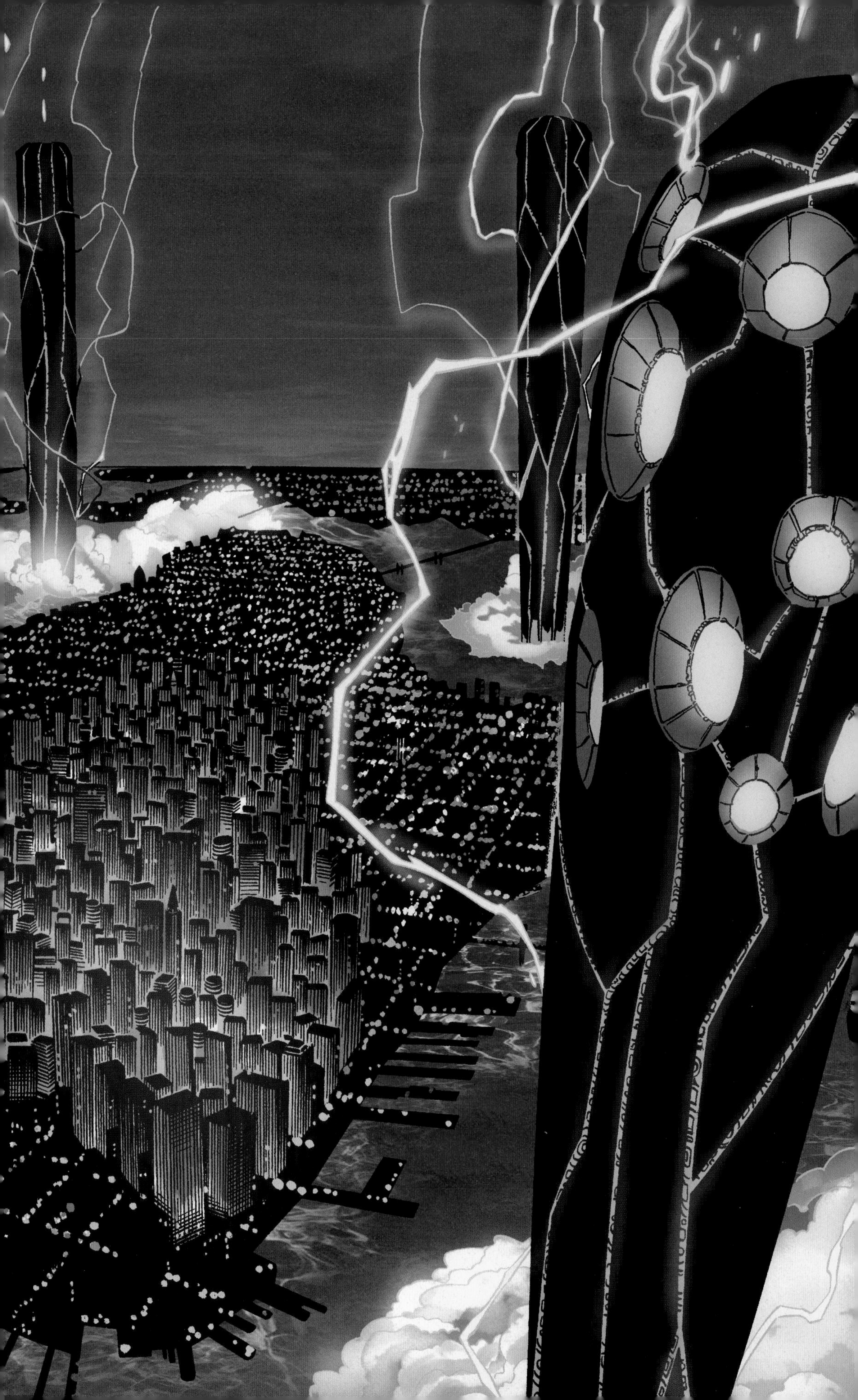

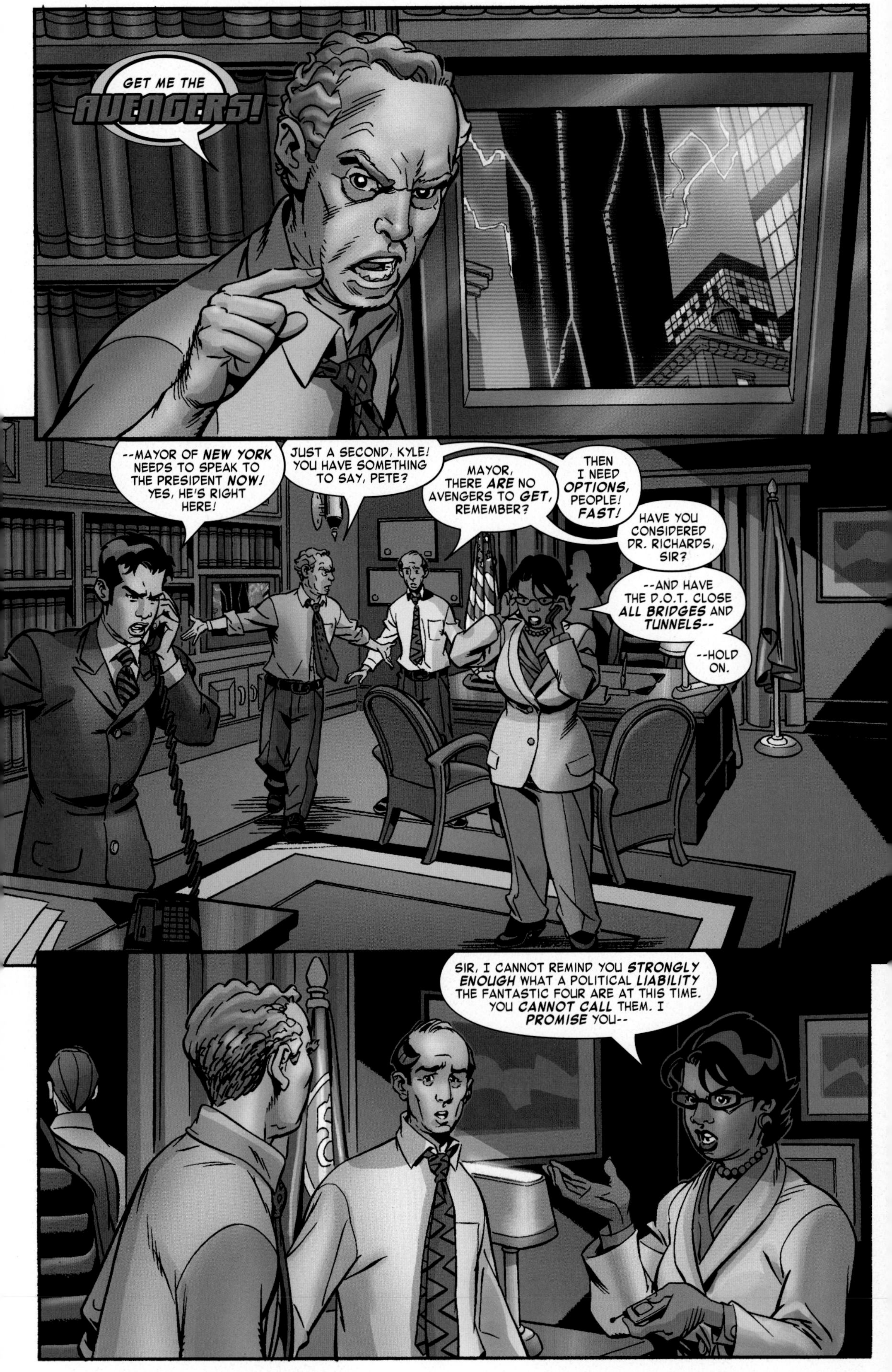
GET ME THE AVENGERS!
--MAYOR OF NEW YORK NEEDS TO SPEAK TO THE PRESIDENT NOW! YES, HE'S RIGHT HERE!
JUST A SECOND, KYLE! YOU HAVE SOMETHING TO SAY, PETE?
MAYOR, THERE ARE NO AVENGERS TO GET, REMEMBER?
THEN I NEED OPTIONS, PEOPLE! FAST!
HAVE YOU CONSIDERED DR. RICHARDS, SIR?
--AND HAVE THE D.O.T. CLOSE ALL BRIDGES AND TUNNELS--
--HOLD ON.
SIR, I CANNOT REMIND YOU STRONGLY ENOUGH WHAT A POLITICAL LIABILITY THE FANTASTIC FOUR ARE AT THIS TIME. YOU CANNOT CALL THEM. I PROMISE YOU--

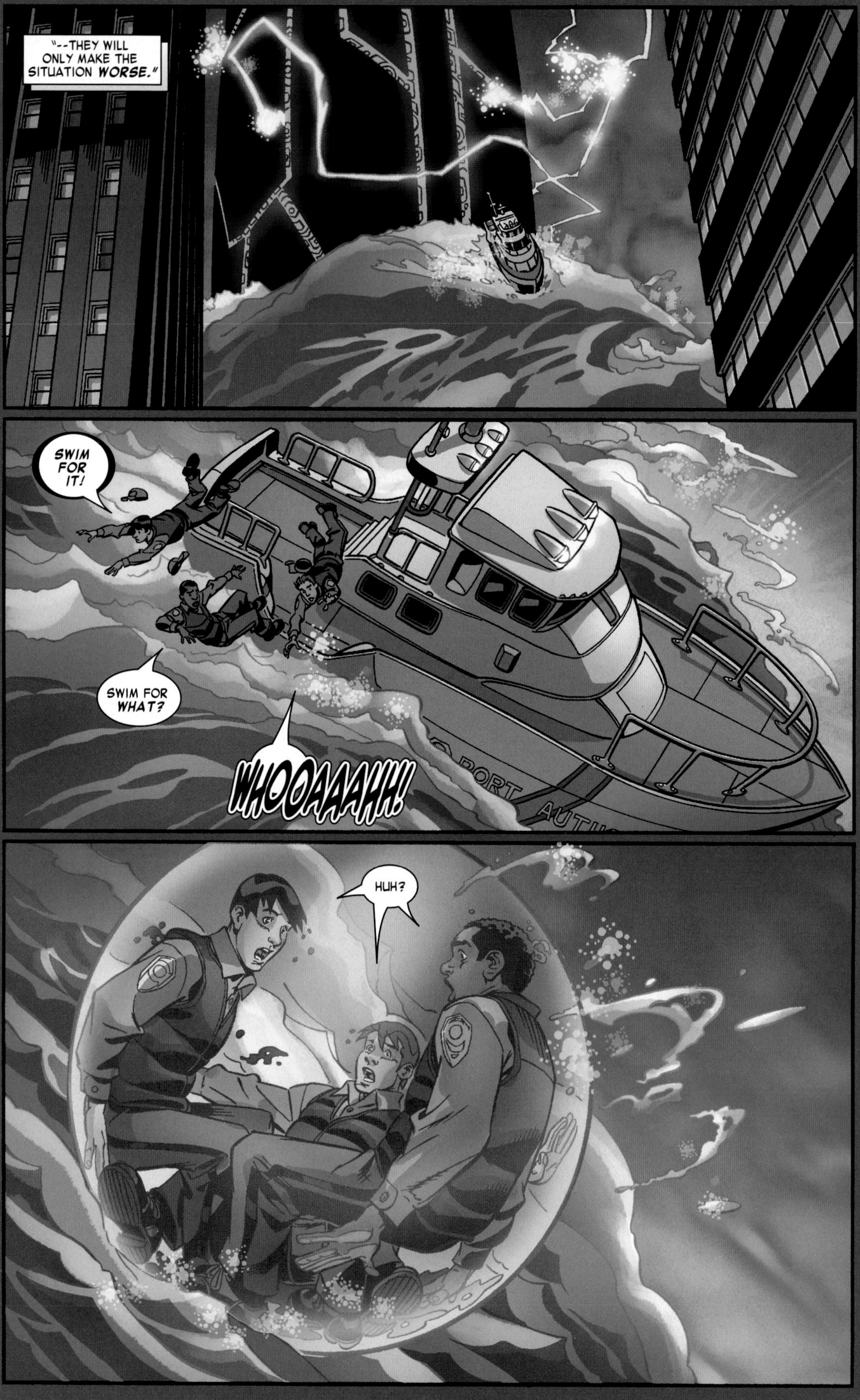
"--THEY WILL ONLY MAKE THE SITUATION WORSE."
SWIM FOR IT!
SWIM FOR WHAT?
WHOOAAAHH!
PORT AUTH
HUH?

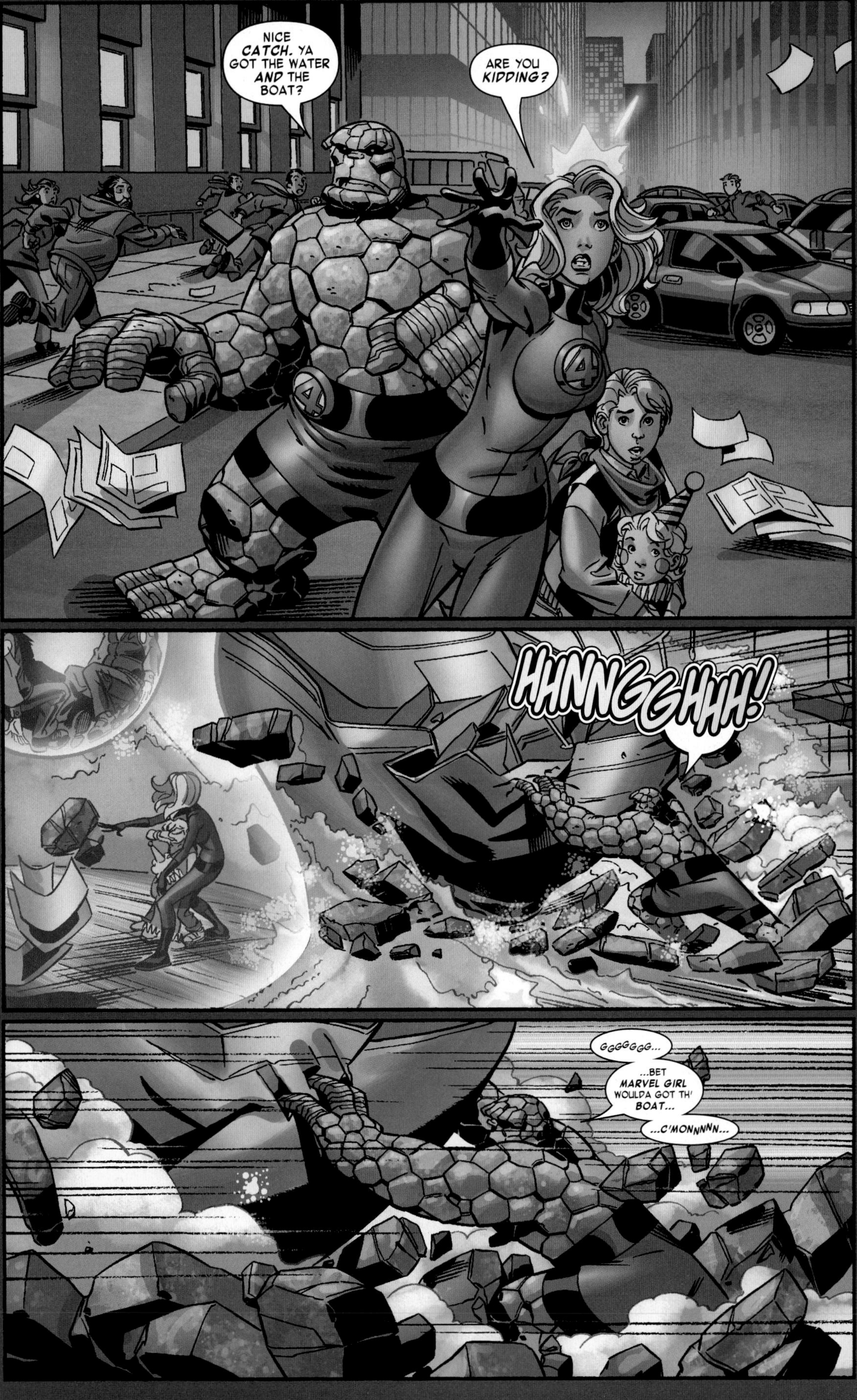
NICE CATCH. YA GOT THE WATER AND THE BOAT?
ARE YOU KIDDING?
HHNNGGHHH!
GGGGGGG...
...BET MARVEL GIRL WOULDA GOT TH' BOAT...
...C'MONNNNN...

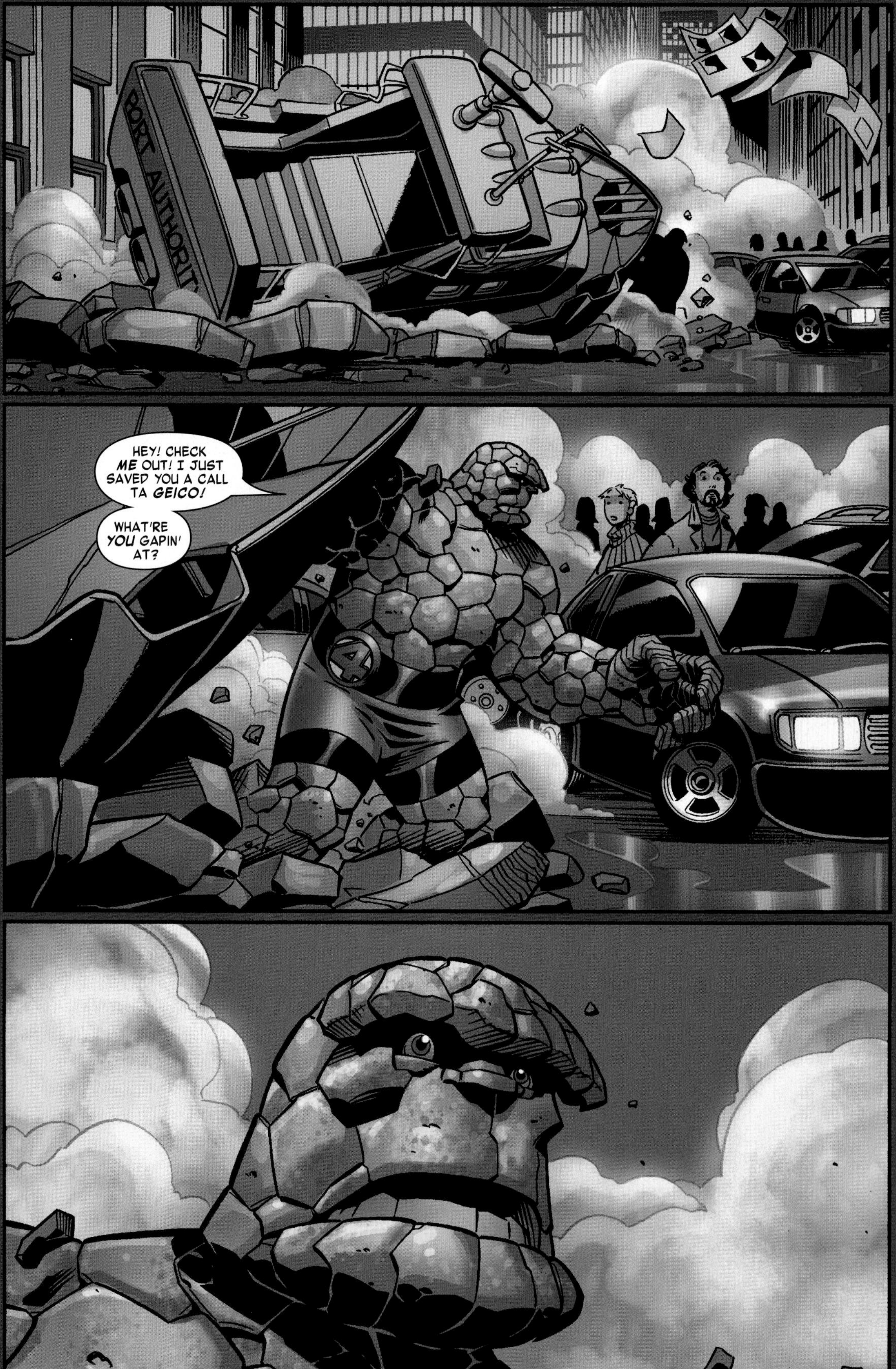
HEY! CHECK ME OUT! I JUST SAVED YOU A CALL TA GEICO!
WHAT'RE YOU GAPIN' AT?

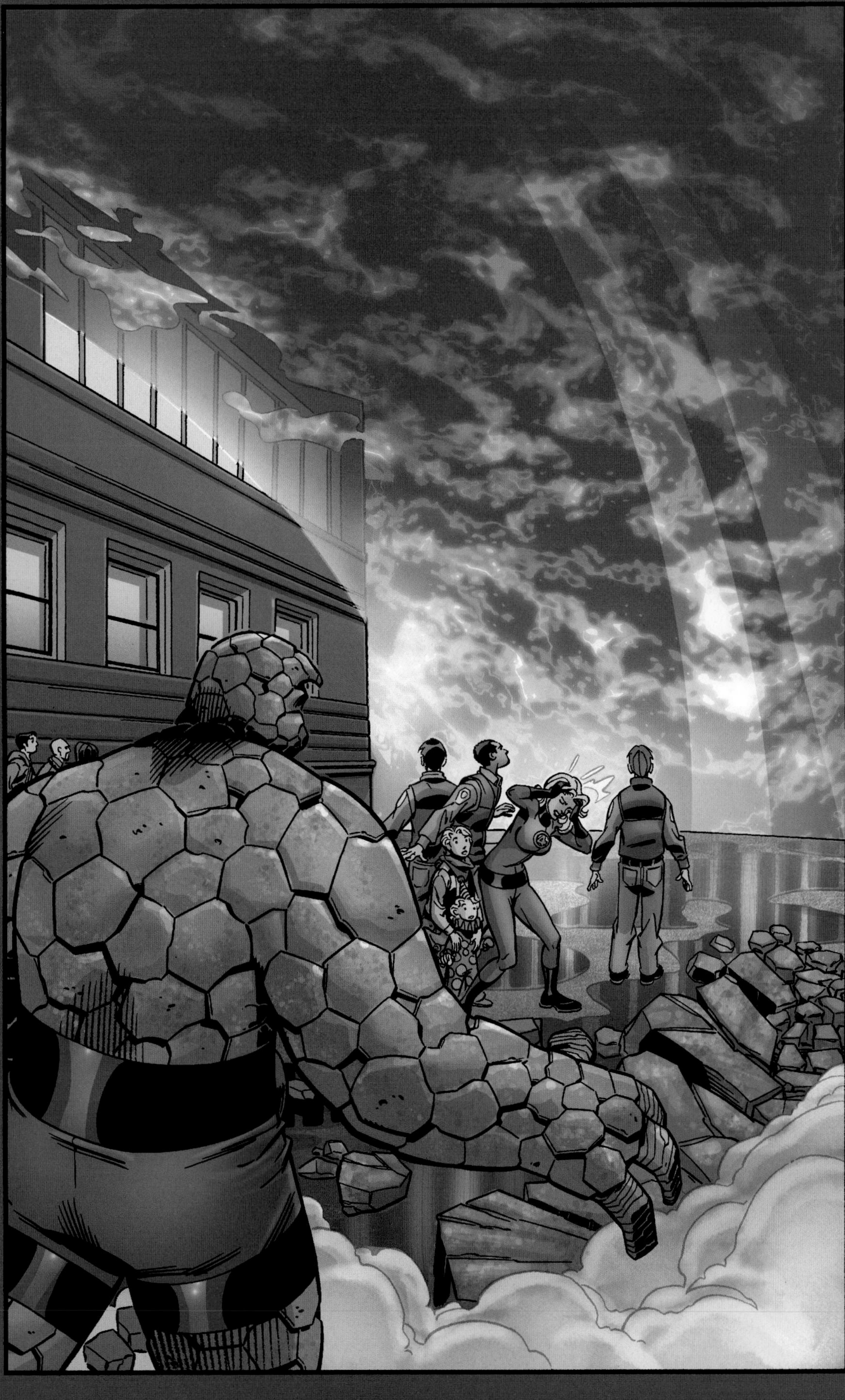

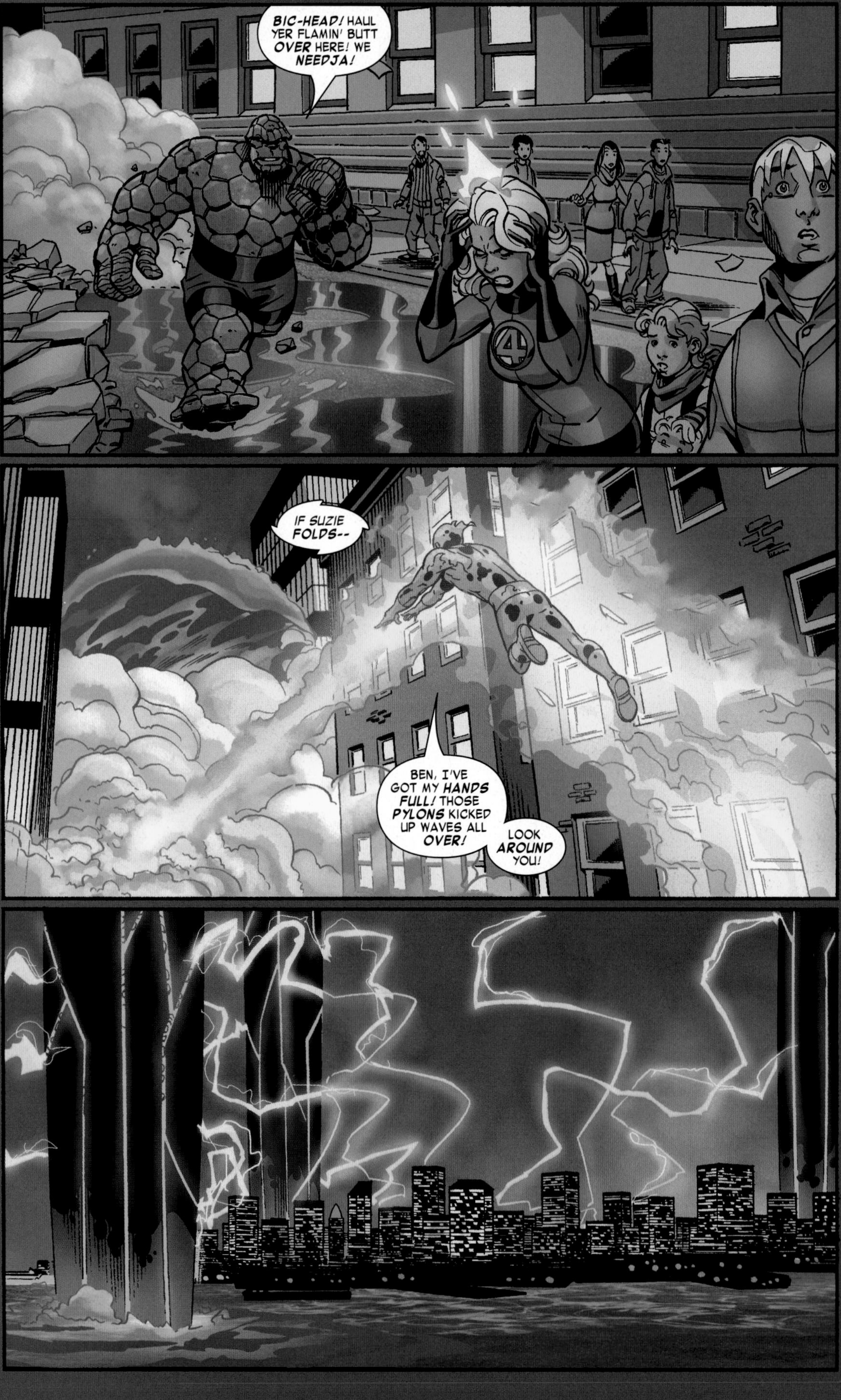
BIG-HEAD! HAUL YER FLAMIN' BUTT OVER HERE! WE NEEDJA!
IF SUZIE FOLDS--
BEN, I'VE GOT MY HANDS FULL! THOSE PYLONS KICKED UP WAVES ALL OVER!
LOOK AROUND YOU!

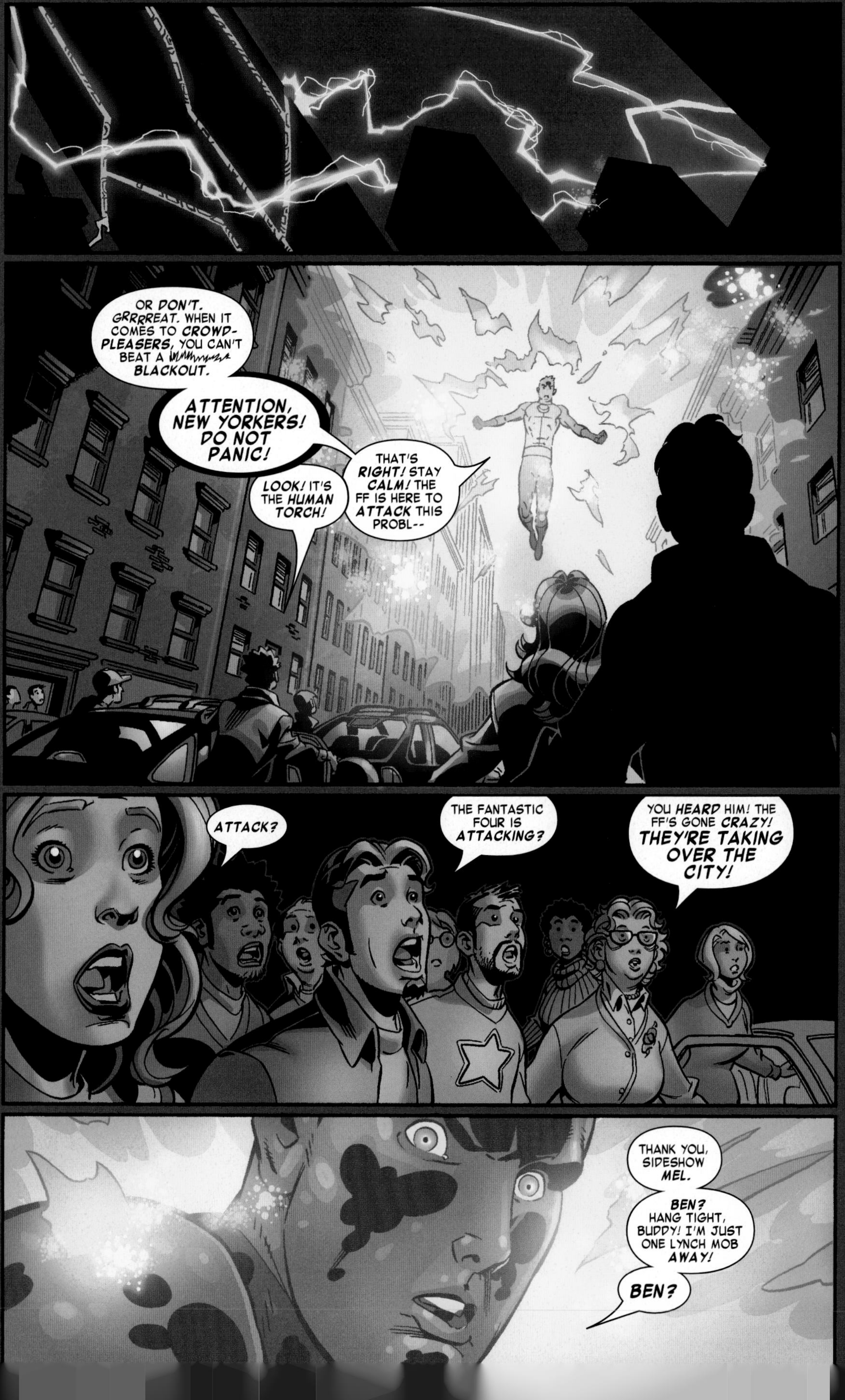
OR DON'T. GRRRREAT. WHEN IT COMES TO CROWD-PLEASERS, YOU CAN'T BEAT A BLACKOUT.
ATTENTION, NEW YORKERS! DO NOT PANIC!
THAT'S RIGHT! STAY CALM! THE FF IS HERE TO ATTACK THIS PROBL--
LOOK! IT'S THE HUMAN TORCH!
ATTACK?
THE FANTASTIC FOUR IS ATTACKING?
YOU HEARD HIM! THE FF'S GONE CRAZY! THEY'RE TAKING OVER THE CITY!
THANK YOU, SIDESHOW MEL.
BEN? HANG TIGHT, BUDDY! I'M JUST ONE LYNCH MOB AWAY!
BEN?

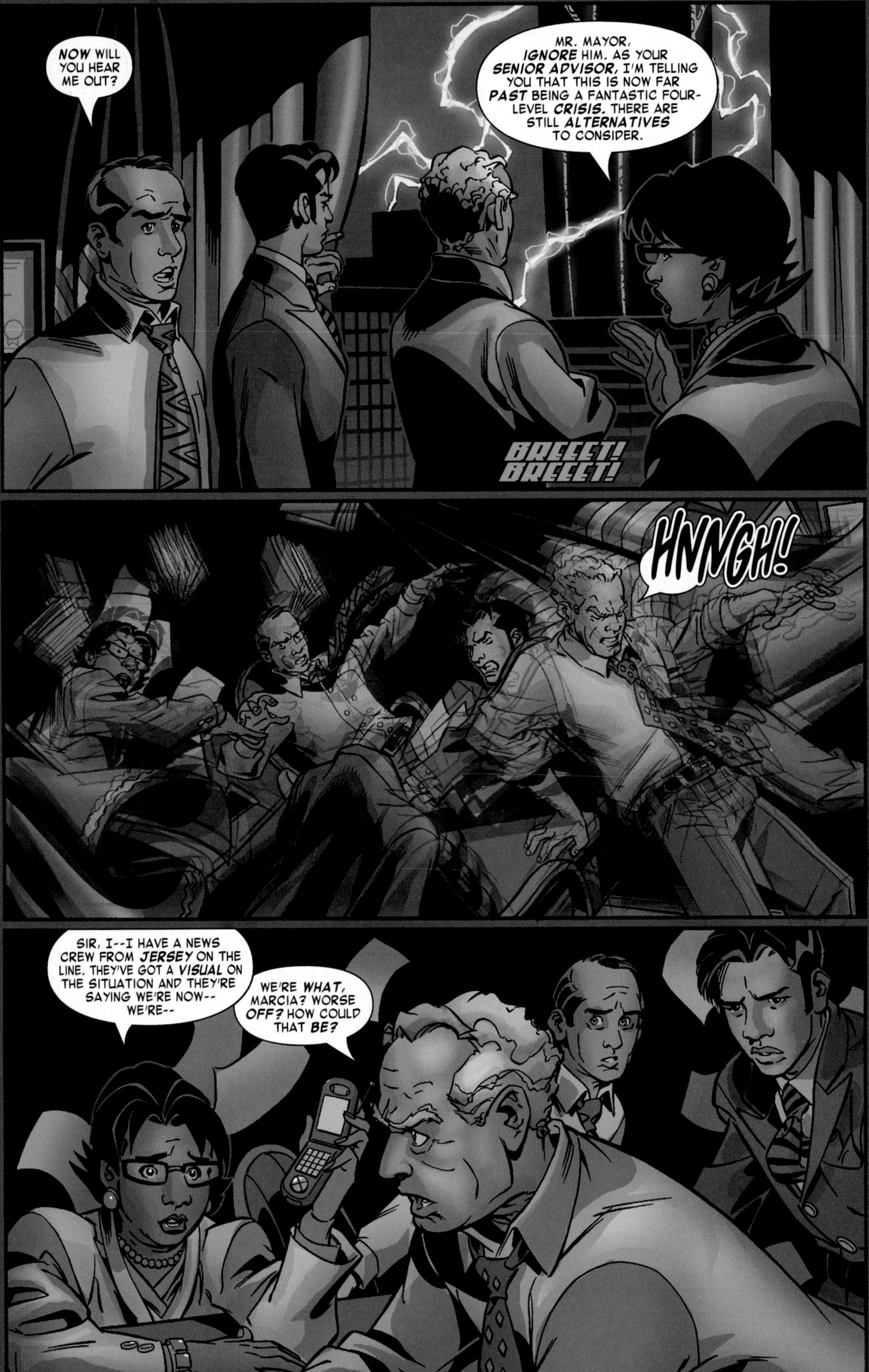
NOW WILL YOU HEAR ME OUT?
MR. MAYOR, IGNORE HIM. AS YOUR SENIOR ADVISOR, I'M TELLING YOU THAT THIS IS NOW FAR PAST BEING A FANTASTIC FOUR-LEVEL CRISIS. THERE ARE STILL ALTERNATIVES TO CONSIDER.
BREEET! BREEET!
HNNGH!
SIR, I--I HAVE A NEWS CREW FROM JERSEY ON THE LINE. THEY'VE GOT A VISUAL ON THE SITUATION AND THEY'RE SAYING WE'RE NOW--WE'RE--
WE'RE WHAT, MARCIA? WORSE OFF? HOW COULD THAT BE?

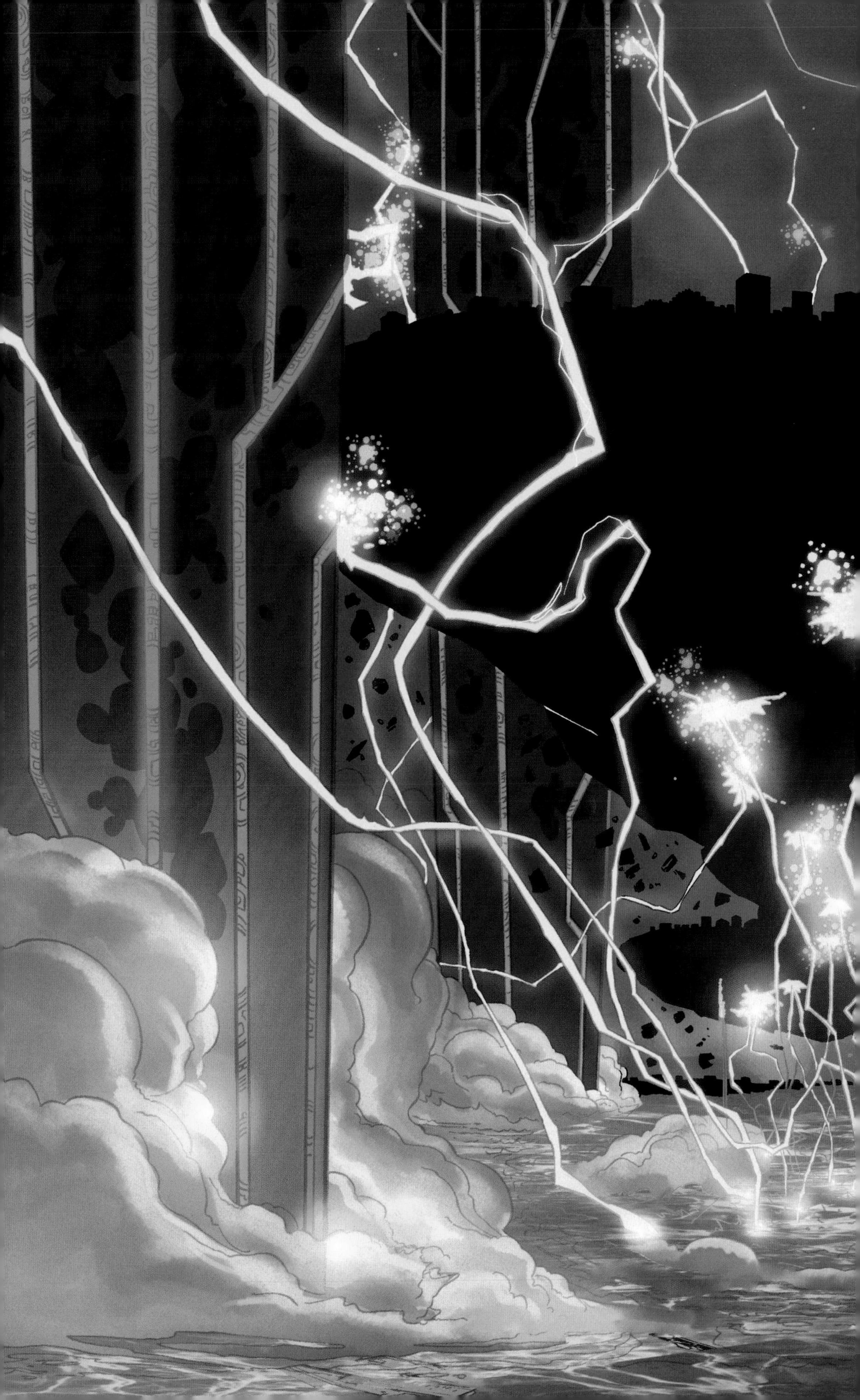

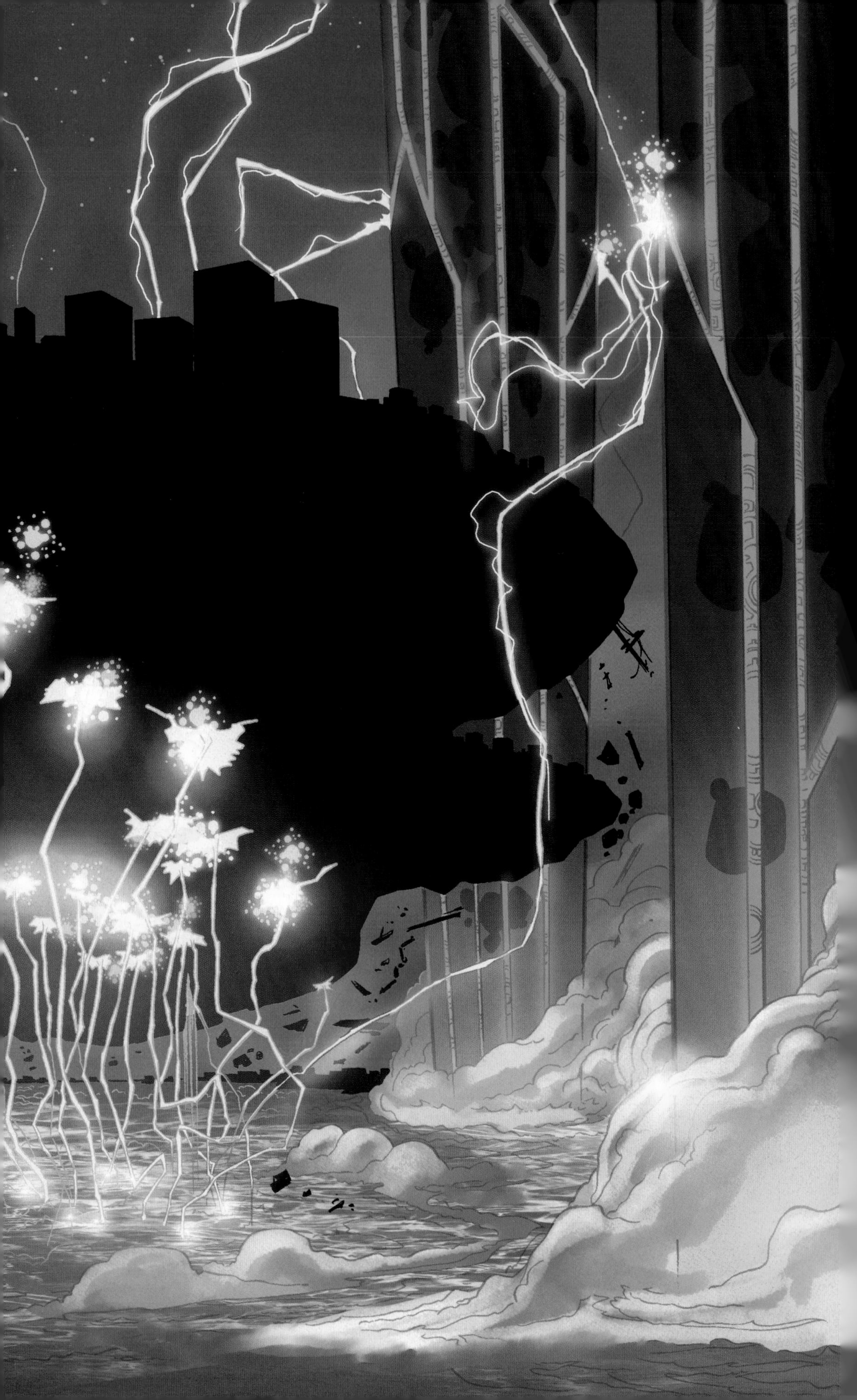

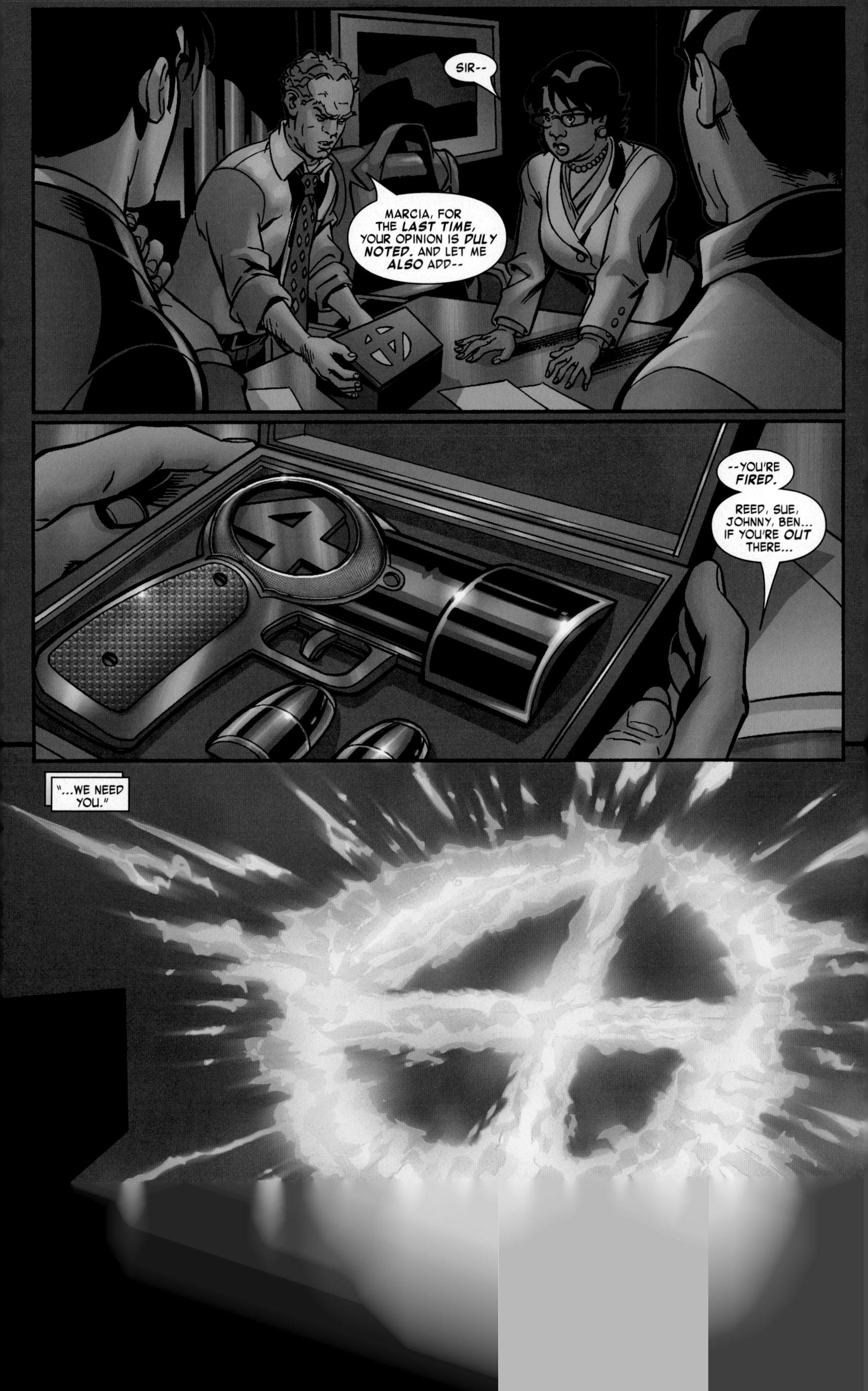
SIR--
MARCIA, FOR THE LAST TIME, YOUR OPINION IS DULY NOTED. AND LET ME ALSO ADD--
--YOU'RE FIRED.
REED, SUE, JOHNNY, BEN... IF YOU'RE OUT THERE...
"...WE NEED YOU."

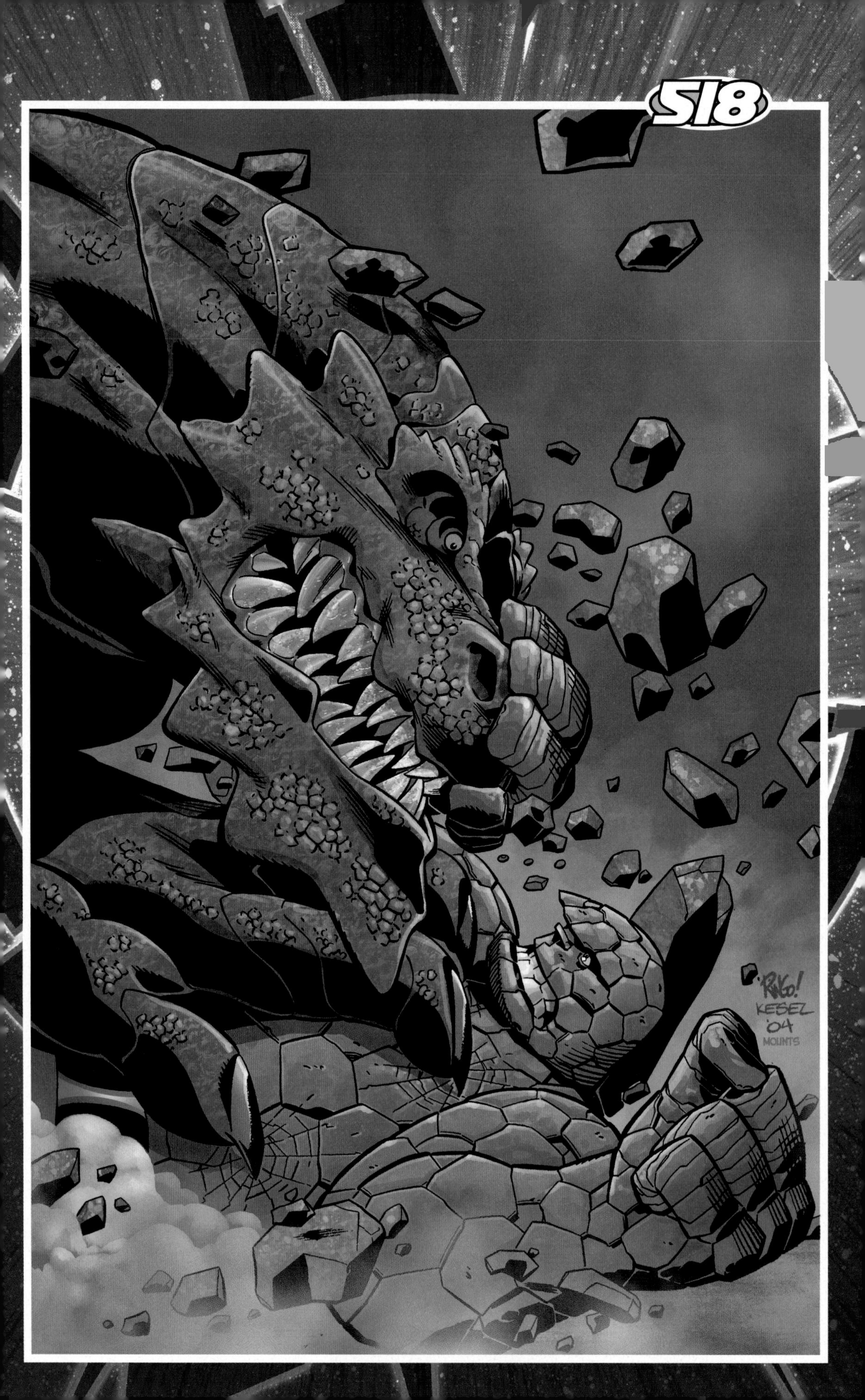
518
RINGO!
KESEL
'04
MOUNTS

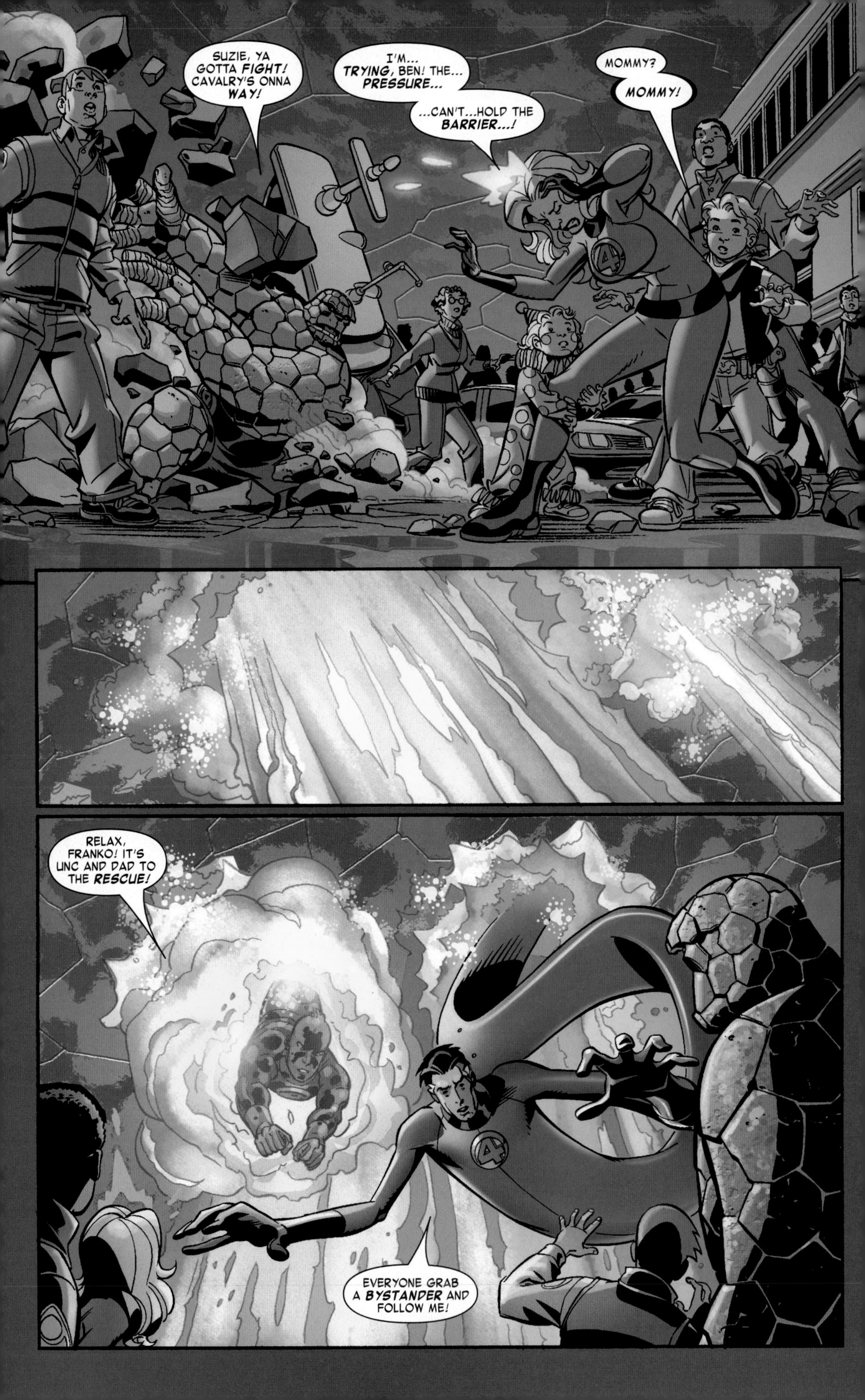
SUZIE, YA GOTTA FIGHT! CAVALRY'S ONNA WAY!
I'M... TRYING, BEN! THE... PRESSURE...
...CAN'T...HOLD THE BARRIER...!
MOMMY?
MOMMY!
RELAX, FRANKO! IT'S UNC AND DAD TO THE RESCUE!
EVERYONE GRAB A BYSTANDER AND FOLLOW ME!

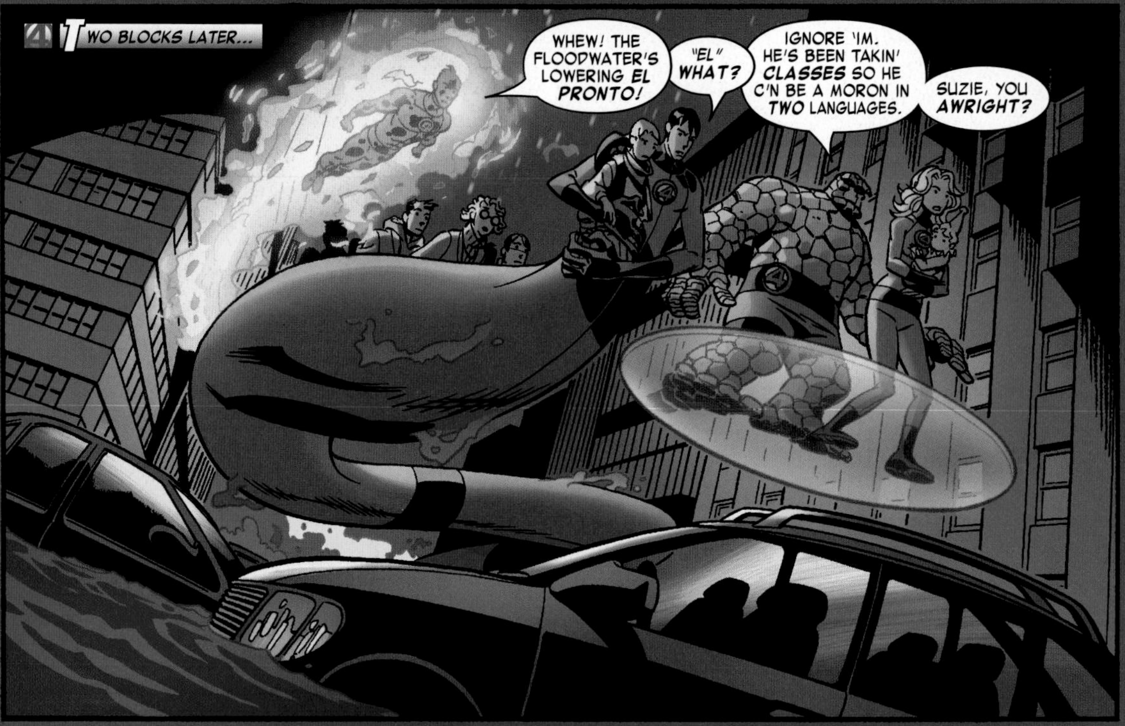
TWO BLOCKS LATER...
WHEW! THE FLOODWATER'S LOWERING EL PRONTO!
"EL" WHAT?
IGNORE 'IM. HE'S BEEN TAKIN' CLASSES SO HE C'N BE A MORON IN TWO LANGUAGES.
SUZIE, YOU AWRIGHT?

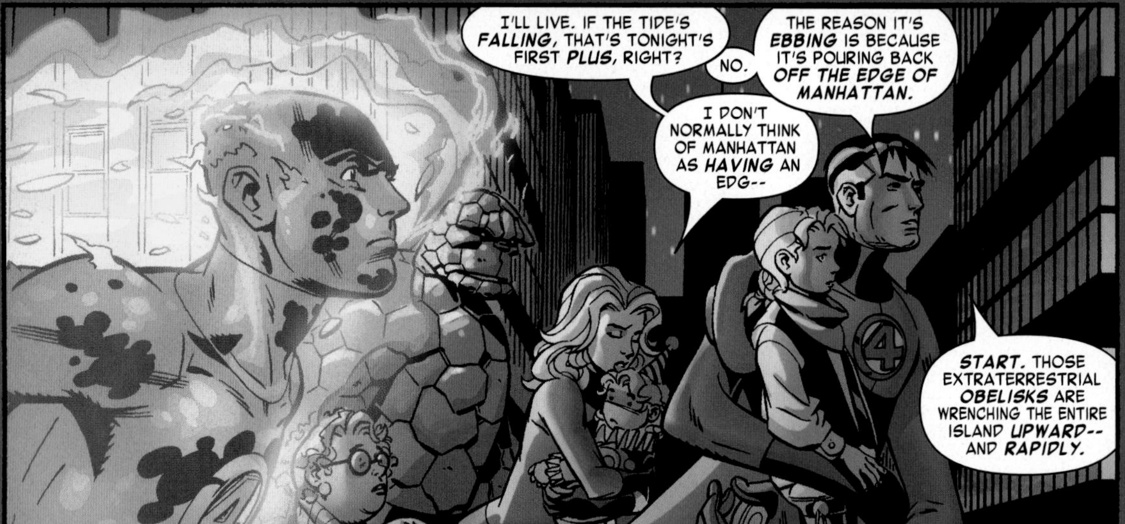
I'LL LIVE. IF THE TIDE'S FALLING, THAT'S TONIGHT'S FIRST PLUS, RIGHT?
NO.
THE REASON IT'S EBBING IS BECAUSE IT'S POURING BACK OFF THE EDGE OF MANHATTAN.
I DON'T NORMALLY THINK OF MANHATTAN AS HAVING AN EDG--
START. THOSE EXTRATERRESTRIAL OBELISKS ARE WRENCHING THE ENTIRE ISLAND UPWARD-- AND RAPIDLY.

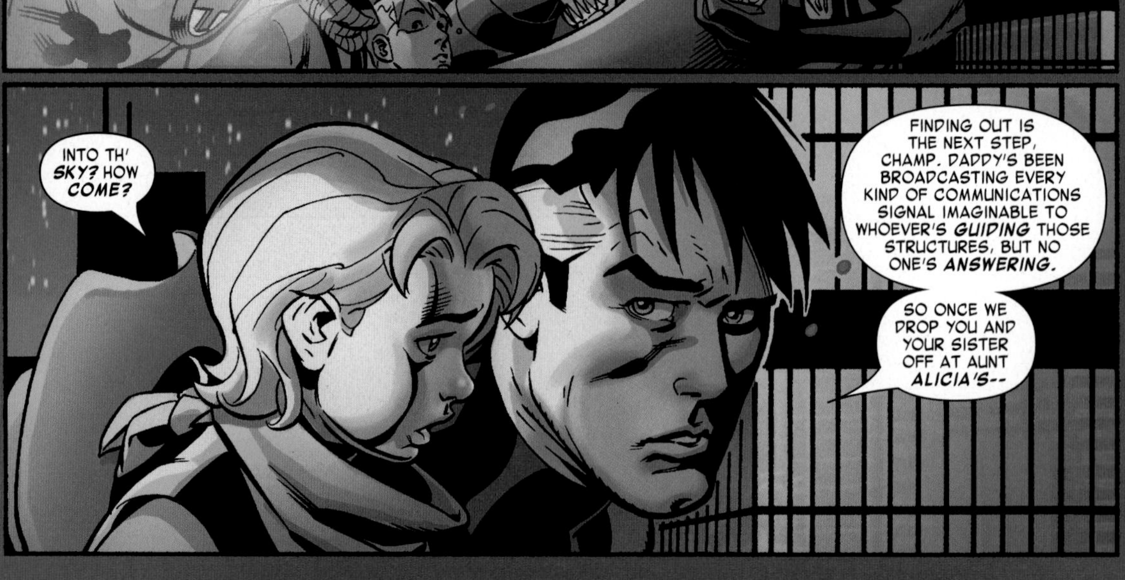
INTO TH' SKY? HOW COME?
FINDING OUT IS THE NEXT STEP, CHAMP. DADDY'S BEEN BROADCASTING EVERY KIND OF COMMUNICATIONS SIGNAL IMAGINABLE TO WHOEVER'S GUIDING THOSE STRUCTURES, BUT NO ONE'S ANSWERING.
SO ONCE WE DROP YOU AND YOUR SISTER OFF AT AUNT ALICIA'S--

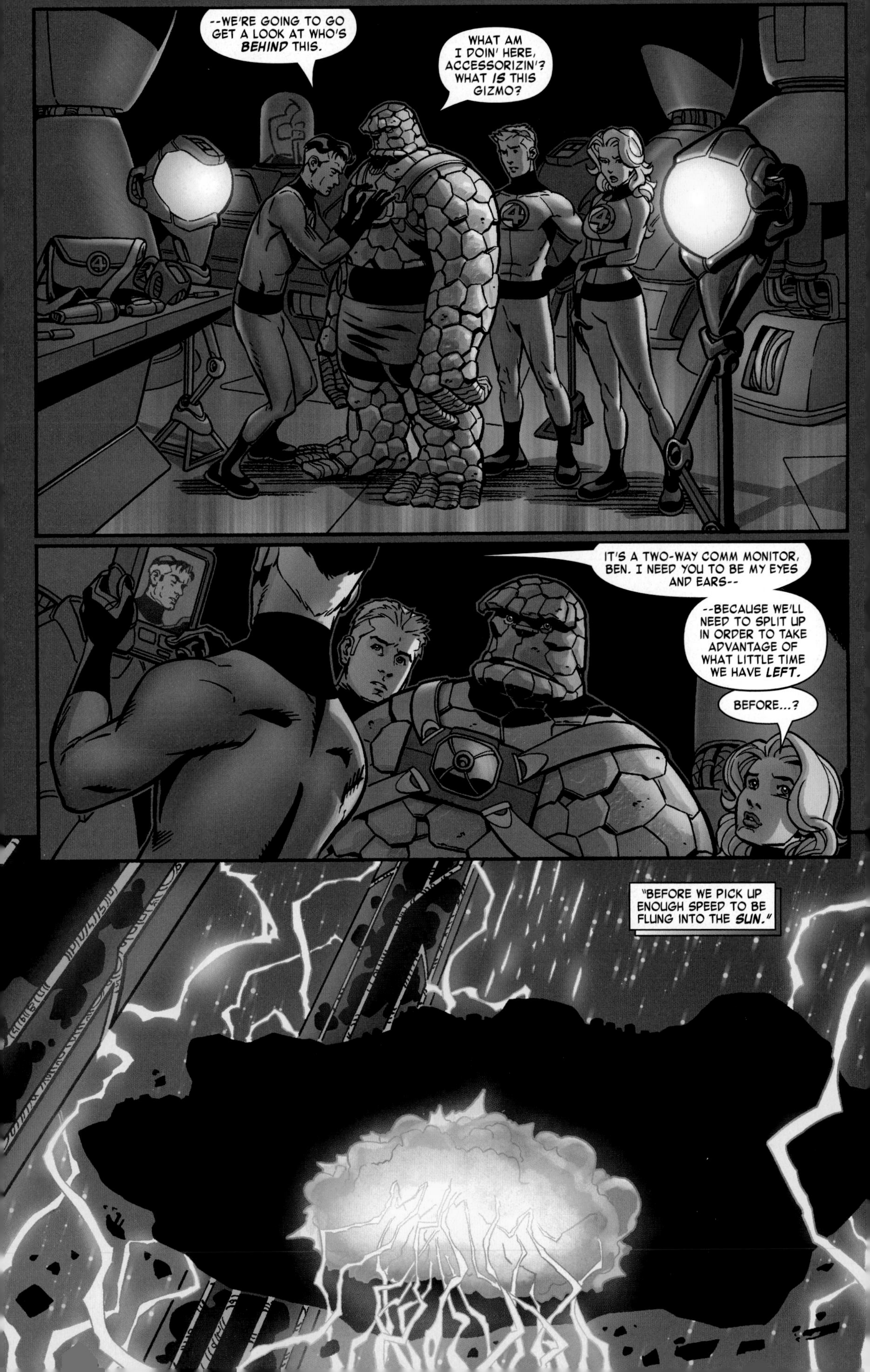
--WE'RE GOING TO GO GET A LOOK AT WHO'S BEHIND THIS.
WHAT AM I DOIN' HERE, ACCESSORIZIN'? WHAT IS THIS GIZMO?
IT'S A TWO-WAY COMM MONITOR, BEN. I NEED YOU TO BE MY EYES AND EARS--
--BECAUSE WE'LL NEED TO SPLIT UP IN ORDER TO TAKE ADVANTAGE OF WHAT LITTLE TIME WE HAVE LEFT.
BEFORE...?
"BEFORE WE PICK UP ENOUGH SPEED TO BE FLUNG INTO THE SUN."

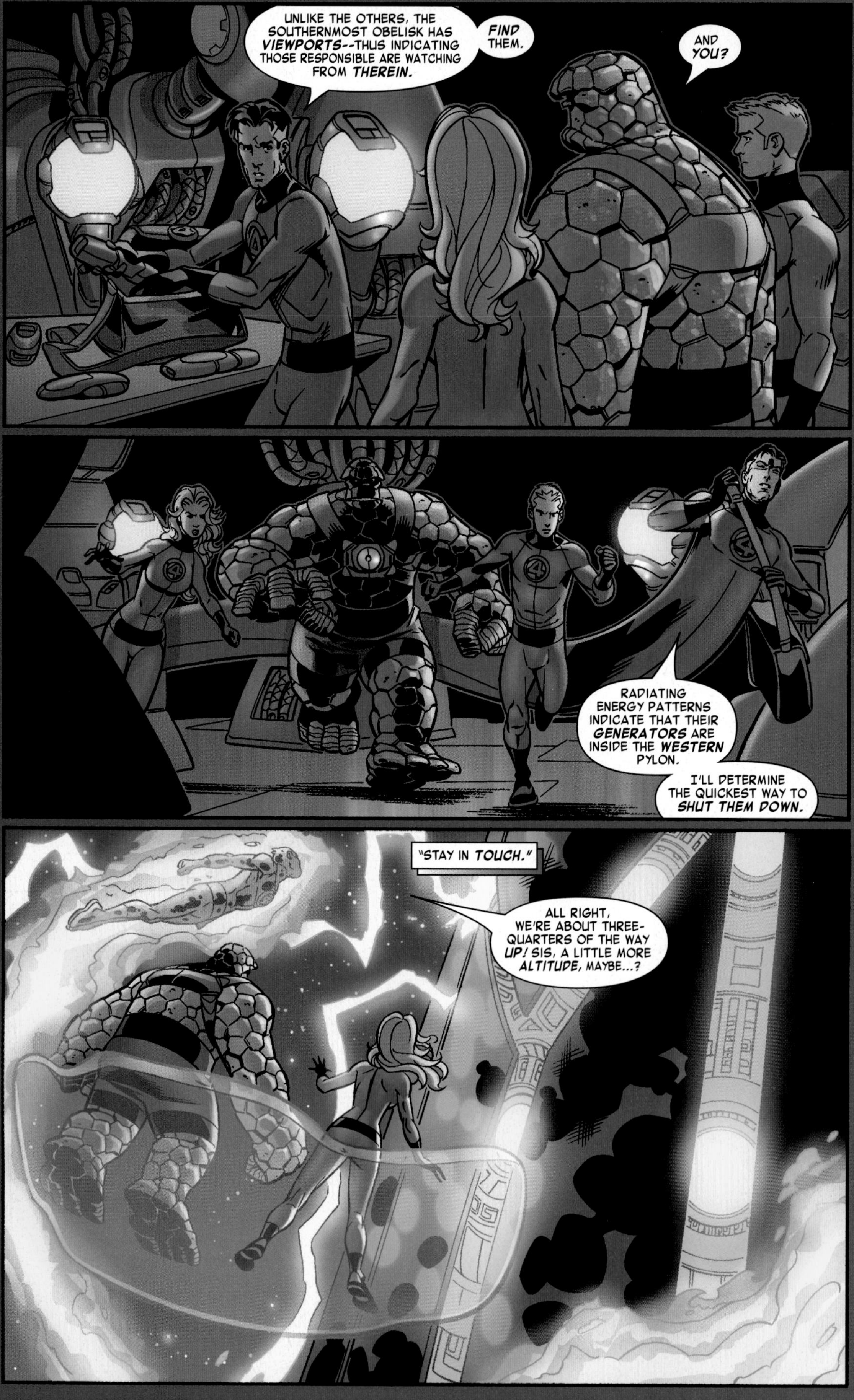
UNLIKE THE OTHERS, THE SOUTHERNMOST OBELISK HAS VIEWPORTS--THUS INDICATING THOSE RESPONSIBLE ARE WATCHING FROM THEREIN.
FIND THEM.
AND YOU?
RADIATING ENERGY PATTERNS INDICATE THAT THEIR GENERATORS ARE INSIDE THE WESTERN PYLON.
I'LL DETERMINE THE QUICKEST WAY TO SHUT THEM DOWN.
"STAY IN TOUCH."
ALL RIGHT, WE'RE ABOUT THREE-QUARTERS OF THE WAY UP! SIS, A LITTLE MORE ALTITUDE, MAYBE...?

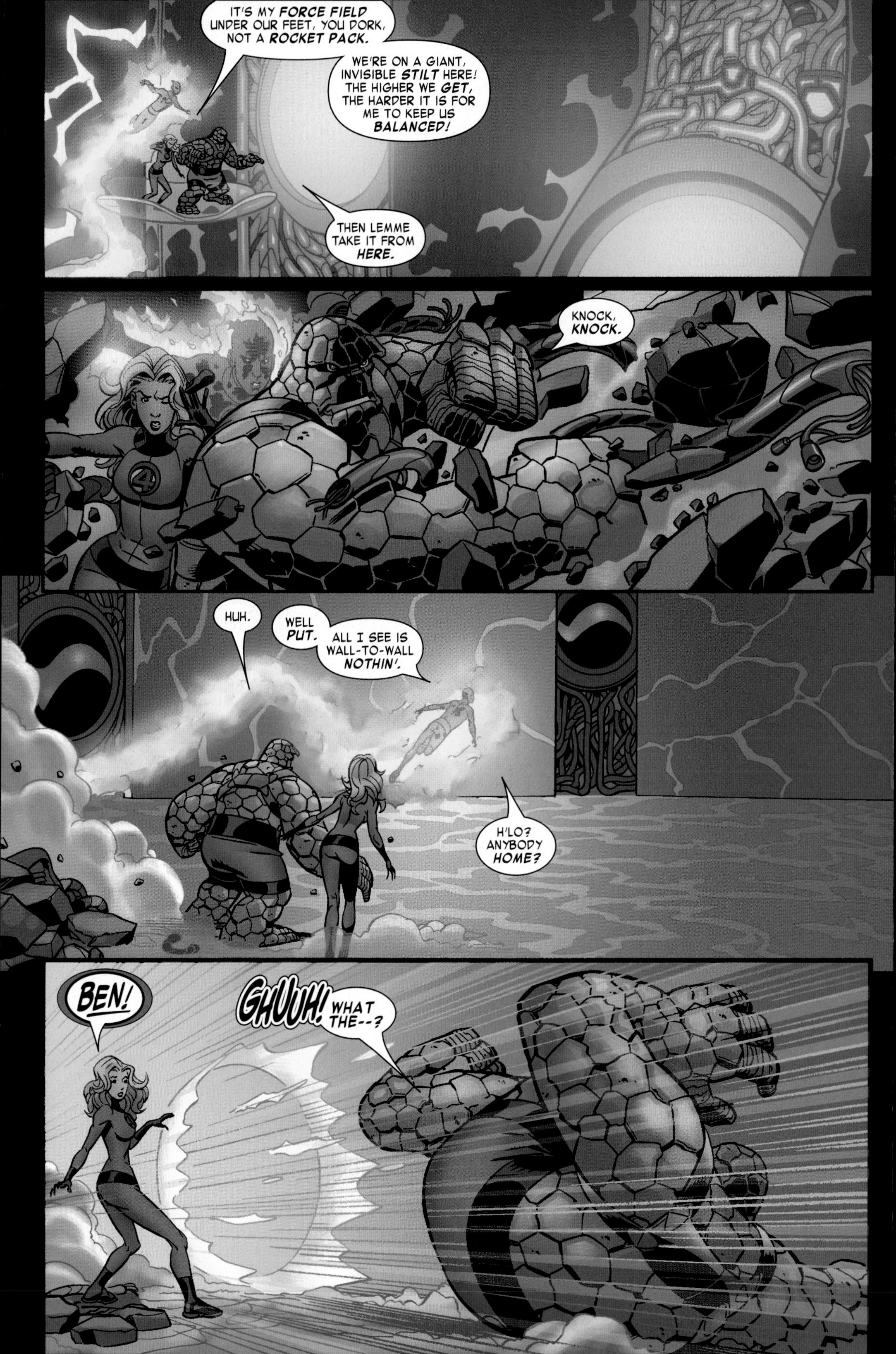
IT'S MY FORCE FIELD UNDER OUR FEET, YOU DORK, NOT A ROCKET PACK.
WE'RE ON A GIANT, INVISIBLE STILT HERE! THE HIGHER WE GET, THE HARDER IT IS FOR ME TO KEEP US BALANCED!
THEN LEMME TAKE IT FROM HERE.
KNOCK, KNOCK.
HUH.
WELL PUT.
ALL I SEE IS WALL-TO-WALL NOTHIN'.
H'LO? ANYBODY HOME?
BEN!
GHUUUH!
WHAT THE--?

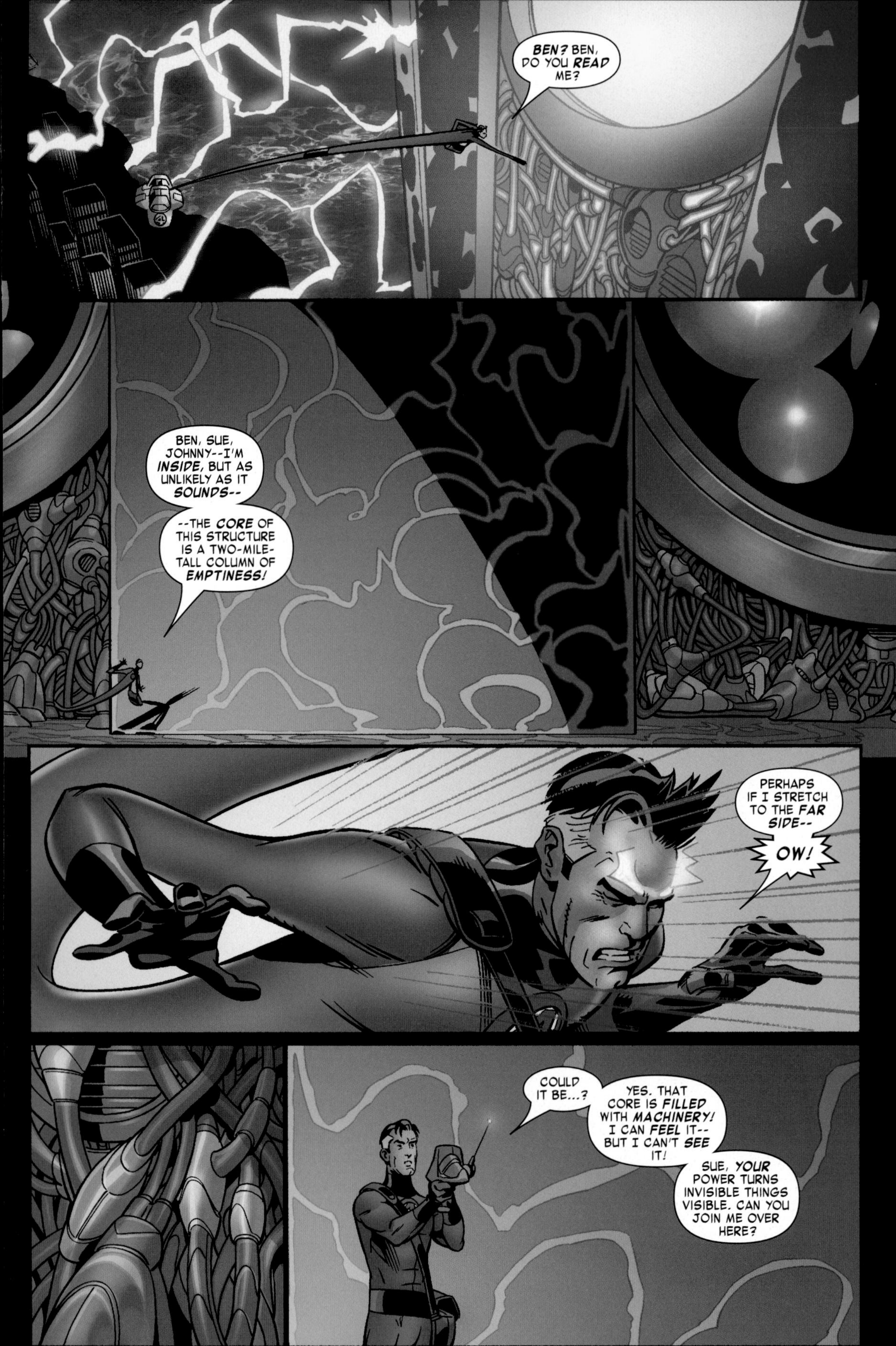
BEN? BEN, DO YOU READ ME?
BEN, SUE, JOHNNY--I'M INSIDE, BUT AS UNLIKELY AS IT SOUNDS--
--THE CORE OF THIS STRUCTURE IS A TWO-MILE-TALL COLUMN OF EMPTINESS!
PERHAPS IF I STRETCH TO THE FAR SIDE--
OW!
COULD IT BE...?
YES. THAT CORE IS FILLED WITH MACHINERY! I CAN FEEL IT-- BUT I CAN'T SEE IT!
SUE, YOUR POWER TURNS INVISIBLE THINGS VISIBLE. CAN YOU JOIN ME OVER HERE?

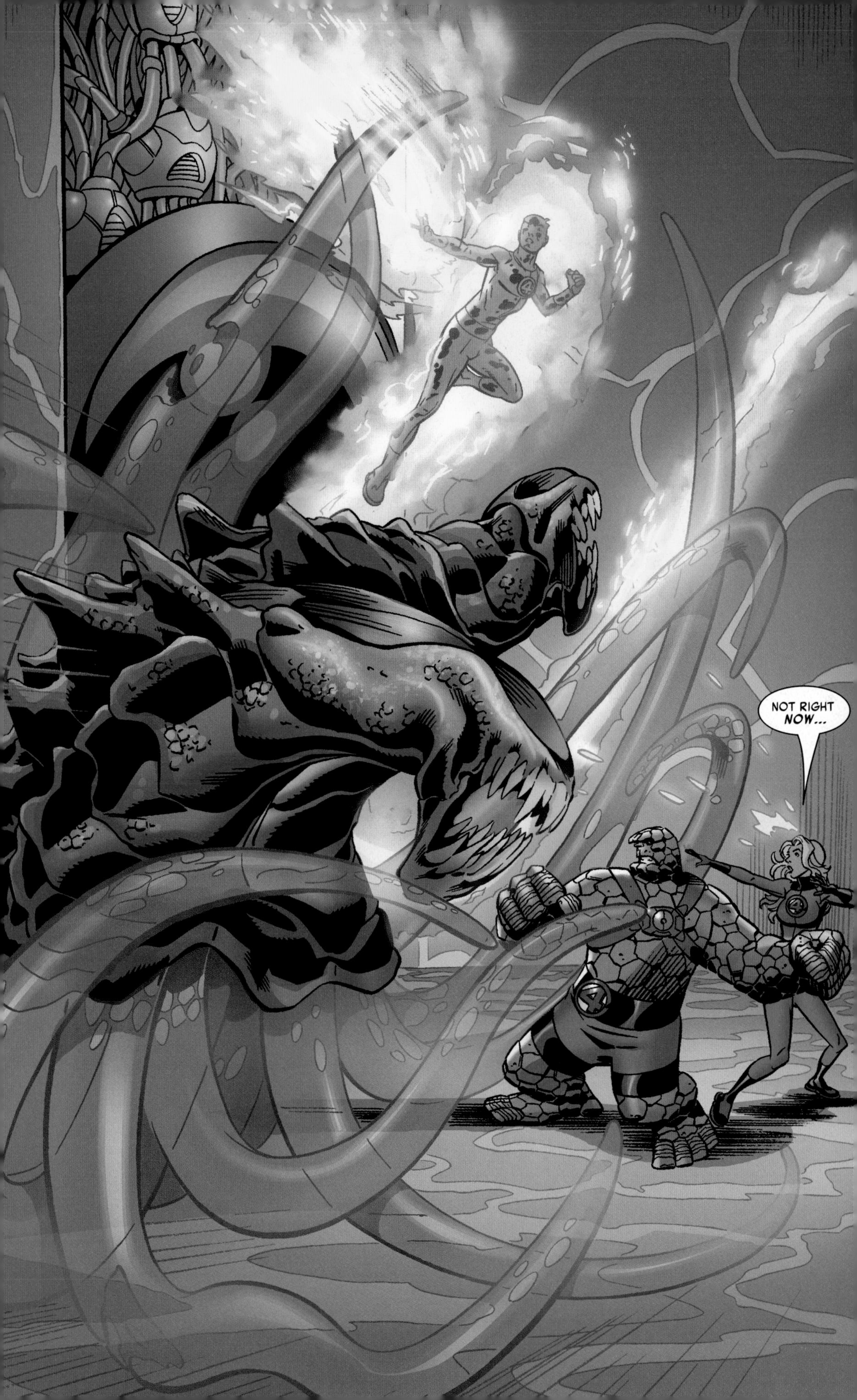
NOT RIGHT NOW...

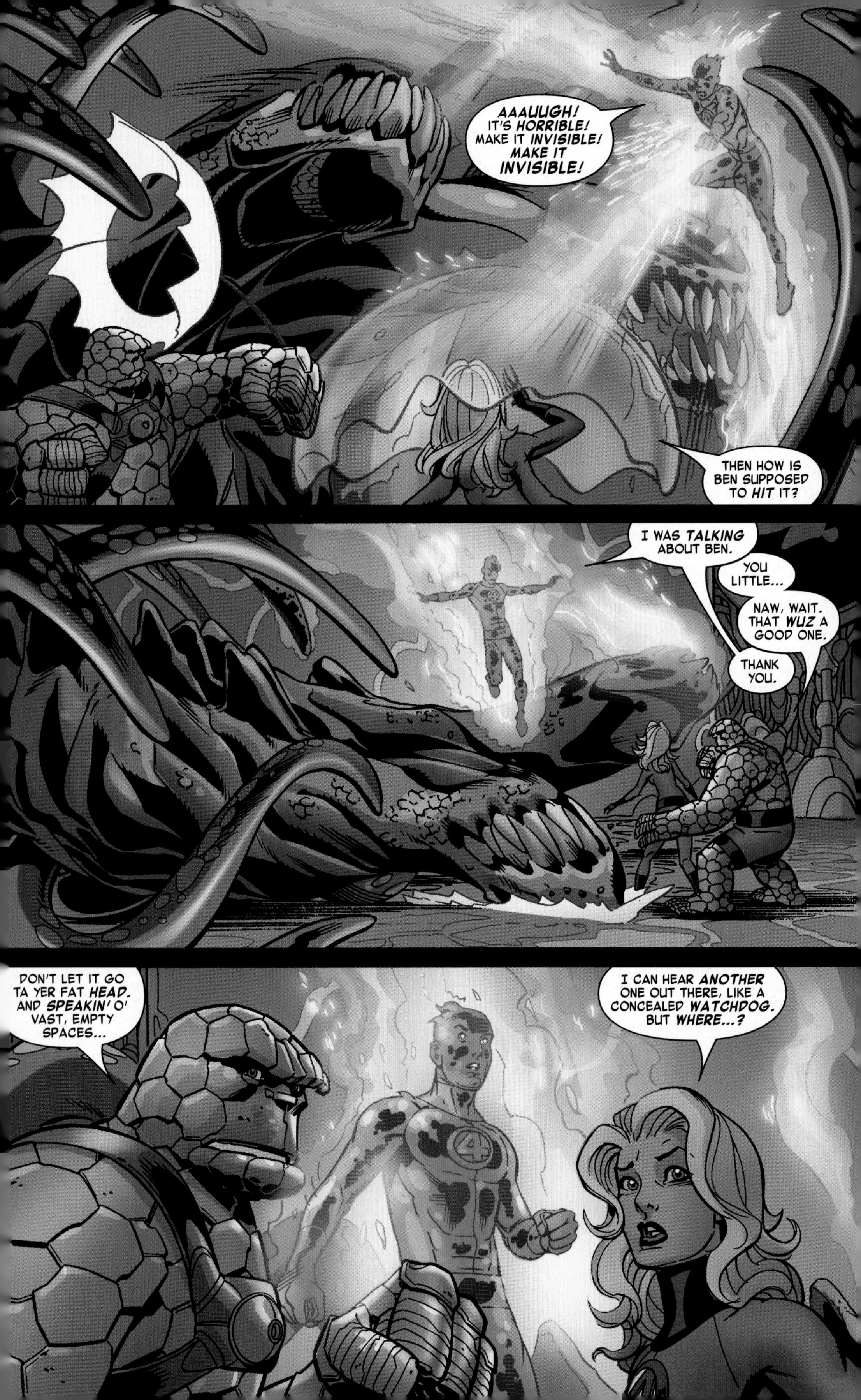
AAAUUGH! IT'S HORRIBLE! MAKE IT INVISIBLE! MAKE IT INVISIBLE!
THEN HOW IS BEN SUPPOSED TO HIT IT?
I WAS TALKING ABOUT BEN.
YOU LITTLE...
NAW, WAIT. THAT WUZ A GOOD ONE.
THANK YOU.
DON'T LET IT GO TA YER FAT HEAD. AND SPEAKIN' O' VAST, EMPTY SPACES...
I CAN HEAR ANOTHER ONE OUT THERE, LIKE A CONCEALED WATCHDOG. BUT WHERE...?

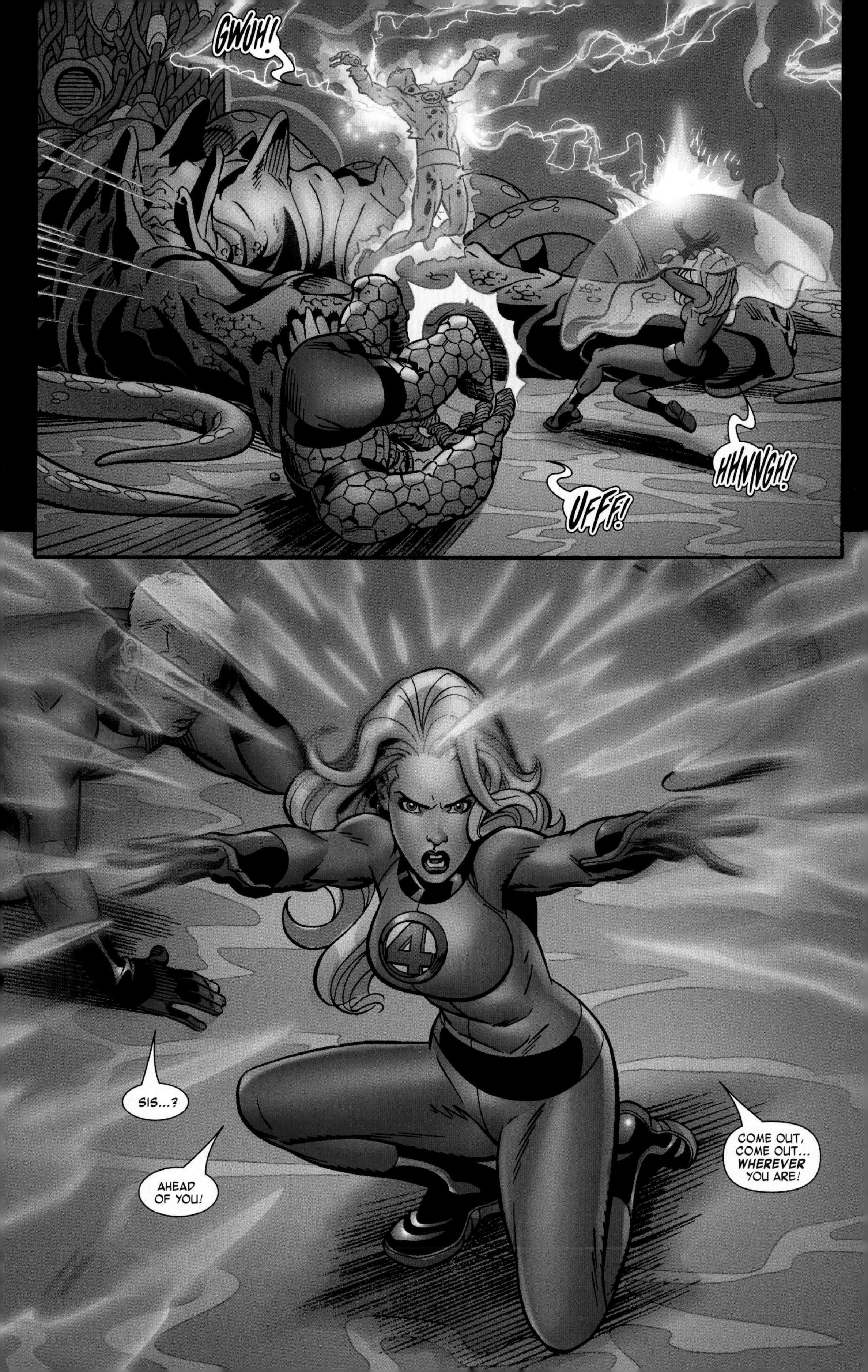
GWOH!
OFFF!
HHNNGH!
SIS...?
AHEAD OF YOU!
COME OUT, COME OUT... WHEREVER YOU ARE!

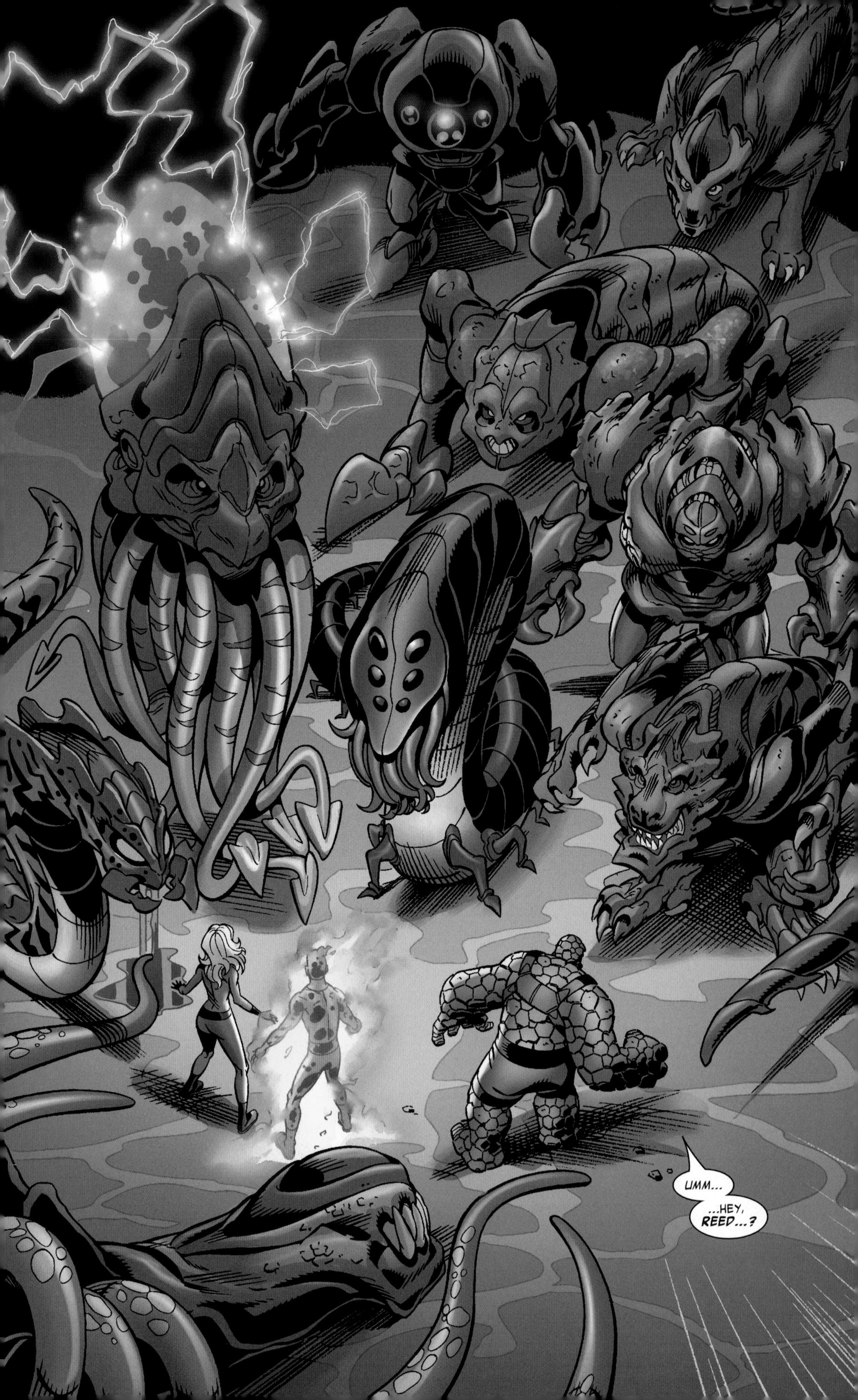
UMM...
...HEY, REED...?

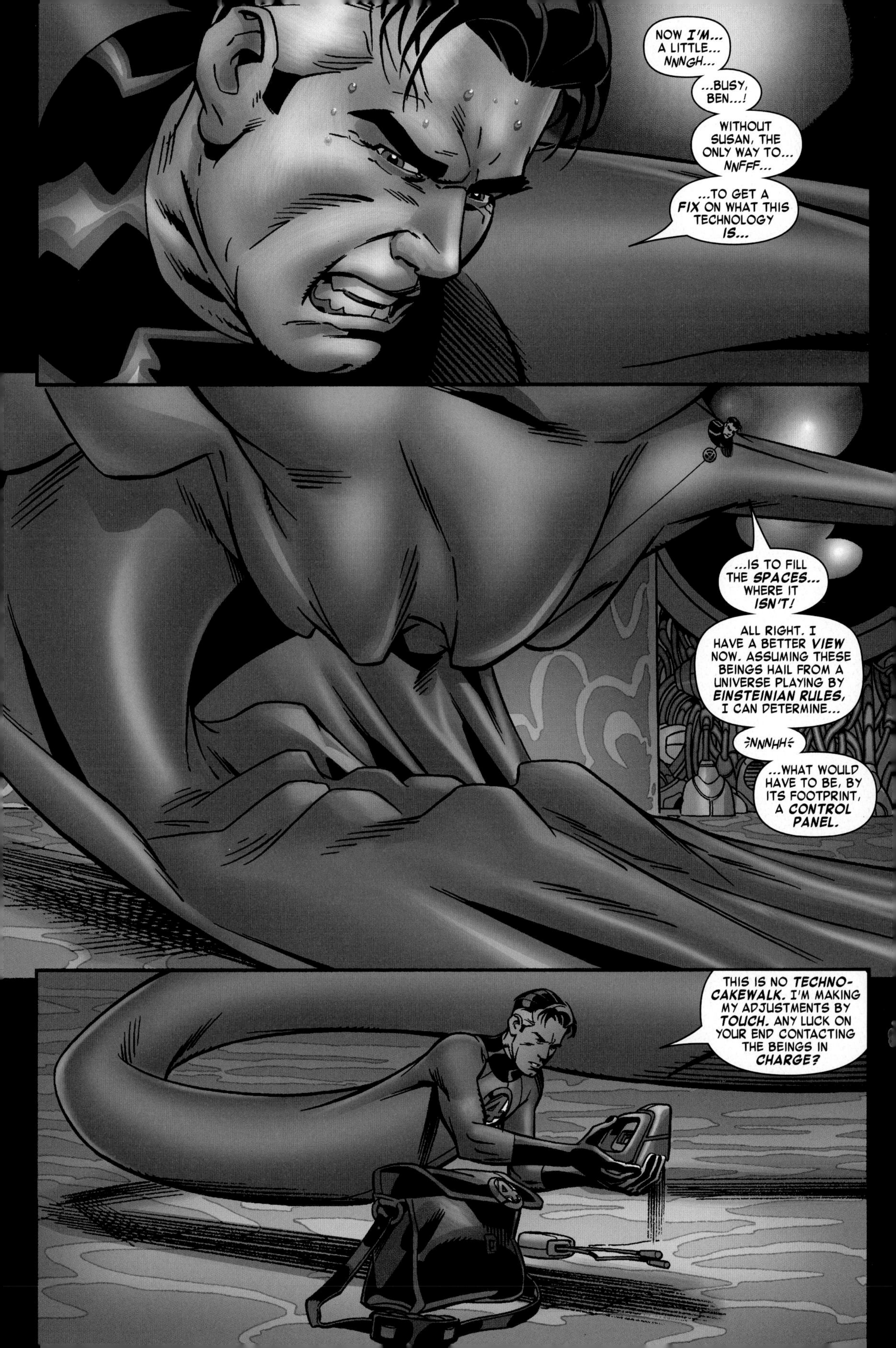
NOW I'M... A LITTLE... NNNGH...
...BUSY, BEN...!
WITHOUT SUSAN, THE ONLY WAY TO... NNFFF...
...TO GET A FIX ON WHAT THIS TECHNOLOGY IS...
...IS TO FILL THE SPACES... WHERE IT ISN'T!
ALL RIGHT. I HAVE A BETTER VIEW NOW. ASSUMING THESE BEINGS HAIL FROM A UNIVERSE PLAYING BY EINSTEINIAN RULES, I CAN DETERMINE...
NNNHH
...WHAT WOULD HAVE TO BE, BY ITS FOOTPRINT, A CONTROL PANEL.
THIS IS NO TECHNO-CAKEWALK. I'M MAKING MY ADJUSTMENTS BY TOUCH. ANY LUCK ON YOUR END CONTACTING THE BEINGS IN CHARGE?

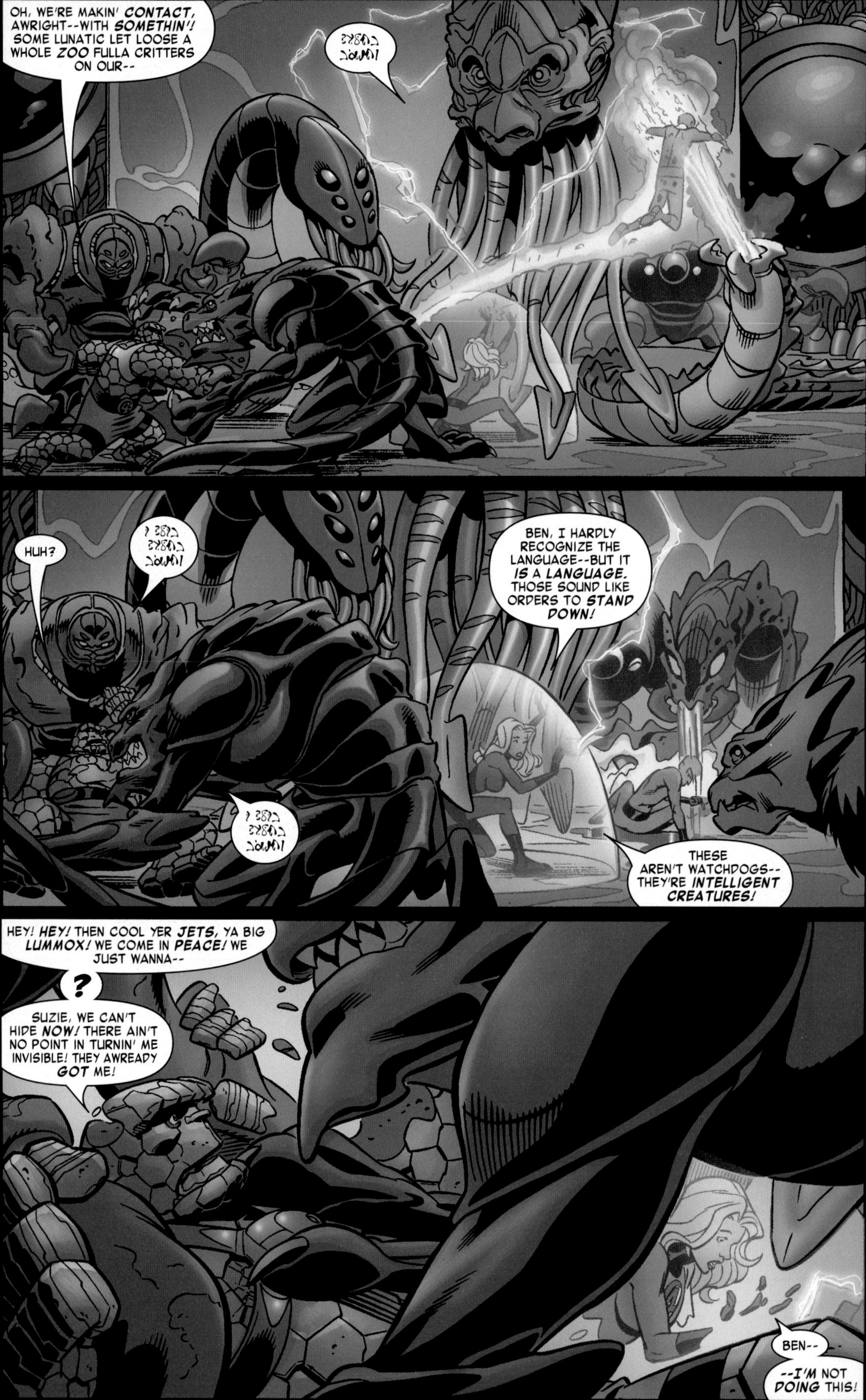
OH, WE'RE MAKIN' CONTACT, AWRIGHT--WITH SOMETHIN'! SOME LUNATIC LET LOOSE A WHOLE ZOO FULLA CRITTERS ON OUR--
HUH?
BEN, I HARDLY RECOGNIZE THE LANGUAGE--BUT IT IS A LANGUAGE. THOSE SOUND LIKE ORDERS TO STAND DOWN!
THESE AREN'T WATCHDOGS--THEY'RE INTELLIGENT CREATURES!
HEY! HEY! THEN COOL YER JETS, YA BIG LUMMOX! WE COME IN PEACE! WE JUST WANNA--
?
SUZIE, WE CAN'T HIDE NOW! THERE AIN'T NO POINT IN TURNIN' ME INVISIBLE! THEY AWREADY GOT ME!
BEN--
--I'M NOT DOING THIS!

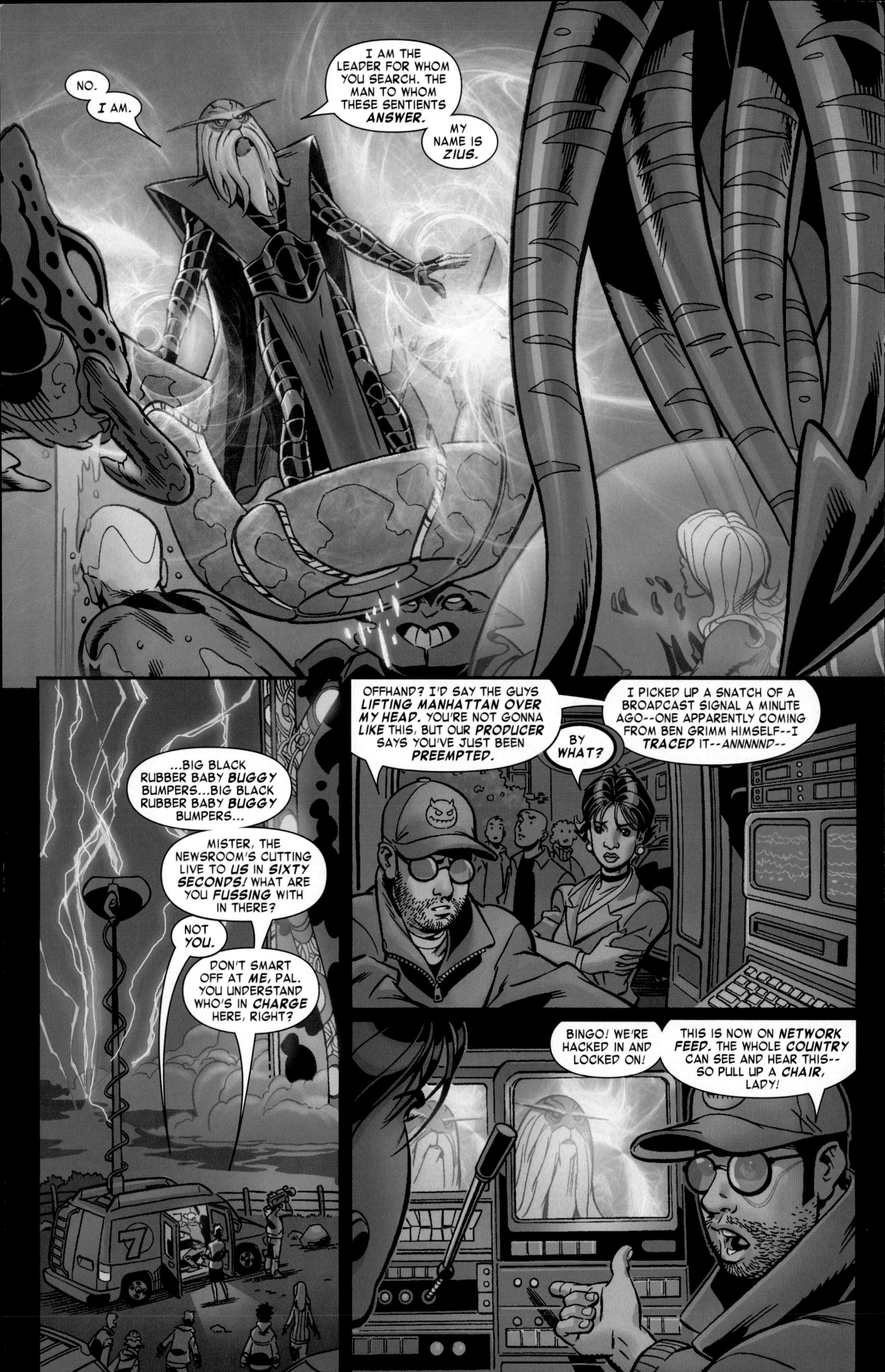
NO.
I AM.
I AM THE LEADER FOR WHOM YOU SEARCH. THE MAN TO WHOM THESE SENTIENTS ANSWER.
MY NAME IS ZIUS.
...BIG BLACK RUBBER BABY BUGGY BUMPERS...BIG BLACK RUBBER BABY BUGGY BUMPERS...
MISTER, THE NEWSROOM'S CUTTING LIVE TO US IN SIXTY SECONDS! WHAT ARE YOU FUSSING WITH IN THERE?
NOT YOU.
DON'T SMART OFF AT ME, PAL. YOU UNDERSTAND WHO'S IN CHARGE HERE, RIGHT?
OFFHAND? I'D SAY THE GUYS LIFTING MANHATTAN OVER MY HEAD. YOU'RE NOT GONNA LIKE THIS, BUT OUR PRODUCER SAYS YOU'VE JUST BEEN PREEMPTED.
BY WHAT?
I PICKED UP A SNATCH OF A BROADCAST SIGNAL A MINUTE AGO--ONE APPARENTLY COMING FROM BEN GRIMM HIMSELF--I TRACED IT--ANNNNND--
BINGO! WE'RE HACKED IN AND LOCKED ON!
THIS IS NOW ON NETWORK FEED. THE WHOLE COUNTRY CAN SEE AND HEAR THIS--SO PULL UP A CHAIR, LADY!
7

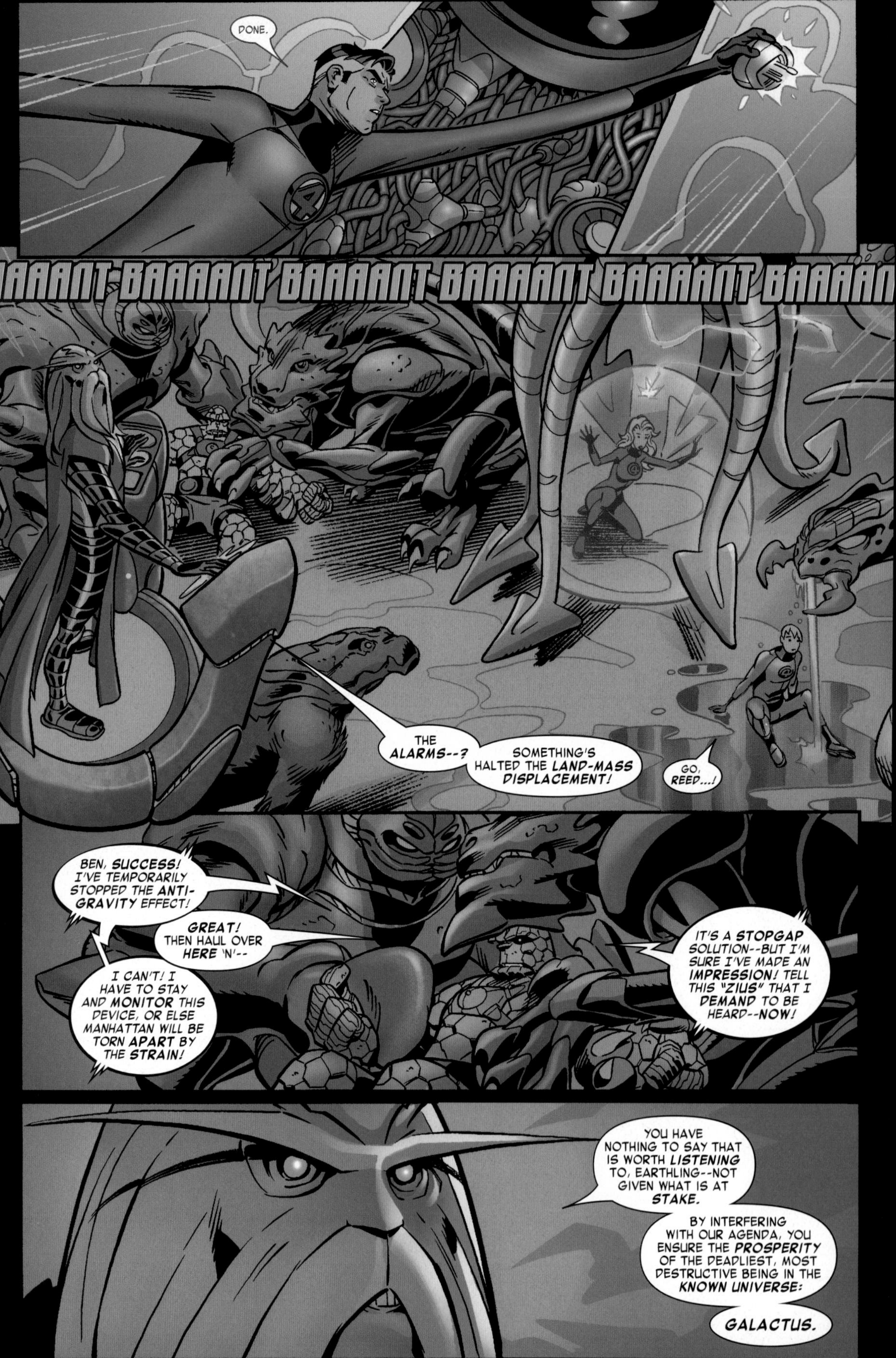
DONE.
BAAAANT BAAAANT BAAAANT BAAAANT BAAAANT BAAAAN
THE ALARMS--?
SOMETHING'S HALTED THE LAND-MASS DISPLACEMENT!
GO, REED...!
BEN, SUCCESS! I'VE TEMPORARILY STOPPED THE ANTI-GRAVITY EFFECT!
GREAT! THEN HAUL OVER HERE 'N'--
I CAN'T! I HAVE TO STAY AND MONITOR THIS DEVICE, OR ELSE MANHATTAN WILL BE TORN APART BY THE STRAIN!
IT'S A STOPGAP SOLUTION--BUT I'M SURE I'VE MADE AN IMPRESSION! TELL THIS "ZIUS" THAT I DEMAND TO BE HEARD--NOW!
YOU HAVE NOTHING TO SAY THAT IS WORTH LISTENING TO, EARTHLING--NOT GIVEN WHAT IS AT STAKE.
BY INTERFERING WITH OUR AGENDA, YOU ENSURE THE PROSPERITY OF THE DEADLIEST, MOST DESTRUCTIVE BEING IN THE KNOWN UNIVERSE:
GALACTUS.

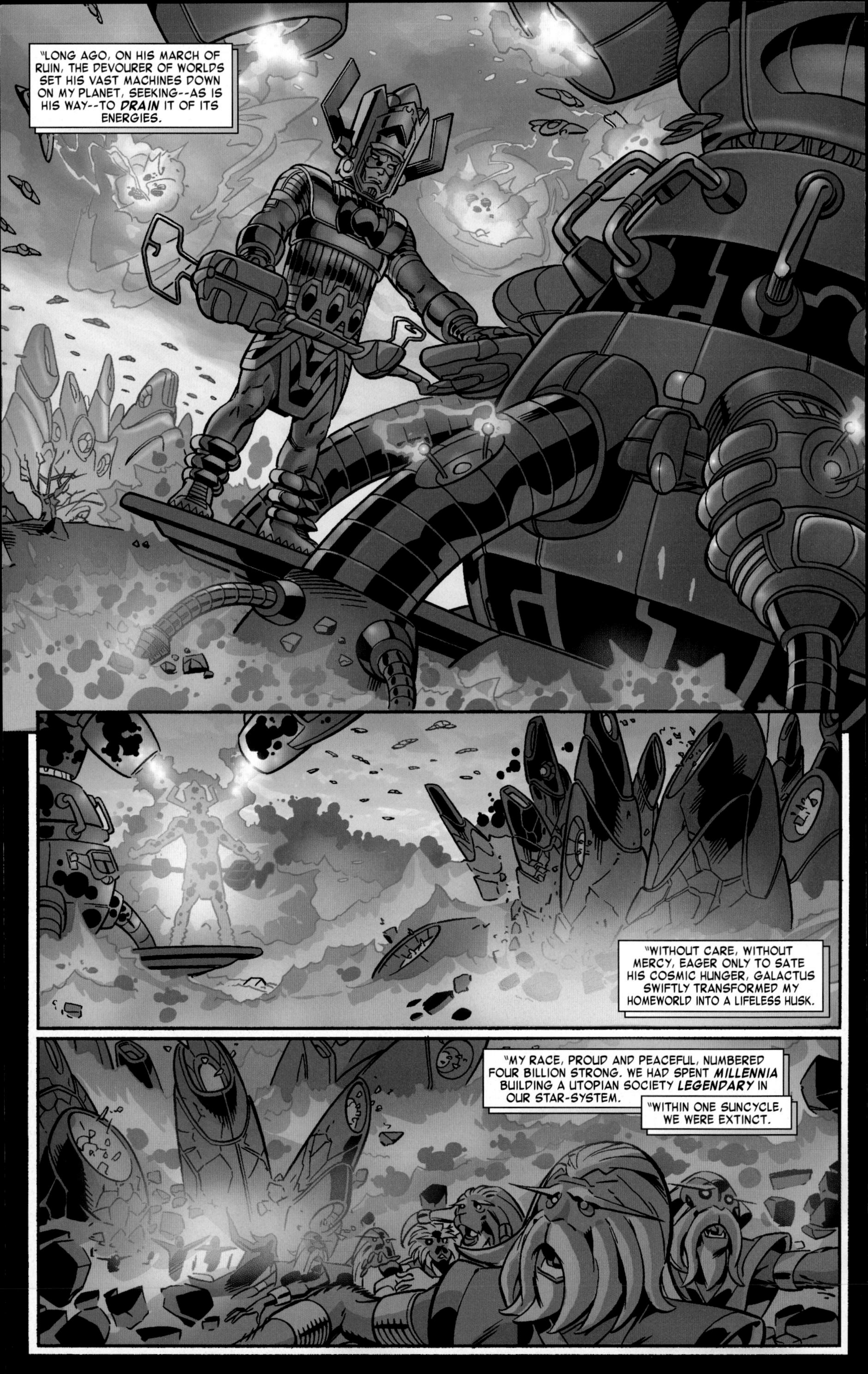
"LONG AGO, ON HIS MARCH OF RUIN, THE DEVOURER OF WORLDS SET HIS VAST MACHINES DOWN ON MY PLANET, SEEKING--AS IS HIS WAY--TO *DRAIN* IT OF ITS ENERGIES.
"WITHOUT CARE, WITHOUT MERCY, EAGER ONLY TO SATE HIS COSMIC HUNGER, GALACTUS SWIFTLY TRANSFORMED MY HOMEWORLD INTO A LIFELESS HUSK.
"MY RACE, PROUD AND PEACEFUL, NUMBERED FOUR BILLION STRONG. WE HAD SPENT *MILLENNIA* BUILDING A UTOPIAN SOCIETY *LEGENDARY* IN OUR STAR-SYSTEM.
"WITHIN ONE SUNCYCLE, WE WERE EXTINCT.

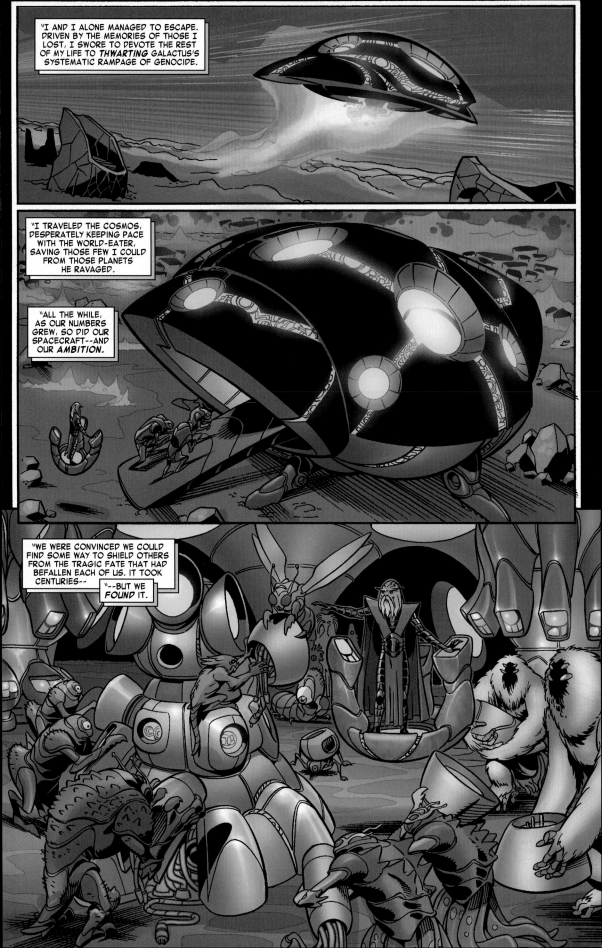

"I AND I ALONE MANAGED TO ESCAPE. DRIVEN BY THE MEMORIES OF THOSE I LOST, I SWORE TO DEVOTE THE REST OF MY LIFE TO *THWARTING* GALACTUS'S SYSTEMATIC RAMPAGE OF GENOCIDE.

"I TRAVELED THE COSMOS, DESPERATELY KEEPING PACE WITH THE WORLD-EATER, SAVING THOSE FEW I COULD FROM THOSE PLANETS HE RAVAGED.

"ALL THE WHILE, AS OUR NUMBERS GREW, SO DID OUR SPACECRAFT--AND OUR *AMBITION*.

"WE WERE CONVINCED WE COULD FIND SOME WAY TO SHIELD OTHERS FROM THE TRAGIC FATE THAT HAD BEFALLEN EACH OF US. IT TOOK CENTURIES--

"--BUT WE *FOUND* IT.

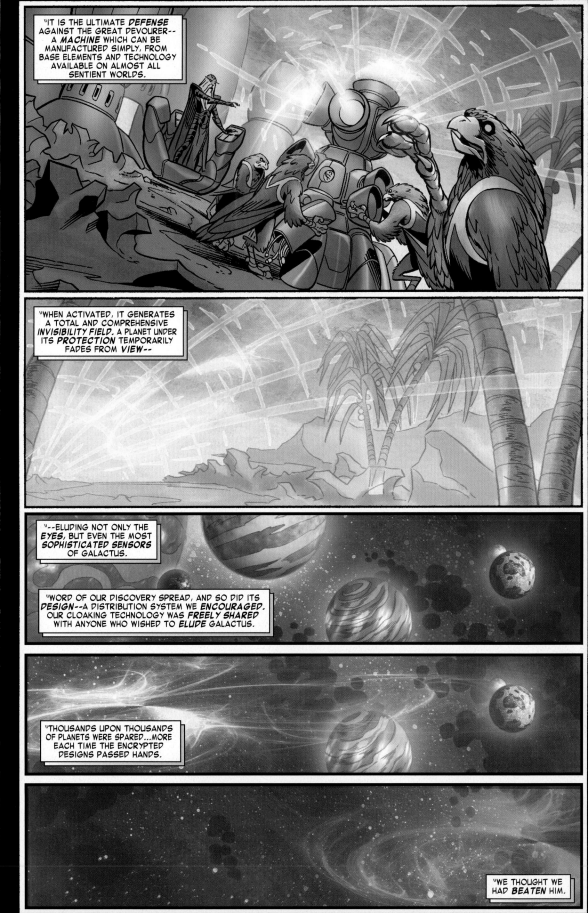

"IT IS THE ULTIMATE *DEFENSE* AGAINST THE GREAT DEVOURER-- A *MACHINE* WHICH CAN BE MANUFACTURED SIMPLY, FROM BASE ELEMENTS AND TECHNOLOGY AVAILABLE ON ALMOST ALL SENTIENT WORLDS.

"WHEN ACTIVATED, IT GENERATES A TOTAL AND COMPREHENSIVE *INVISIBILITY FIELD.* A PLANET UNDER ITS *PROTECTION* TEMPORARILY FADES FROM *VIEW*--

"--ELUDING NOT ONLY THE *EYES,* BUT EVEN THE MOST *SOPHISTICATED SENSORS* OF GALACTUS.

"WORD OF OUR DISCOVERY SPREAD, AND SO DID ITS *DESIGN*--A DISTRIBUTION SYSTEM WE *ENCOURAGED.* OUR CLOAKING TECHNOLOGY WAS *FREELY SHARED* WITH ANYONE WHO WISHED TO *ELUDE* GALACTUS.

"THOUSANDS UPON THOUSANDS OF PLANETS WERE SPARED...MORE EACH TIME THE ENCRYPTED DESIGNS PASSED HANDS.

"WE THOUGHT WE HAD *BEATEN* HIM.

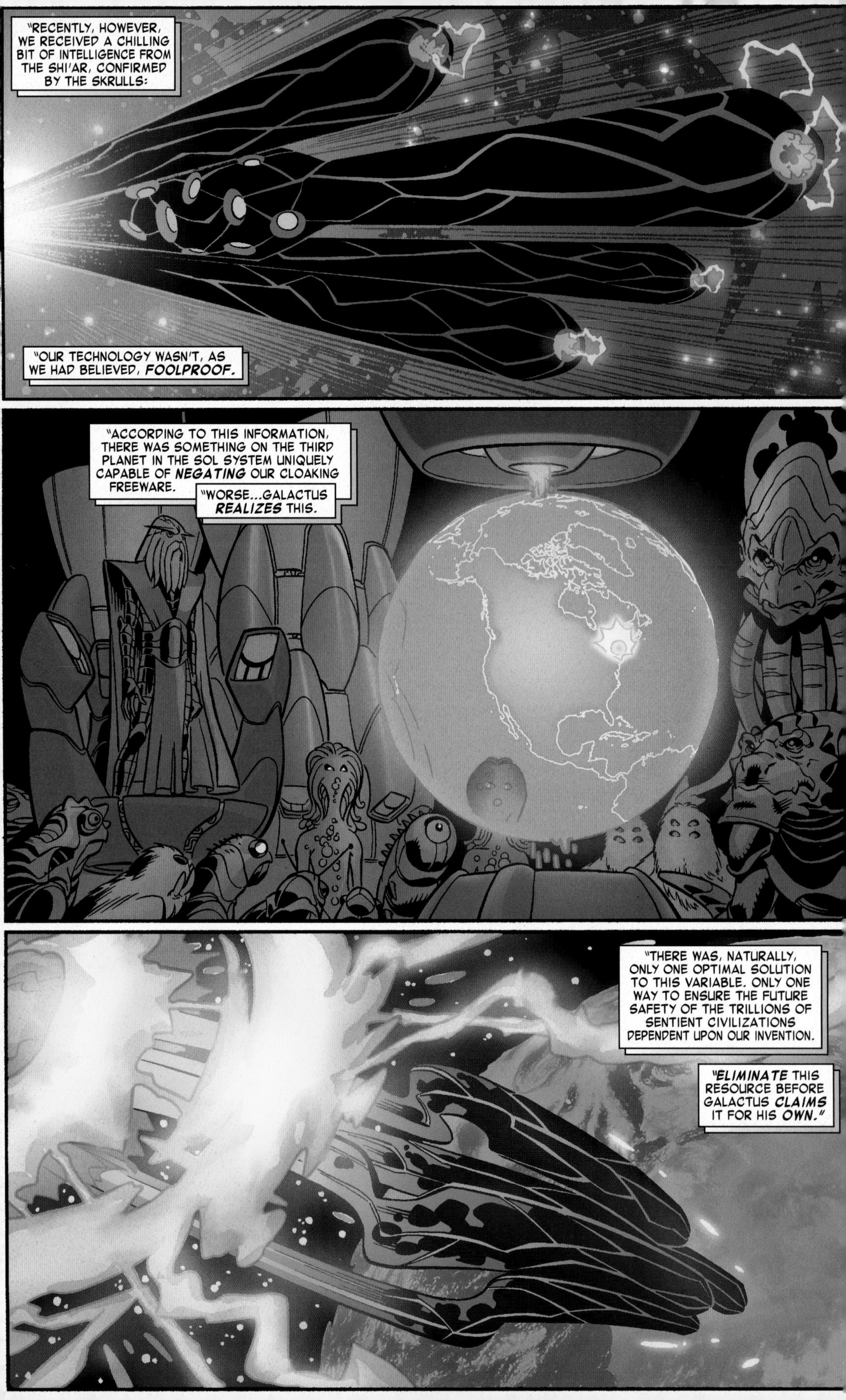
"RECENTLY, HOWEVER, WE RECEIVED A CHILLING BIT OF INTELLIGENCE FROM THE SHI'AR, CONFIRMED BY THE SKRULLS:
"OUR TECHNOLOGY WASN'T, AS WE HAD BELIEVED, FOOLPROOF.
"ACCORDING TO THIS INFORMATION, THERE WAS SOMETHING ON THE THIRD PLANET IN THE SOL SYSTEM UNIQUELY CAPABLE OF NEGATING OUR CLOAKING FREEWARE.
"WORSE...GALACTUS REALIZES THIS.
"THERE WAS, NATURALLY, ONLY ONE OPTIMAL SOLUTION TO THIS VARIABLE. ONLY ONE WAY TO ENSURE THE FUTURE SAFETY OF THE TRILLIONS OF SENTIENT CIVILIZATIONS DEPENDENT UPON OUR INVENTION.
"ELIMINATE THIS RESOURCE BEFORE GALACTUS CLAIMS IT FOR HIS OWN."

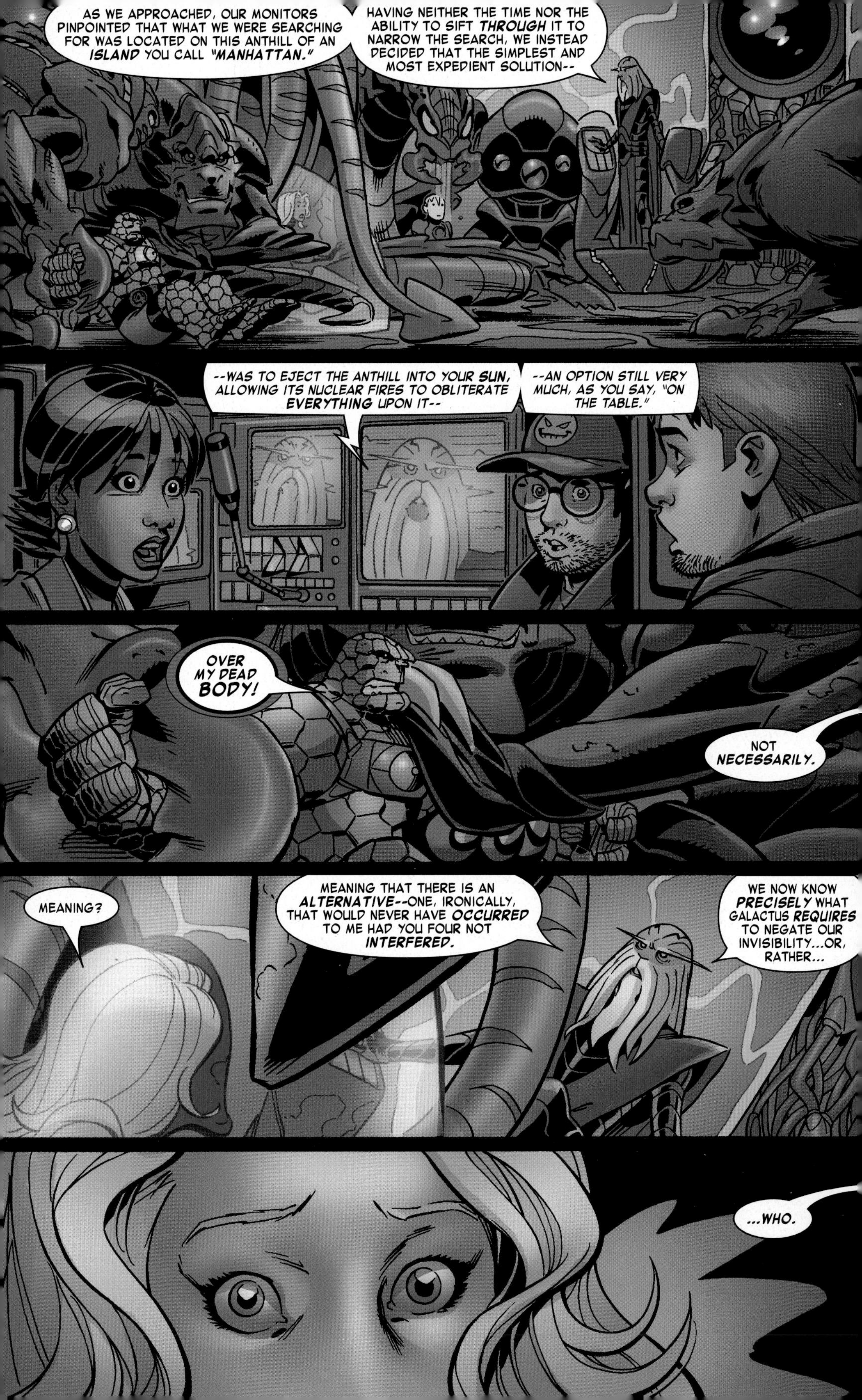
AS WE APPROACHED, OUR MONITORS PINPOINTED THAT WHAT WE WERE SEARCHING FOR WAS LOCATED ON THIS ANTHILL OF AN ISLAND YOU CALL "MANHATTAN."
HAVING NEITHER THE TIME NOR THE ABILITY TO SIFT THROUGH IT TO NARROW THE SEARCH, WE INSTEAD DECIDED THAT THE SIMPLEST AND MOST EXPEDIENT SOLUTION--
--WAS TO EJECT THE ANTHILL INTO YOUR SUN, ALLOWING ITS NUCLEAR FIRES TO OBLITERATE EVERYTHING UPON IT--
--AN OPTION STILL VERY MUCH, AS YOU SAY, "ON THE TABLE."
OVER MY DEAD BODY!
NOT NECESSARILY.
MEANING?
MEANING THAT THERE IS AN ALTERNATIVE--ONE, IRONICALLY, THAT WOULD NEVER HAVE OCCURRED TO ME HAD YOU FOUR NOT INTERFERED.
WE NOW KNOW PRECISELY WHAT GALACTUS REQUIRES TO NEGATE OUR INVISIBILITY...OR, RATHER...
...WHO.

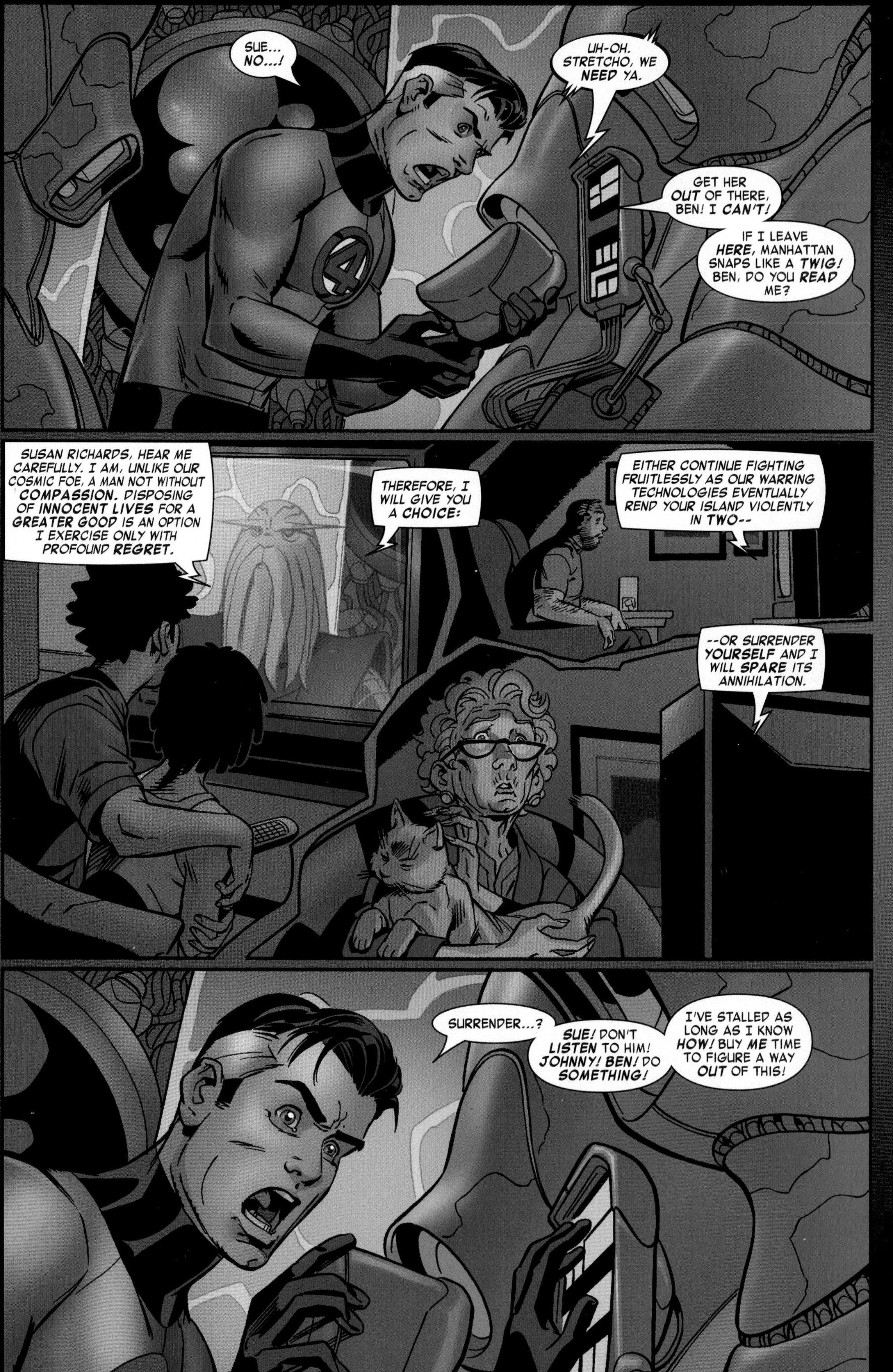
SUE... NO...!
UH-OH. STRETCHO, WE NEED YA.
GET HER OUT OF THERE, BEN! I CAN'T!
IF I LEAVE HERE, MANHATTAN SNAPS LIKE A TWIG! BEN, DO YOU READ ME?
SUSAN RICHARDS, HEAR ME CAREFULLY. I AM, UNLIKE OUR COSMIC FOE, A MAN NOT WITHOUT COMPASSION. DISPOSING OF INNOCENT LIVES FOR A GREATER GOOD IS AN OPTION I EXERCISE ONLY WITH PROFOUND REGRET.
THEREFORE, I WILL GIVE YOU A CHOICE:
EITHER CONTINUE FIGHTING FRUITLESSLY AS OUR WARRING TECHNOLOGIES EVENTUALLY REND YOUR ISLAND VIOLENTLY IN TWO--
--OR SURRENDER YOURSELF AND I WILL SPARE ITS ANNIHILATION.
SURRENDER...?
SUE! DON'T LISTEN TO HIM! JOHNNY! BEN! DO SOMETHING!
I'VE STALLED AS LONG AS I KNOW HOW! BUY ME TIME TO FIGURE A WAY OUT OF THIS!

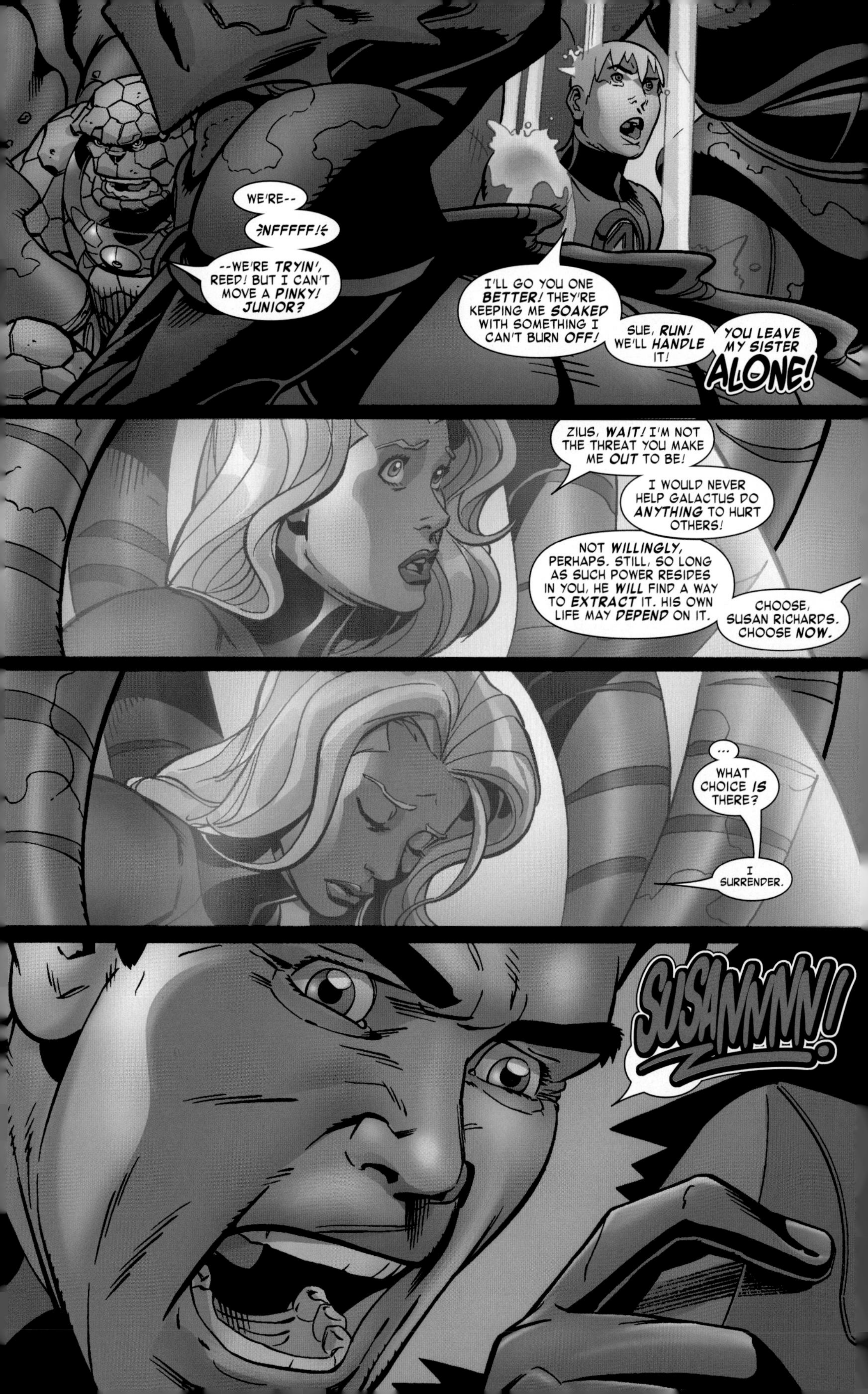
WE'RE--
NFFFFF!
--WE'RE TRYIN', REED! BUT I CAN'T MOVE A PINKY! JUNIOR?
I'LL GO YOU ONE BETTER! THEY'RE KEEPING ME SOAKED WITH SOMETHING I CAN'T BURN OFF!
SUE, RUN! WE'LL HANDLE IT!
YOU LEAVE MY SISTER ALONE!
ZIUS, WAIT! I'M NOT THE THREAT YOU MAKE ME OUT TO BE!
I WOULD NEVER HELP GALACTUS DO ANYTHING TO HURT OTHERS!
NOT WILLINGLY, PERHAPS. STILL, SO LONG AS SUCH POWER RESIDES IN YOU, HE WILL FIND A WAY TO EXTRACT IT. HIS OWN LIFE MAY DEPEND ON IT.
CHOOSE, SUSAN RICHARDS. CHOOSE NOW.
...
WHAT CHOICE IS THERE?
I SURRENDER.
SUSANNNN!

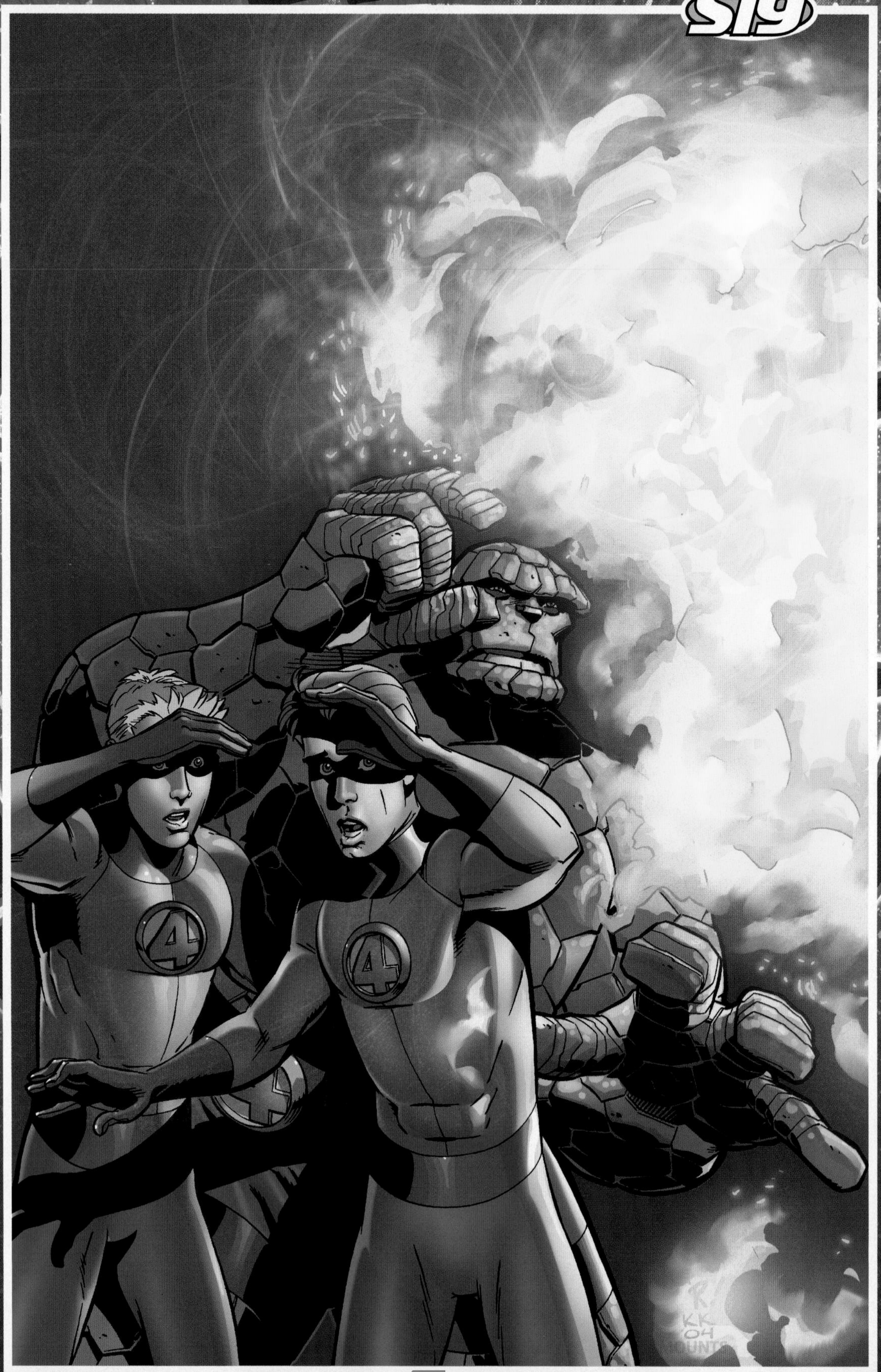
519

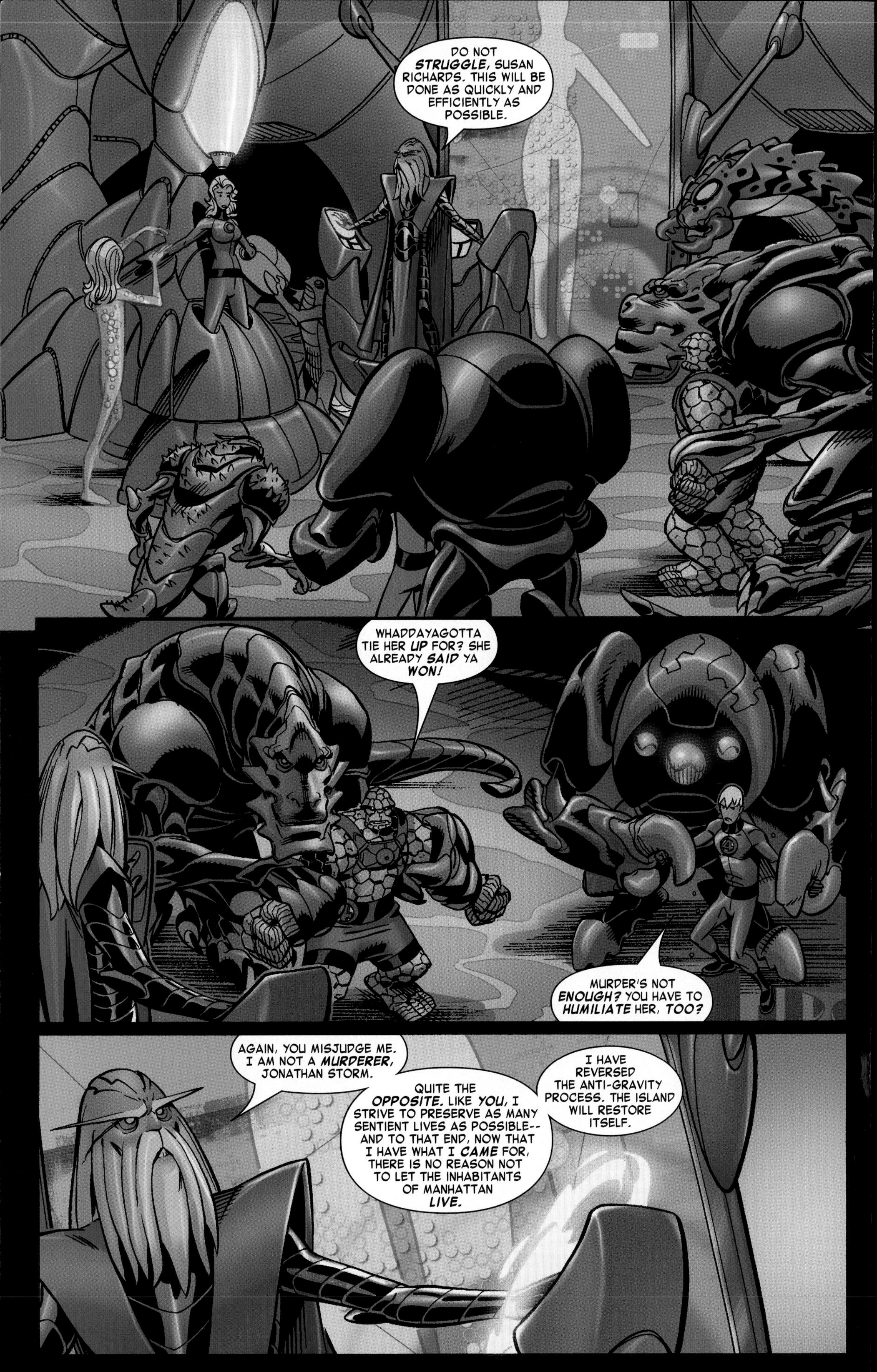
DO NOT STRUGGLE, SUSAN RICHARDS. THIS WILL BE DONE AS QUICKLY AND EFFICIENTLY AS POSSIBLE.
WHADDAYAGOTTA TIE HER UP FOR? SHE ALREADY SAID YA WON!
MURDER'S NOT ENOUGH? YOU HAVE TO HUMILIATE HER, TOO?
AGAIN, YOU MISJUDGE ME. I AM NOT A MURDERER, JONATHAN STORM.
QUITE THE OPPOSITE. LIKE YOU, I STRIVE TO PRESERVE AS MANY SENTIENT LIVES AS POSSIBLE-- AND TO THAT END, NOW THAT I HAVE WHAT I CAME FOR, THERE IS NO REASON NOT TO LET THE INHABITANTS OF MANHATTAN LIVE.
I HAVE REVERSED THE ANTI-GRAVITY PROCESS. THE ISLAND WILL RESTORE ITSELF.

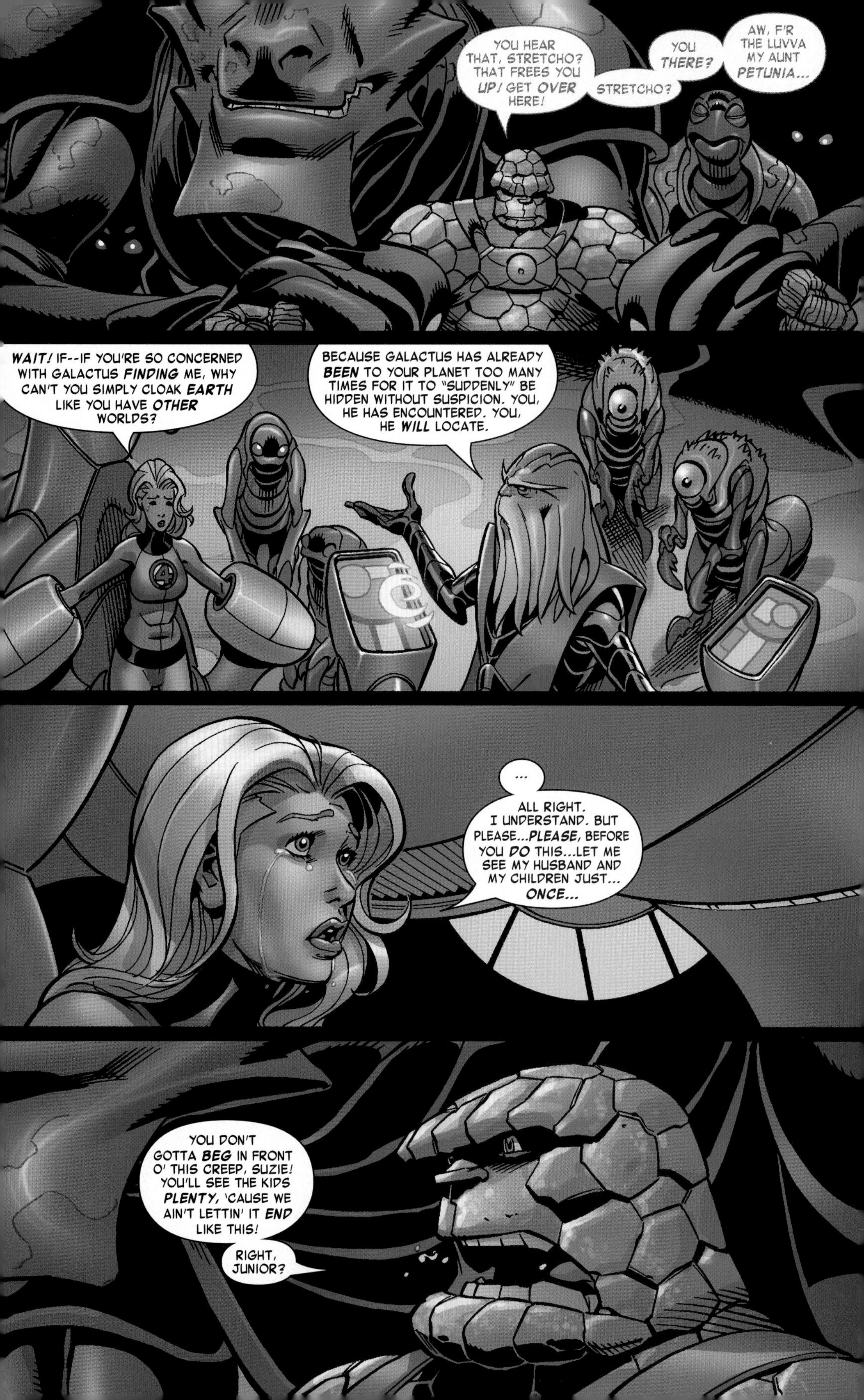
YOU HEAR THAT, STRETCHO? THAT FREES YOU UP! GET OVER HERE!
STRETCHO?
YOU THERE?
AW, F'R THE LUVVA MY AUNT PETUNIA...
WAIT! IF--IF YOU'RE SO CONCERNED WITH GALACTUS FINDING ME, WHY CAN'T YOU SIMPLY CLOAK EARTH LIKE YOU HAVE OTHER WORLDS?
BECAUSE GALACTUS HAS ALREADY BEEN TO YOUR PLANET TOO MANY TIMES FOR IT TO "SUDDENLY" BE HIDDEN WITHOUT SUSPICION. YOU, HE HAS ENCOUNTERED. YOU, HE WILL LOCATE.
...
ALL RIGHT. I UNDERSTAND. BUT PLEASE...PLEASE, BEFORE YOU DO THIS...LET ME SEE MY HUSBAND AND MY CHILDREN JUST... ONCE...
YOU DON'T GOTTA BEG IN FRONT O' THIS CREEP, SUZIE! YOU'LL SEE THE KIDS PLENTY, 'CAUSE WE AIN'T LETTIN' IT END LIKE THIS!
RIGHT, JUNIOR?

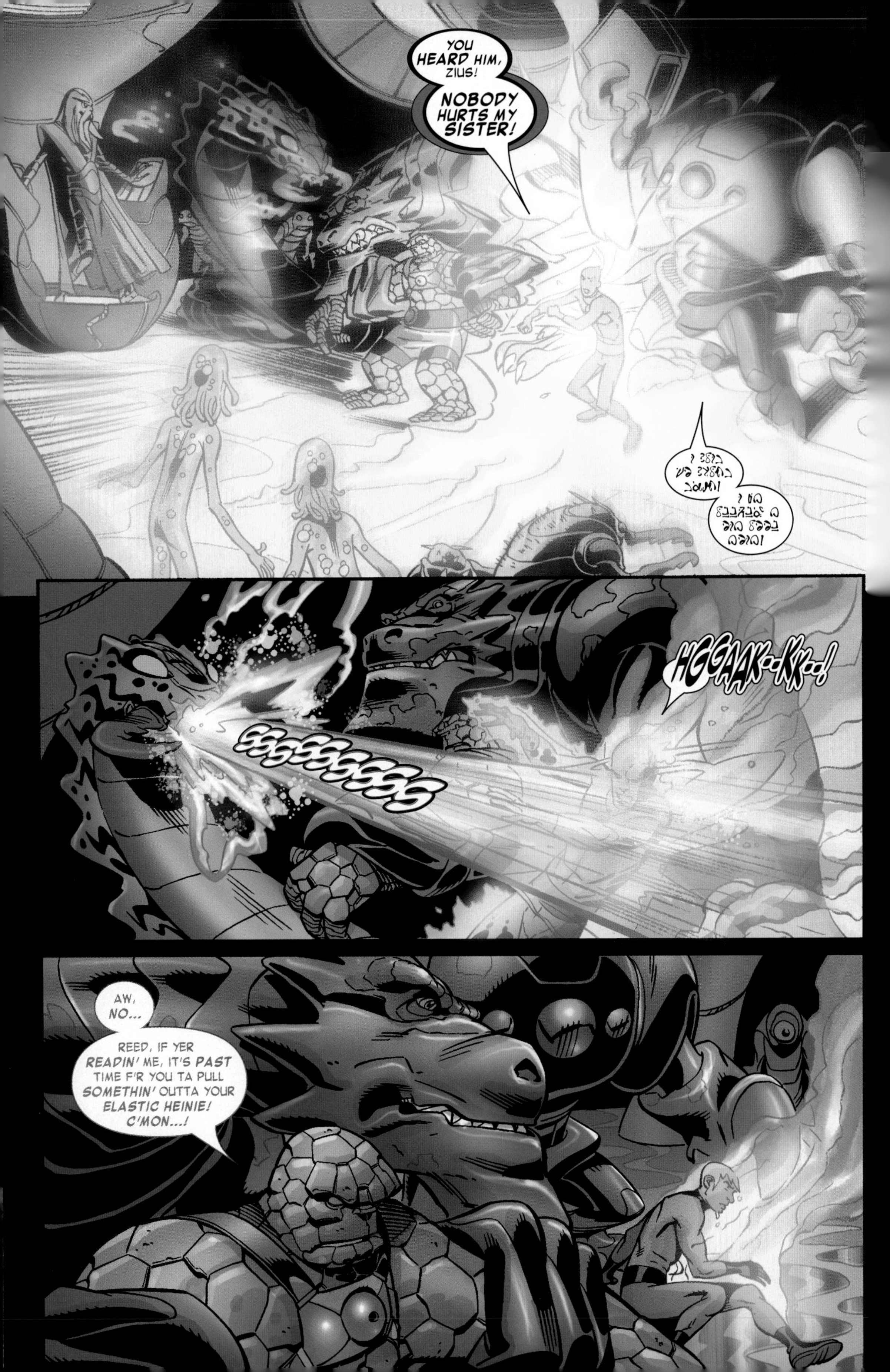
YOU HEARD HIM, ZIUS!
NOBODY HURTS MY SISTER!
HGGAAK--KK--!
SSSSSSSSSS
AW, NO...
REED, IF YER READIN' ME, IT'S PAST TIME F'R YOU TA PULL SOMETHIN' OUTTA YOUR ELASTIC HEINIE! C'MON...!

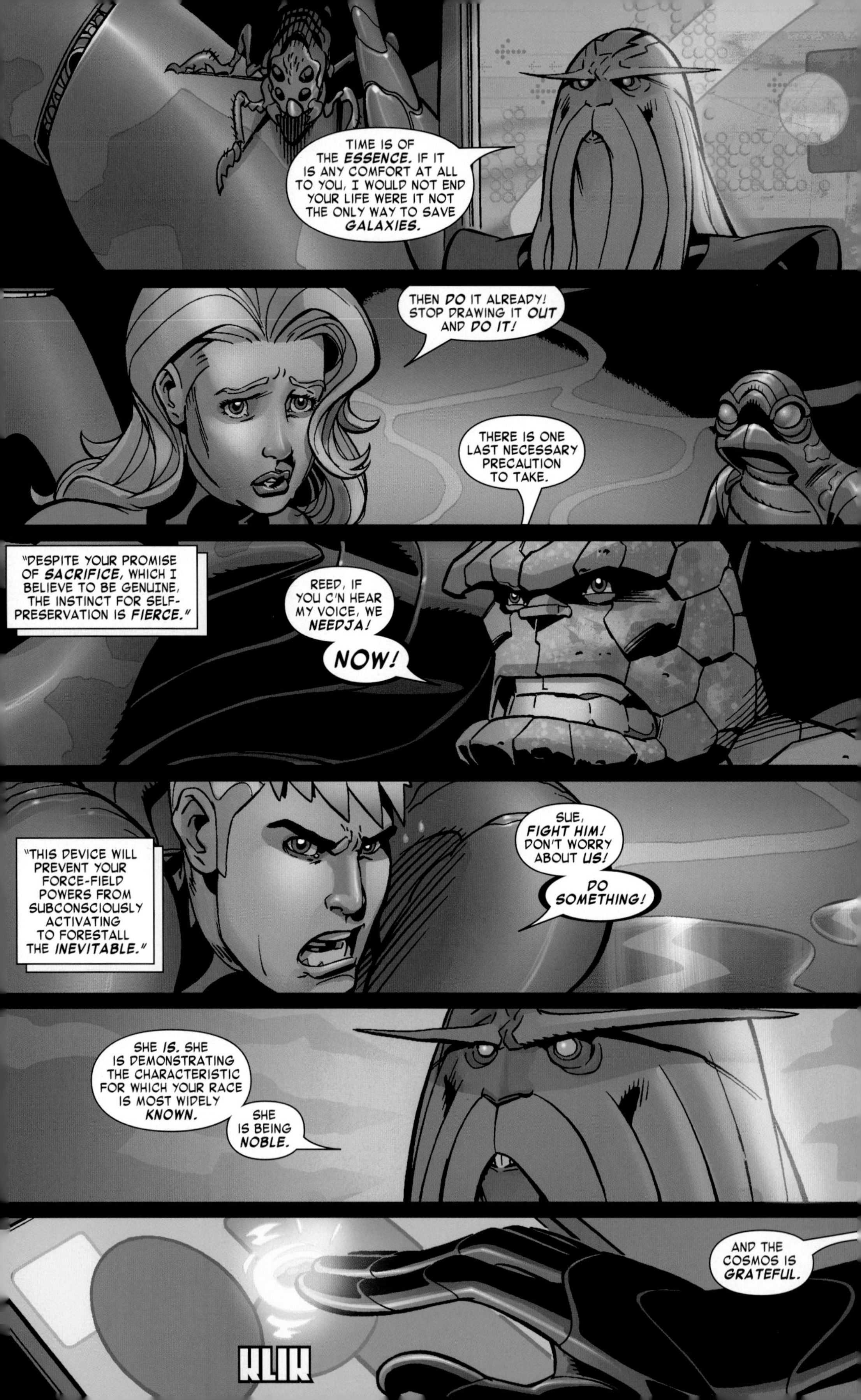
TIME IS OF THE ESSENCE. IF IT IS ANY COMFORT AT ALL TO YOU, I WOULD NOT END YOUR LIFE WERE IT NOT THE ONLY WAY TO SAVE GALAXIES.
THEN DO IT ALREADY! STOP DRAWING IT OUT AND DO IT!
THERE IS ONE LAST NECESSARY PRECAUTION TO TAKE.
"DESPITE YOUR PROMISE OF SACRIFICE, WHICH I BELIEVE TO BE GENUINE, THE INSTINCT FOR SELF-PRESERVATION IS FIERCE."
REED, IF YOU C'N HEAR MY VOICE, WE NEEDJA!
NOW!
"THIS DEVICE WILL PREVENT YOUR FORCE-FIELD POWERS FROM SUBCONSCIOUSLY ACTIVATING TO FORESTALL THE INEVITABLE."
SUE, FIGHT HIM! DON'T WORRY ABOUT US!
DO SOMETHING!
SHE IS. SHE IS DEMONSTRATING THE CHARACTERISTIC FOR WHICH YOUR RACE IS MOST WIDELY KNOWN.
SHE IS BEING NOBLE.
AND THE COSMOS IS GRATEFUL.
KLIK

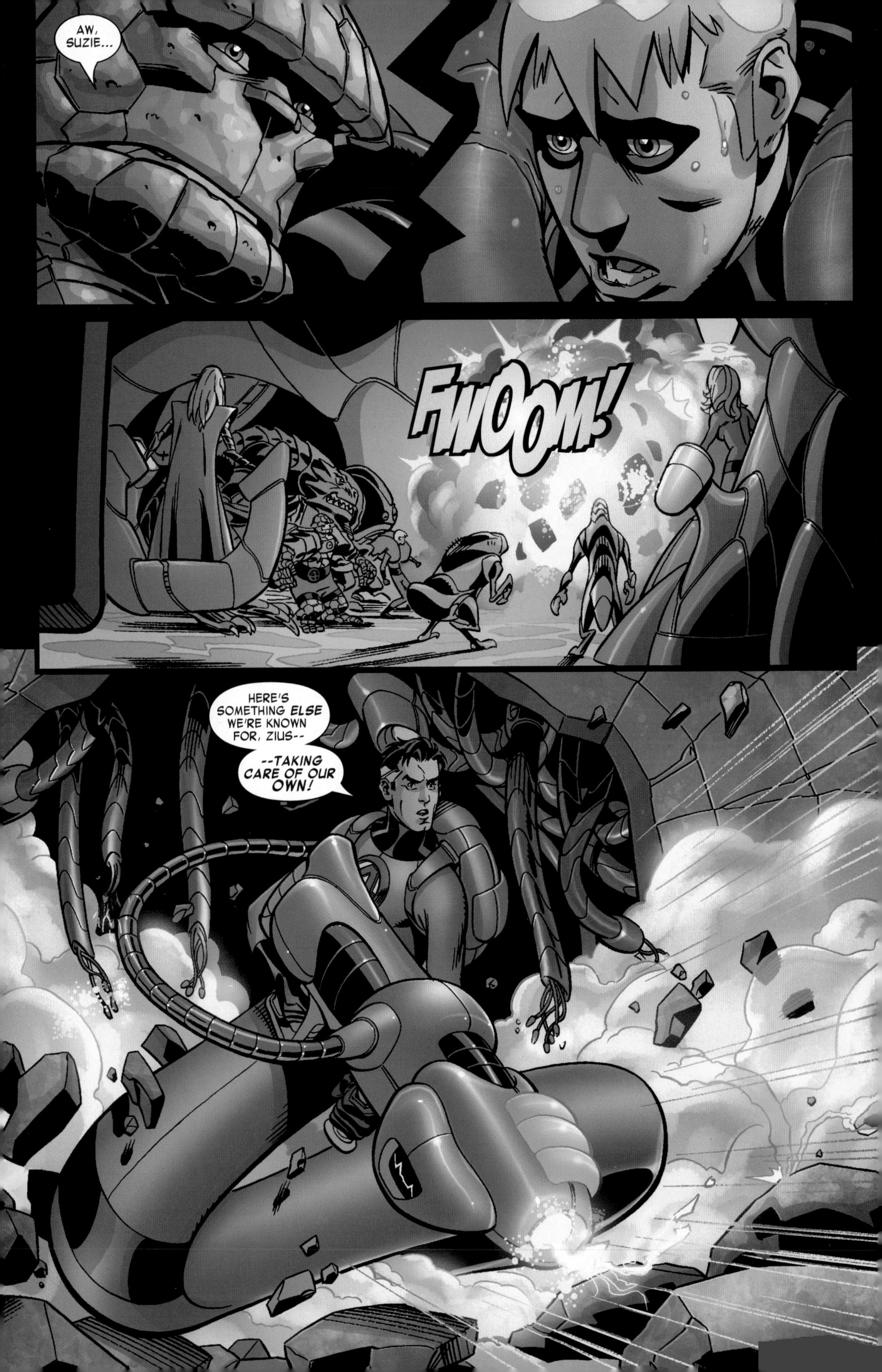
AW, SUZIE...
FWOOM!
HERE'S SOMETHING ELSE WE'RE KNOWN FOR, ZIUS--
--TAKING CARE OF OUR OWN!

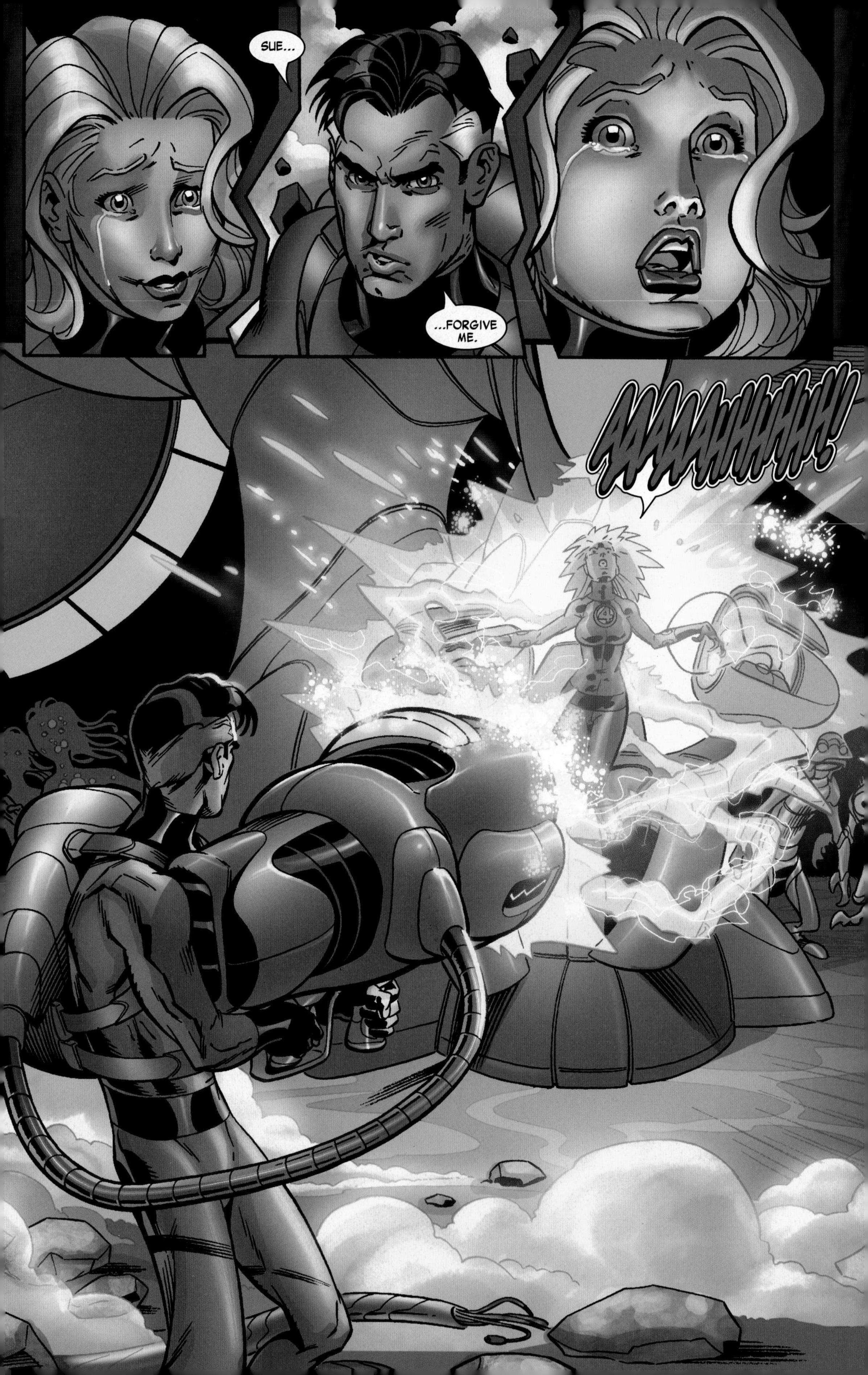
SUE...
...FORGIVE ME.
AAAAAHHHHHH!

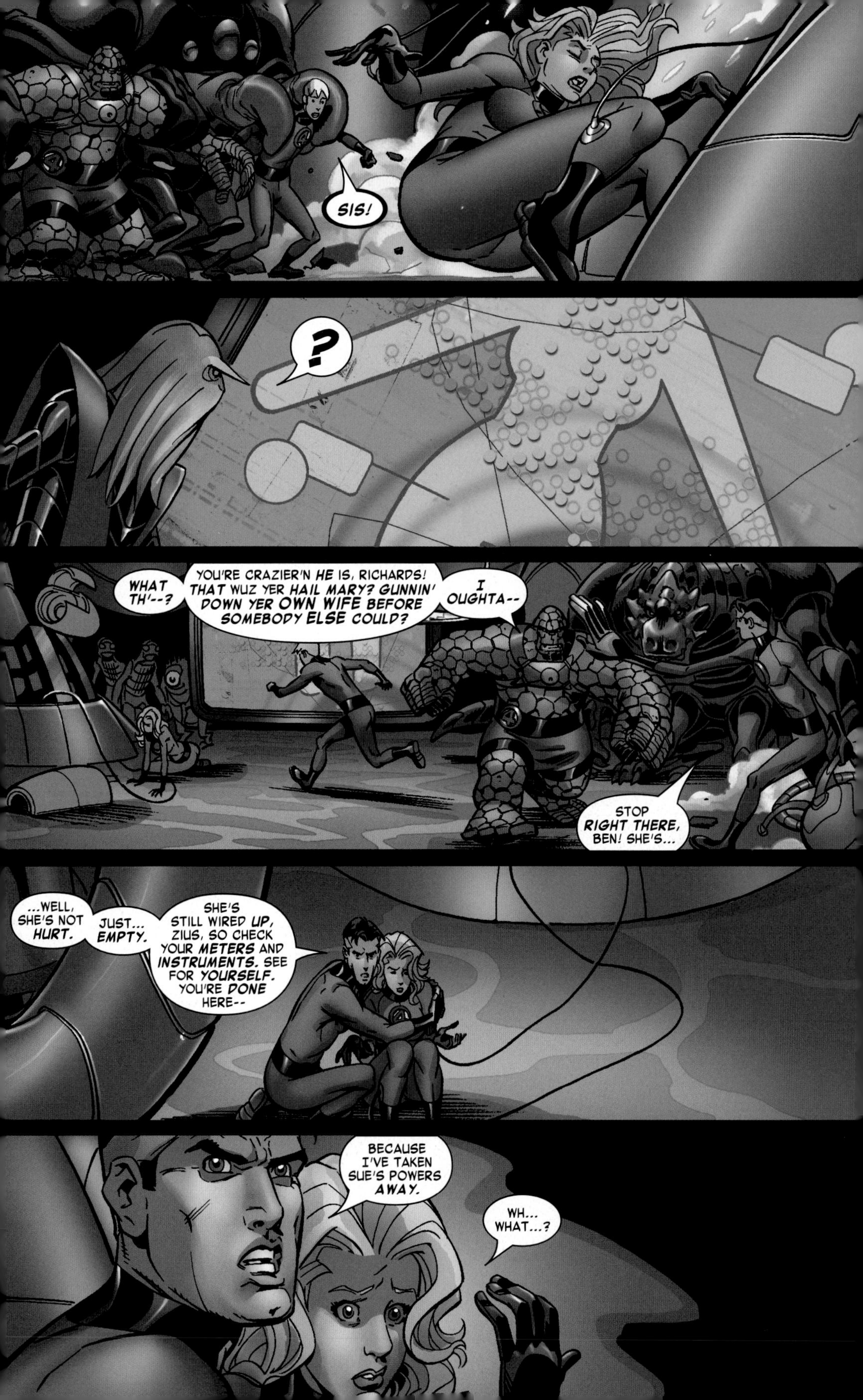
SIS!
?
WHAT TH'--?
YOU'RE CRAZIER'N HE IS, RICHARDS! THAT WUZ YER HAIL MARY? GUNNIN' DOWN YER OWN WIFE BEFORE SOMEBODY ELSE COULD?
I OUGHTA--
STOP RIGHT THERE, BEN! SHE'S...
...WELL, SHE'S NOT HURT.
JUST... EMPTY.
SHE'S STILL WIRED UP, ZIUS, SO CHECK YOUR METERS AND INSTRUMENTS. SEE FOR YOURSELF. YOU'RE DONE HERE--
BECAUSE I'VE TAKEN SUE'S POWERS AWAY.
WH... WHAT...?

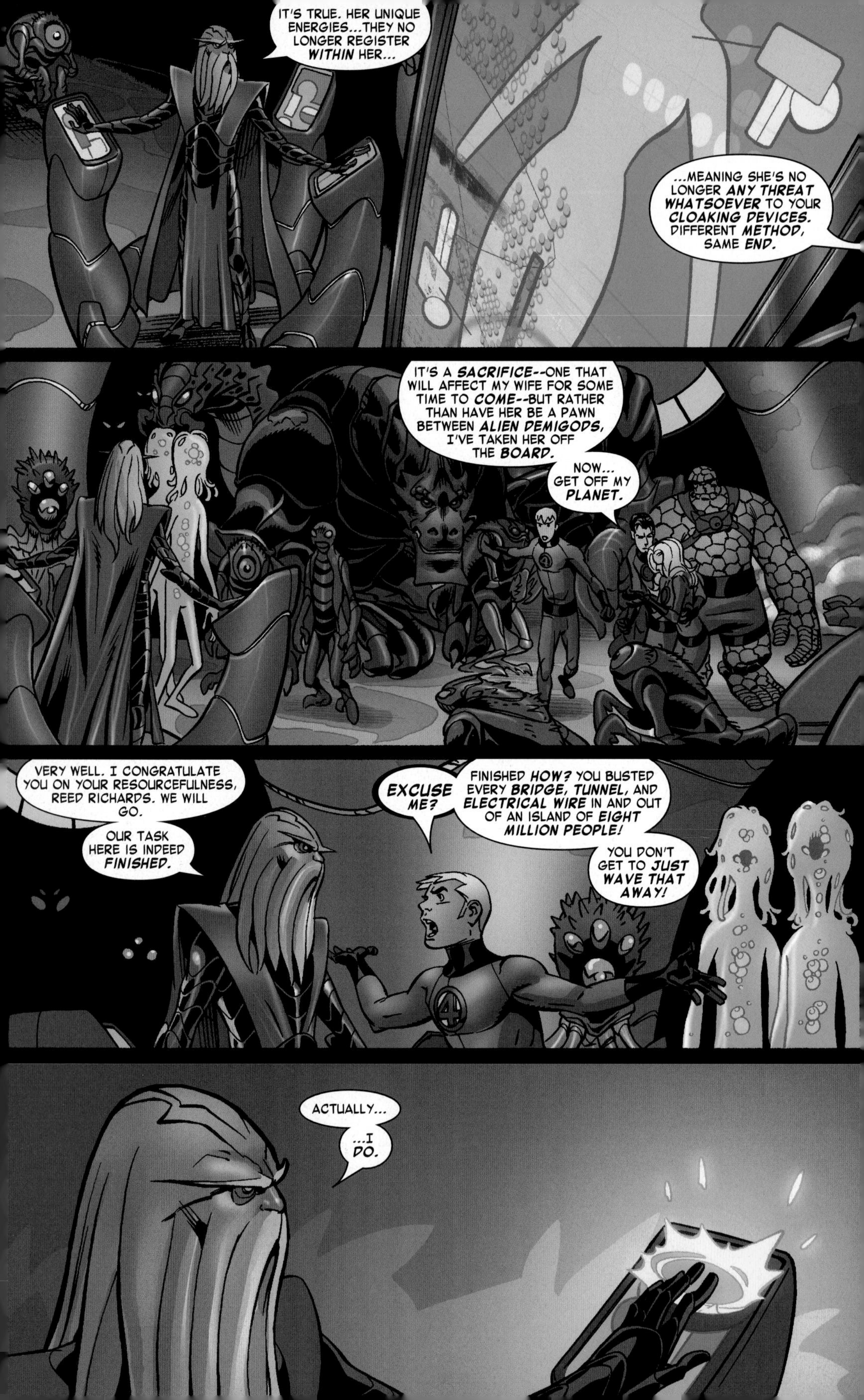
IT'S TRUE. HER UNIQUE ENERGIES...THEY NO LONGER REGISTER WITHIN HER...
...MEANING SHE'S NO LONGER ANY THREAT WHATSOEVER TO YOUR CLOAKING DEVICES. DIFFERENT METHOD, SAME END.
IT'S A SACRIFICE--ONE THAT WILL AFFECT MY WIFE FOR SOME TIME TO COME--BUT RATHER THAN HAVE HER BE A PAWN BETWEEN ALIEN DEMIGODS, I'VE TAKEN HER OFF THE BOARD.
NOW... GET OFF MY PLANET.
VERY WELL. I CONGRATULATE YOU ON YOUR RESOURCEFULNESS, REED RICHARDS. WE WILL GO.
OUR TASK HERE IS INDEED FINISHED.
EXCUSE ME?
FINISHED HOW? YOU BUSTED EVERY BRIDGE, TUNNEL, AND ELECTRICAL WIRE IN AND OUT OF AN ISLAND OF EIGHT MILLION PEOPLE!
YOU DON'T GET TO JUST WAVE THAT AWAY!
ACTUALLY...
...I DO.

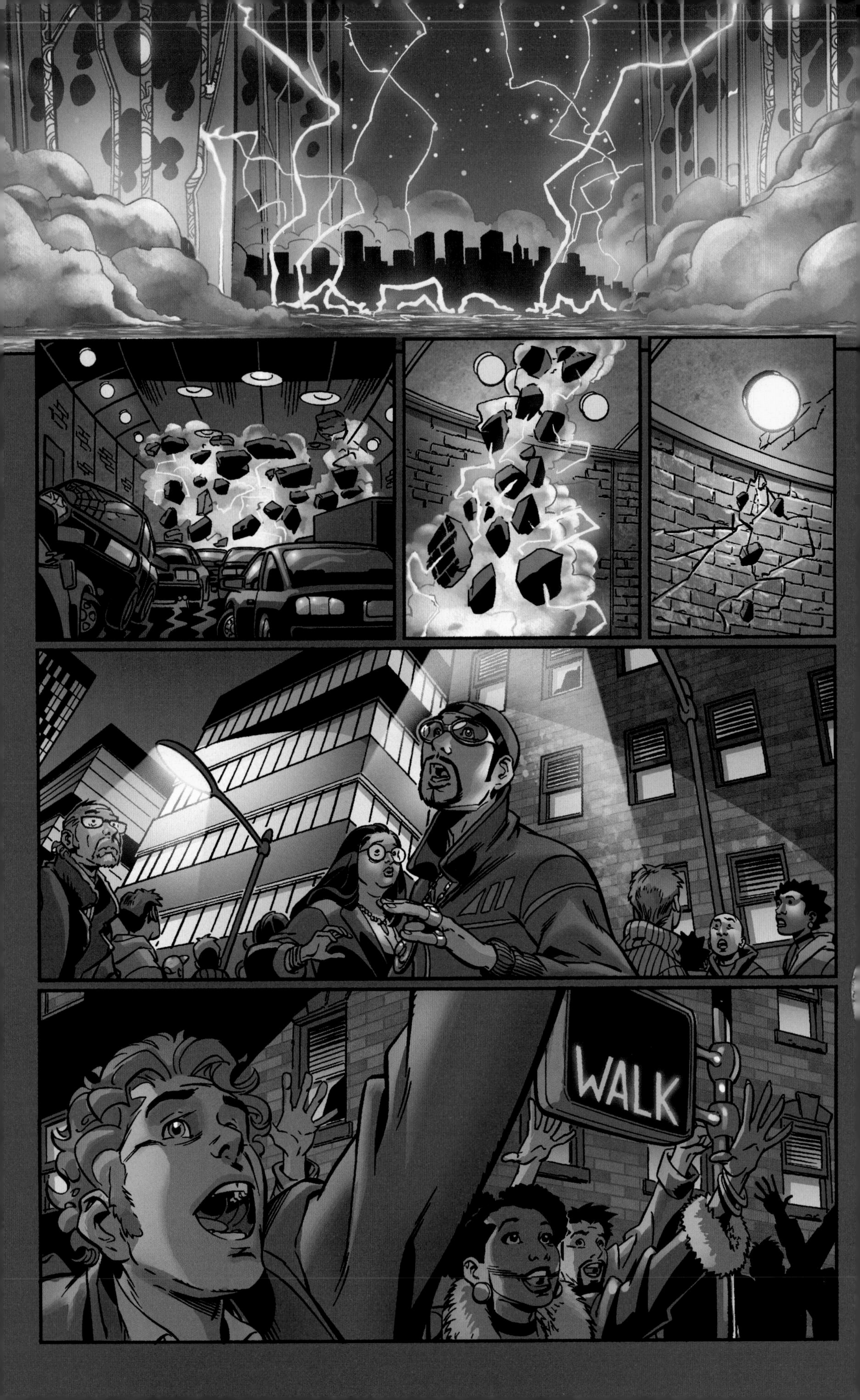
WALK

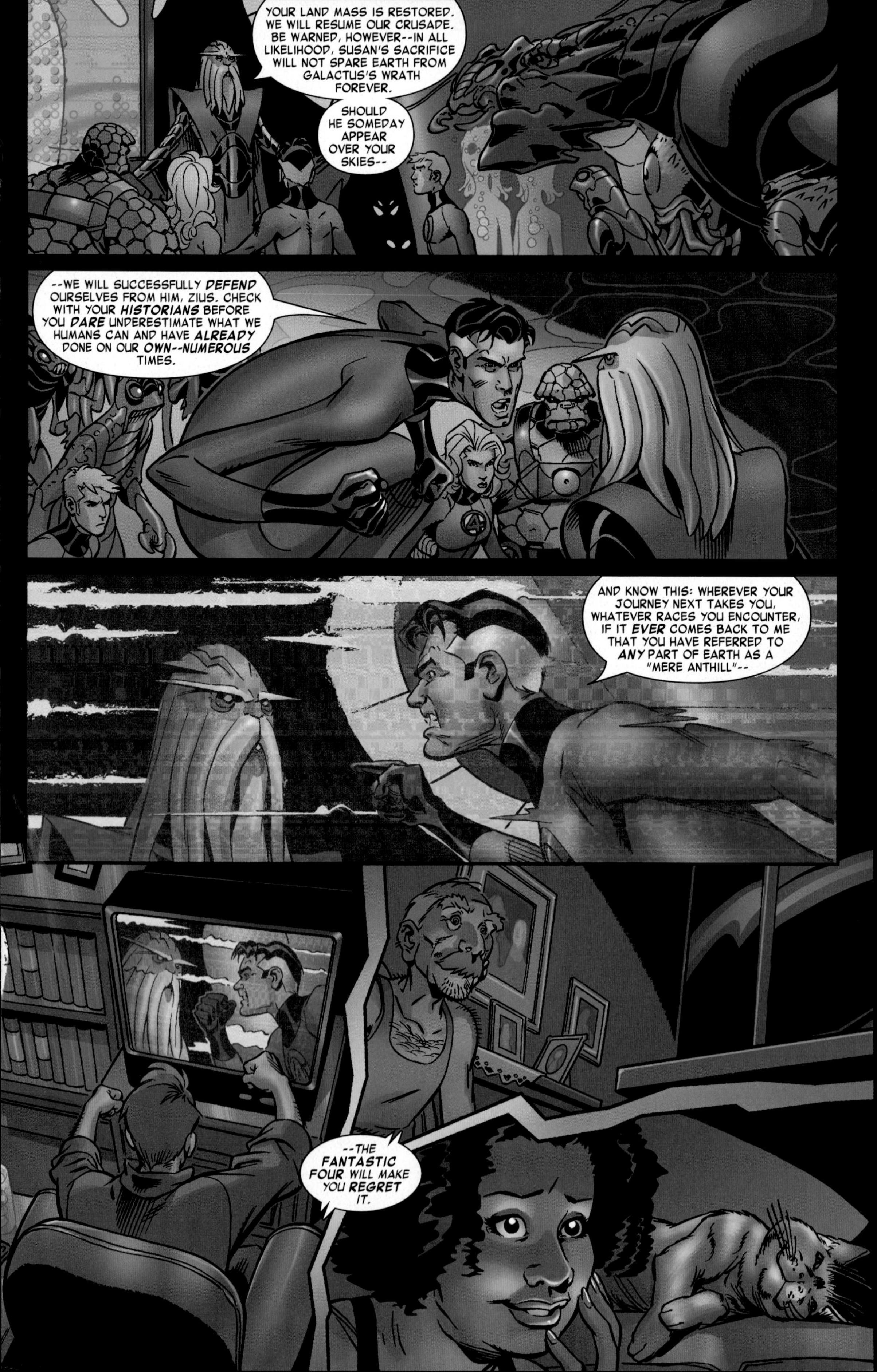
YOUR LAND MASS IS RESTORED. WE WILL RESUME OUR CRUSADE. BE WARNED, HOWEVER--IN ALL LIKELIHOOD, SUSAN'S SACRIFICE WILL NOT SPARE EARTH FROM GALACTUS'S WRATH FOREVER.
SHOULD HE SOMEDAY APPEAR OVER YOUR SKIES--
--WE WILL SUCCESSFULLY DEFEND OURSELVES FROM HIM, ZIUS. CHECK WITH YOUR HISTORIANS BEFORE YOU DARE UNDERESTIMATE WHAT WE HUMANS CAN AND HAVE ALREADY DONE ON OUR OWN--NUMEROUS TIMES.
AND KNOW THIS: WHEREVER YOUR JOURNEY NEXT TAKES YOU, WHATEVER RACES YOU ENCOUNTER, IF IT EVER COMES BACK TO ME THAT YOU HAVE REFERRED TO ANY PART OF EARTH AS A "MERE ANTHILL"--
--THE FANTASTIC FOUR WILL MAKE YOU REGRET IT.

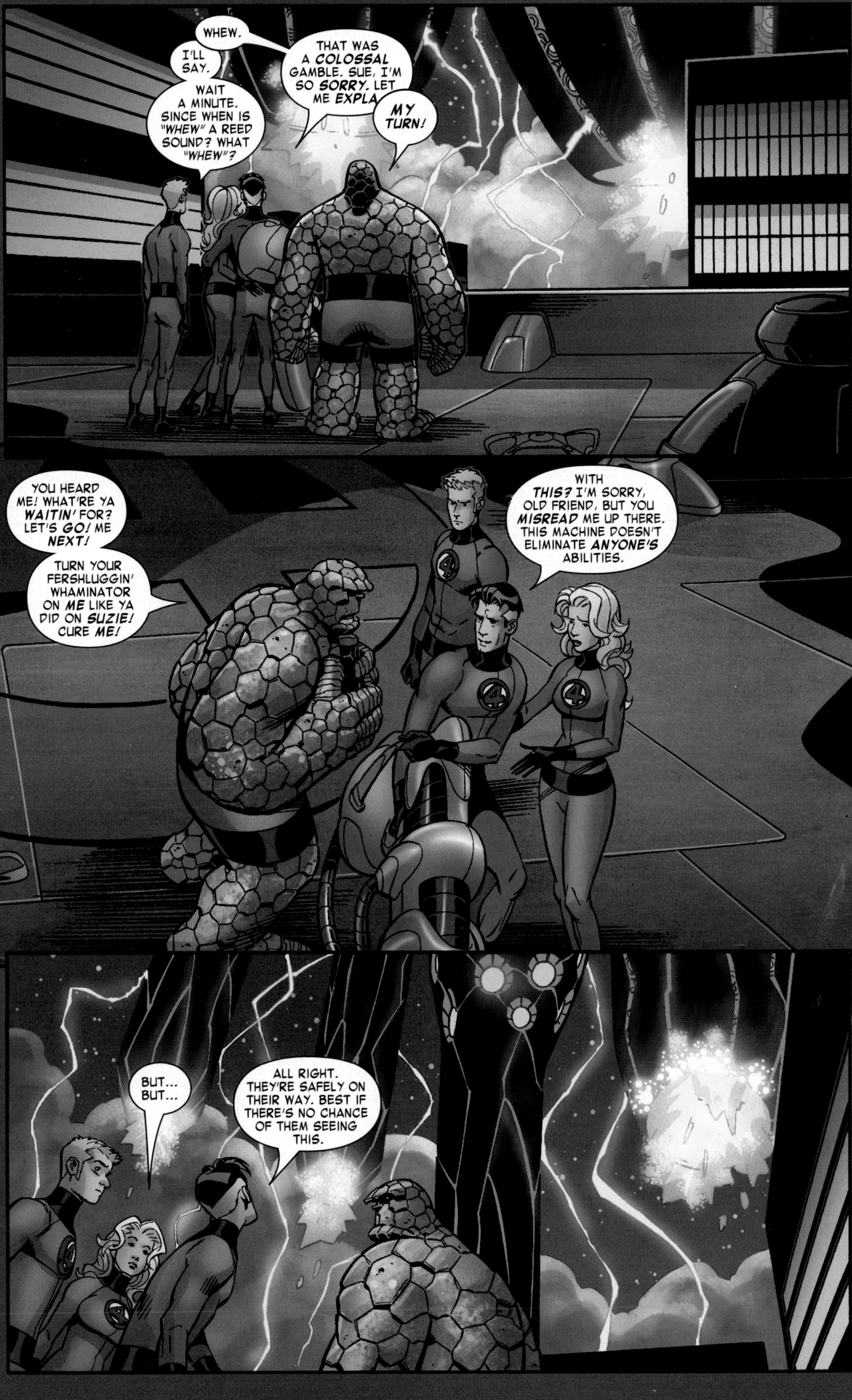
WHEW.
I'LL SAY.
THAT WAS A COLOSSAL GAMBLE. SUE, I'M SO SORRY. LET ME EXPLA
WAIT A MINUTE. SINCE WHEN IS "WHEW" A REED SOUND? WHAT "WHEW"?
MY TURN!
YOU HEARD ME! WHAT'RE YA WAITIN' FOR? LET'S GO! ME NEXT!
TURN YOUR FERSHLUGGIN' WHAMINATOR ON ME LIKE YA DID ON SUZIE! CURE ME!
WITH THIS? I'M SORRY, OLD FRIEND, BUT YOU MISREAD ME UP THERE. THIS MACHINE DOESN'T ELIMINATE ANYONE'S ABILITIES.
BUT... BUT...
ALL RIGHT. THEY'RE SAFELY ON THEIR WAY. BEST IF THERE'S NO CHANCE OF THEM SEEING THIS.

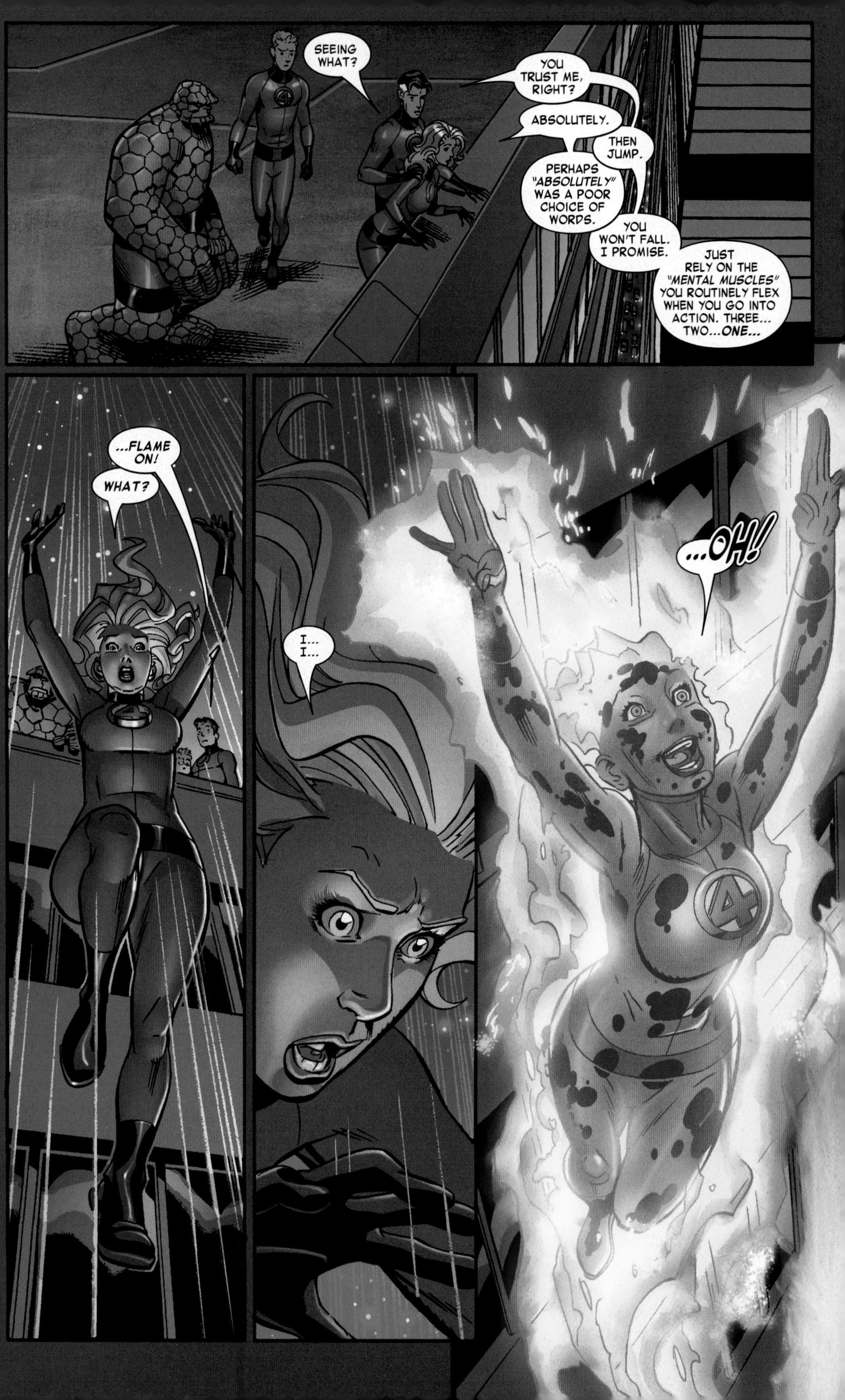
SEEING WHAT?
YOU TRUST ME, RIGHT?
ABSOLUTELY.
THEN JUMP.
PERHAPS "ABSOLUTELY" WAS A POOR CHOICE OF WORDS.
YOU WON'T FALL. I PROMISE.
JUST RELY ON THE "MENTAL MUSCLES" YOU ROUTINELY FLEX WHEN YOU GO INTO ACTION. THREE... TWO...ONE...
...FLAME ON!
WHAT?
I... I...
...OH!

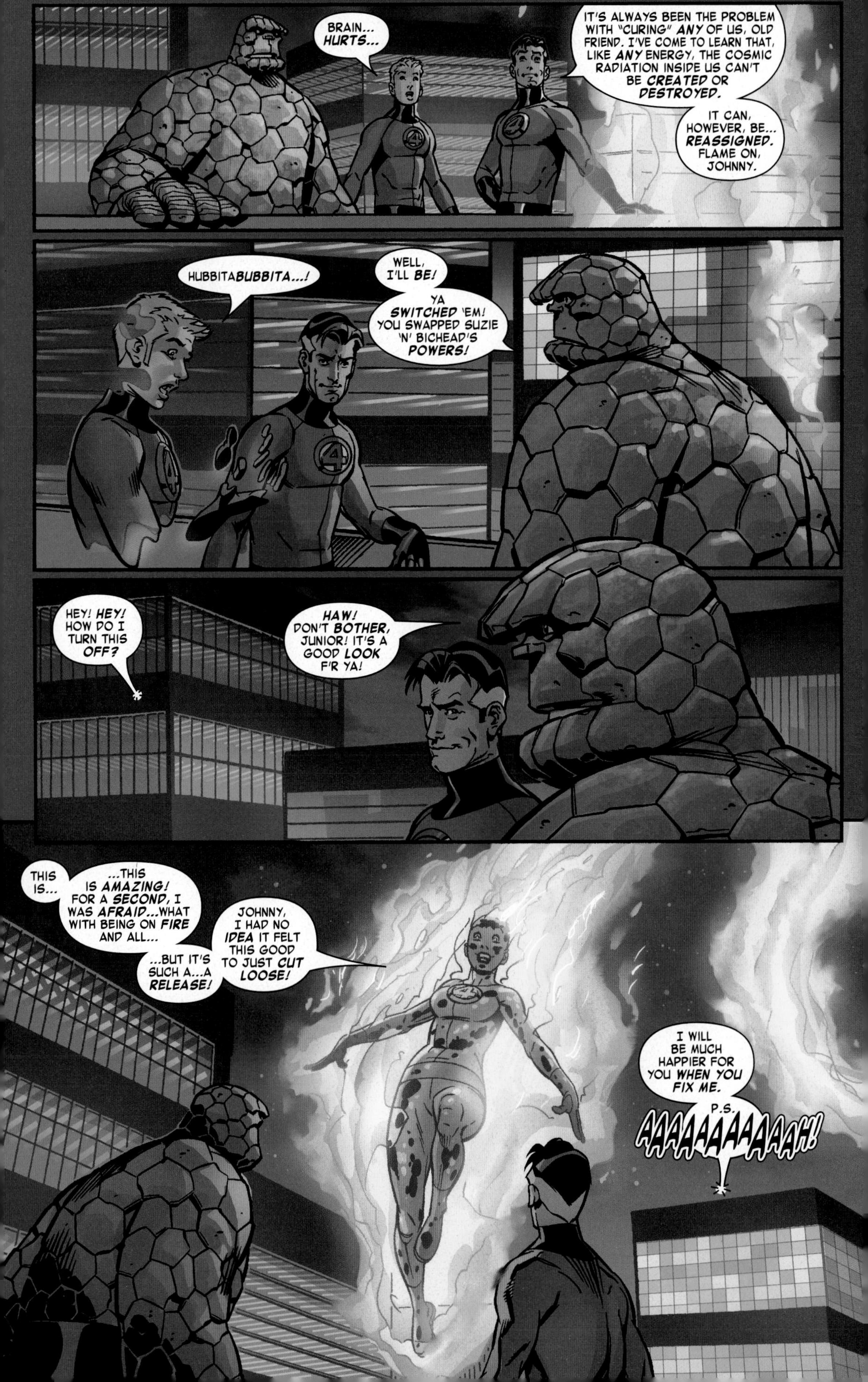
BRAIN... HURTS...
IT'S ALWAYS BEEN THE PROBLEM WITH "CURING" ANY OF US, OLD FRIEND. I'VE COME TO LEARN THAT, LIKE ANY ENERGY, THE COSMIC RADIATION INSIDE US CAN'T BE CREATED OR DESTROYED.
IT CAN, HOWEVER, BE... REASSIGNED. FLAME ON, JOHNNY.
HUBBITABUBBITA...!
WELL, I'LL BE!
YA SWITCHED 'EM! YOU SWAPPED SUZIE 'N' BICHEAD'S POWERS!
HEY! HEY! HOW DO I TURN THIS OFF?
HAW! DON'T BOTHER, JUNIOR! IT'S A GOOD LOOK F'R YA!
THIS IS...
...THIS IS AMAZING! FOR A SECOND, I WAS AFRAID...WHAT WITH BEING ON FIRE AND ALL...
...BUT IT'S SUCH A...A RELEASE!
JOHNNY, I HAD NO IDEA IT FELT THIS GOOD TO JUST CUT LOOSE!
I WILL BE MUCH HAPPIER FOR YOU WHEN YOU FIX ME.
P.S.
AAAAAAAAAAAH!

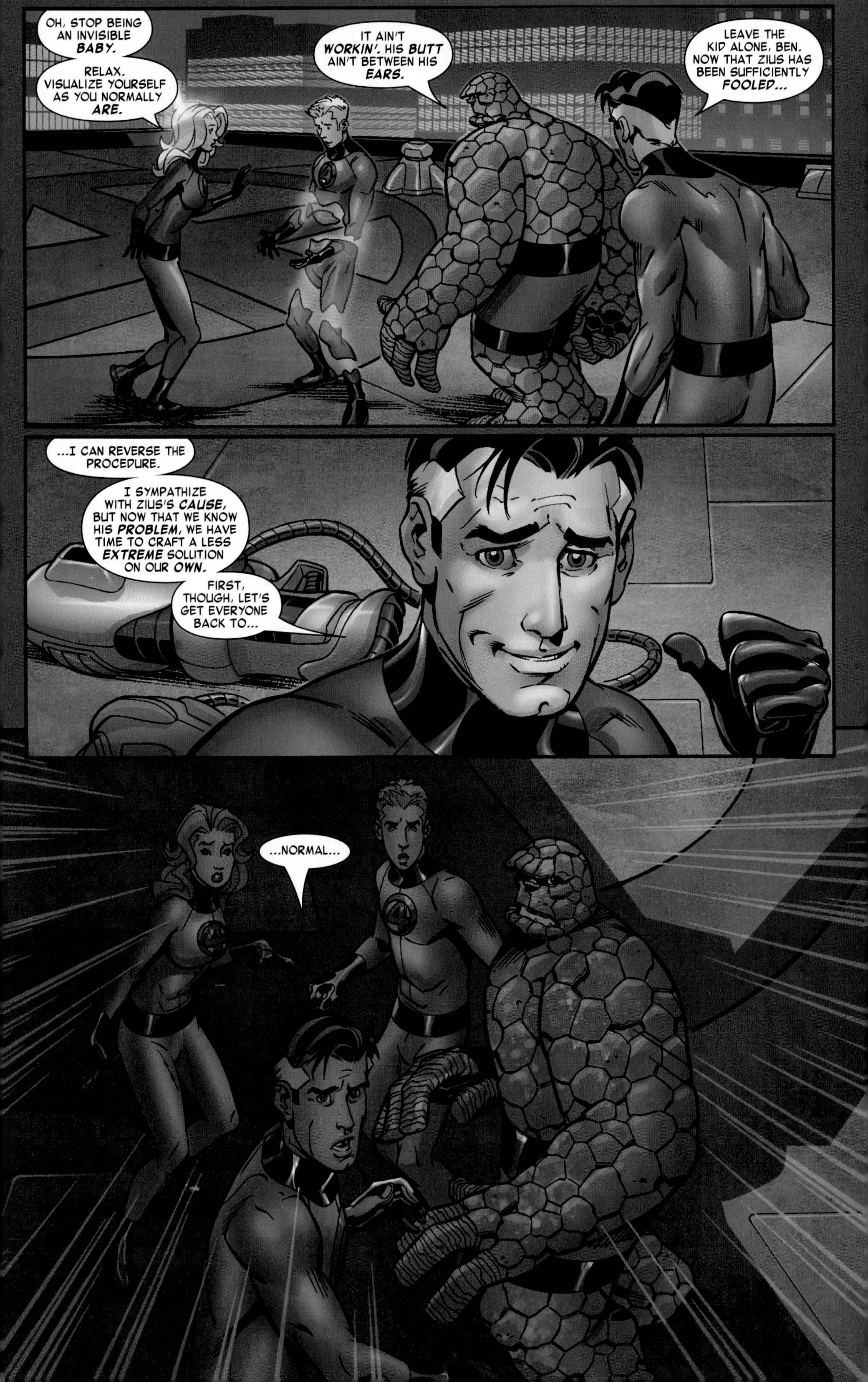
OH, STOP BEING AN INVISIBLE BABY.
RELAX. VISUALIZE YOURSELF AS YOU NORMALLY ARE.
IT AIN'T WORKIN'. HIS BUTT AIN'T BETWEEN HIS EARS.
LEAVE THE KID ALONE, BEN. NOW THAT ZIUS HAS BEEN SUFFICIENTLY FOOLED...
...I CAN REVERSE THE PROCEDURE.
I SYMPATHIZE WITH ZIUS'S CAUSE, BUT NOW THAT WE KNOW HIS PROBLEM, WE HAVE TIME TO CRAFT A LESS EXTREME SOLUTION ON OUR OWN.
FIRST, THOUGH, LET'S GET EVERYONE BACK TO...
...NORMAL...

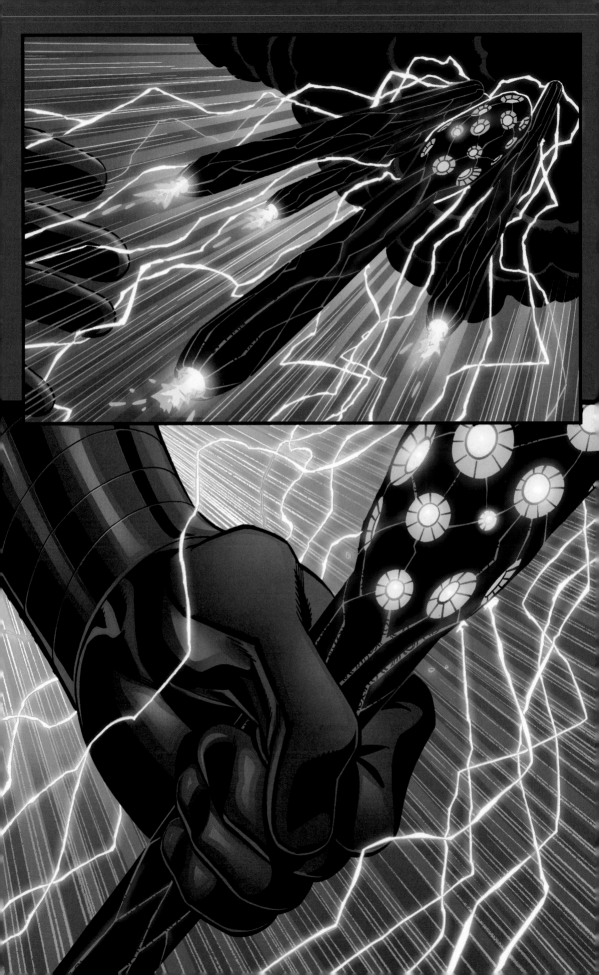

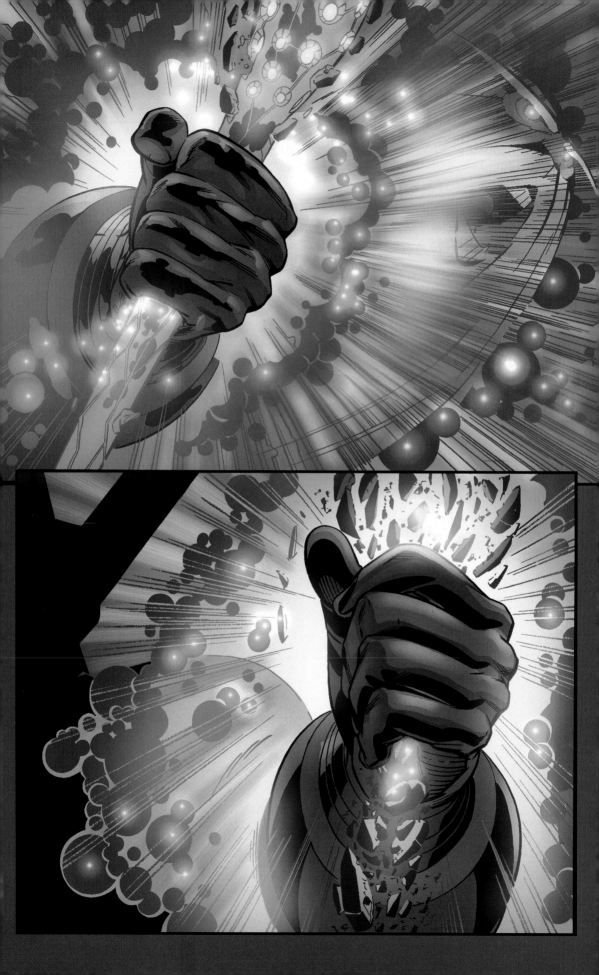

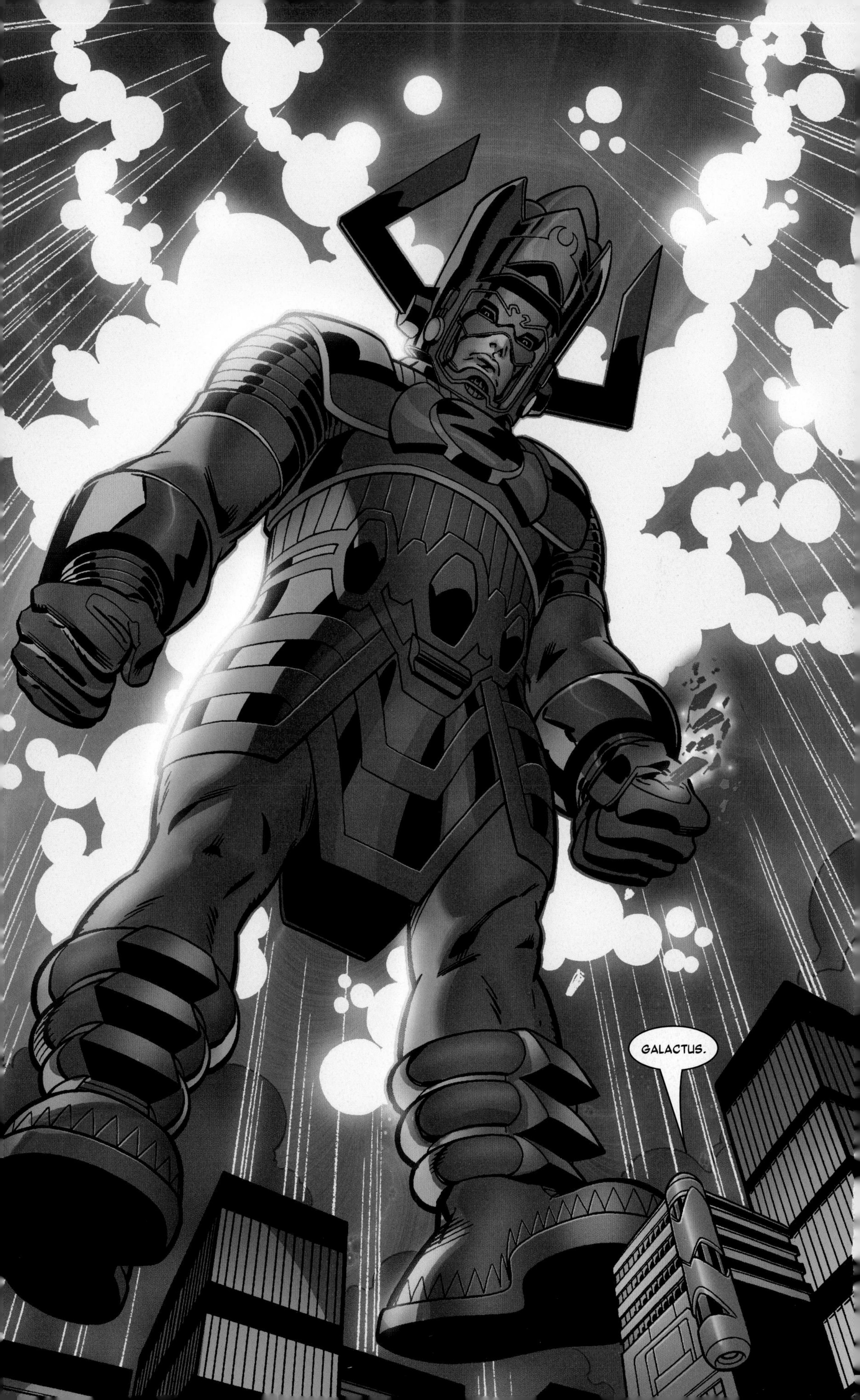
GALACTUS.

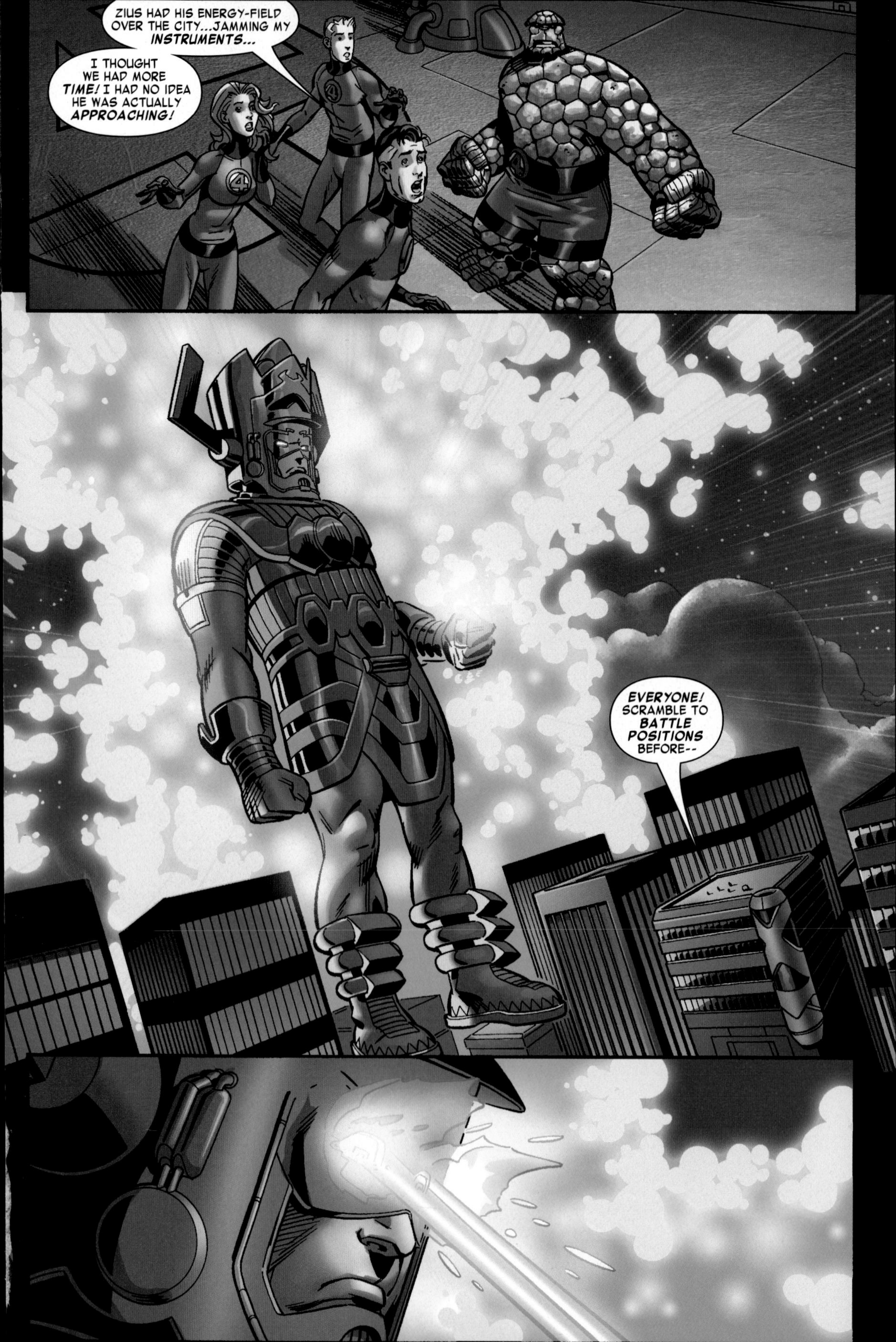
ZIUS HAD HIS ENERGY-FIELD OVER THE CITY...JAMMING MY INSTRUMENTS...
I THOUGHT WE HAD MORE TIME! I HAD NO IDEA HE WAS ACTUALLY APPROACHING!
EVERYONE! SCRAMBLE TO BATTLE POSITIONS BEFORE--

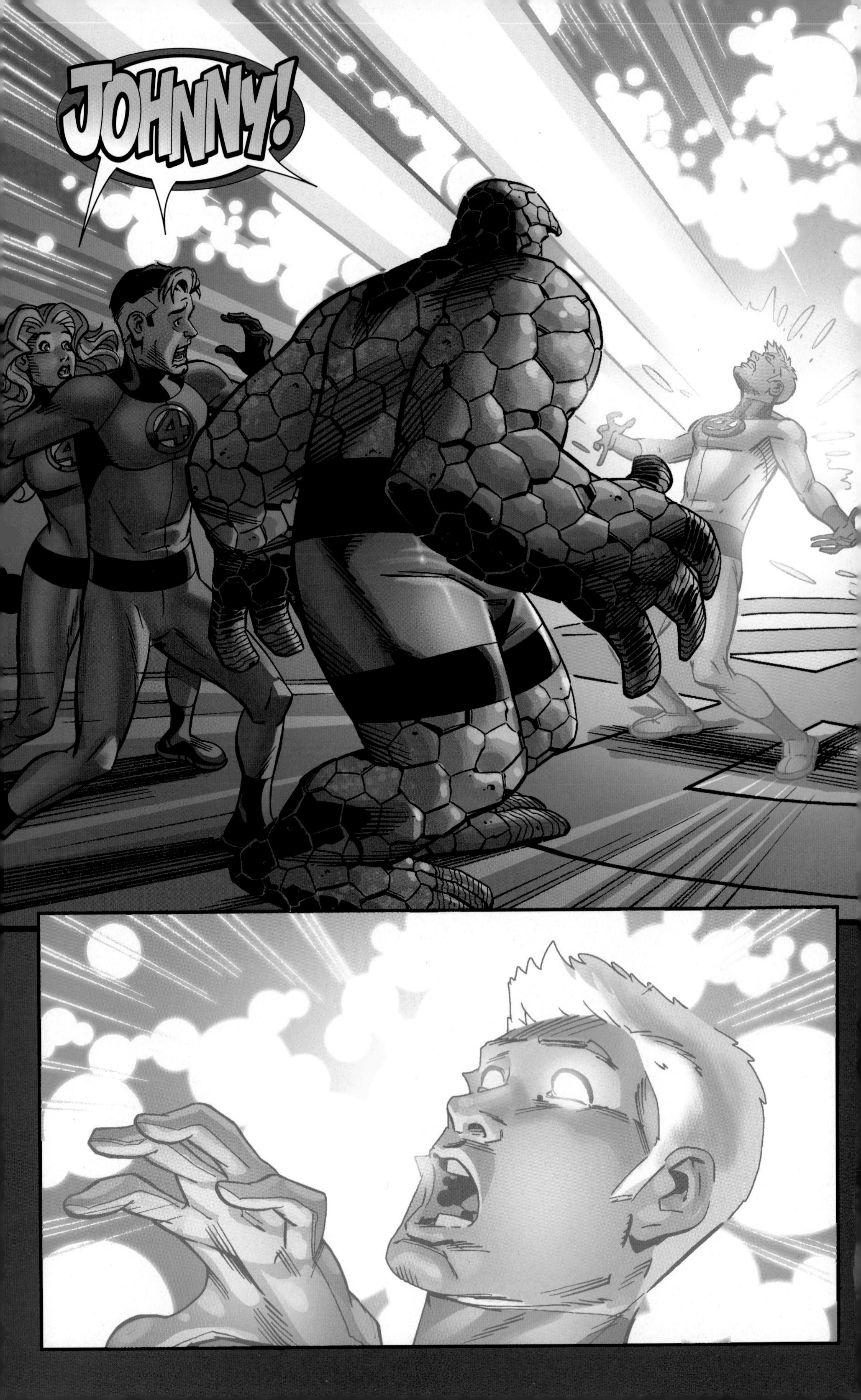
JOHNNY!

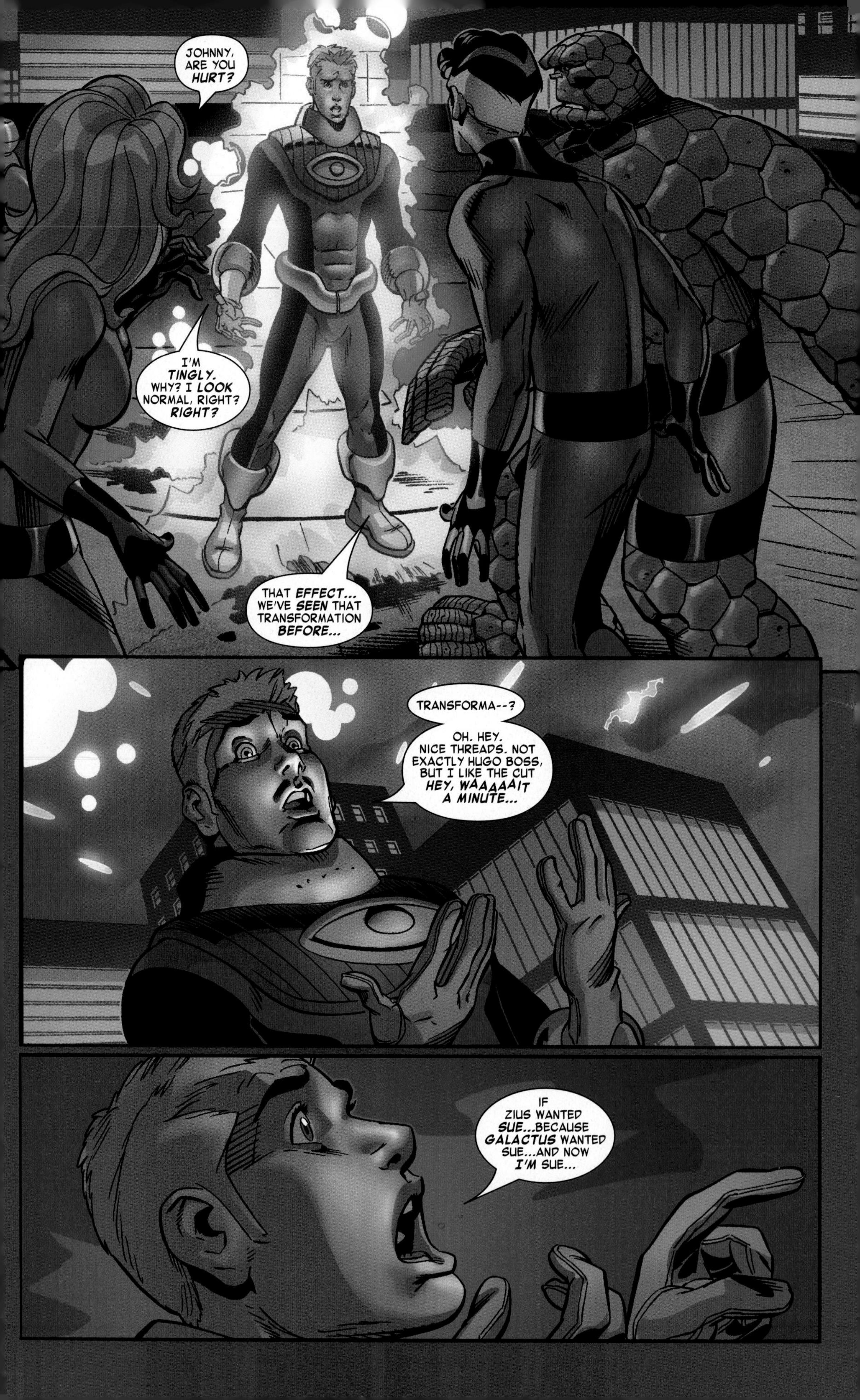
JOHNNY, ARE YOU HURT?
I'M TINGLY. WHY? I LOOK NORMAL, RIGHT? RIGHT?
THAT EFFECT... WE'VE SEEN THAT TRANSFORMATION BEFORE...
TRANSFORMA--?
OH. HEY. NICE THREADS. NOT EXACTLY HUGO BOSS, BUT I LIKE THE CUT HEY, WAAAAAIT A MINUTE...
IF ZIUS WANTED SUE...BECAUSE GALACTUS WANTED SUE...AND NOW I'M SUE...

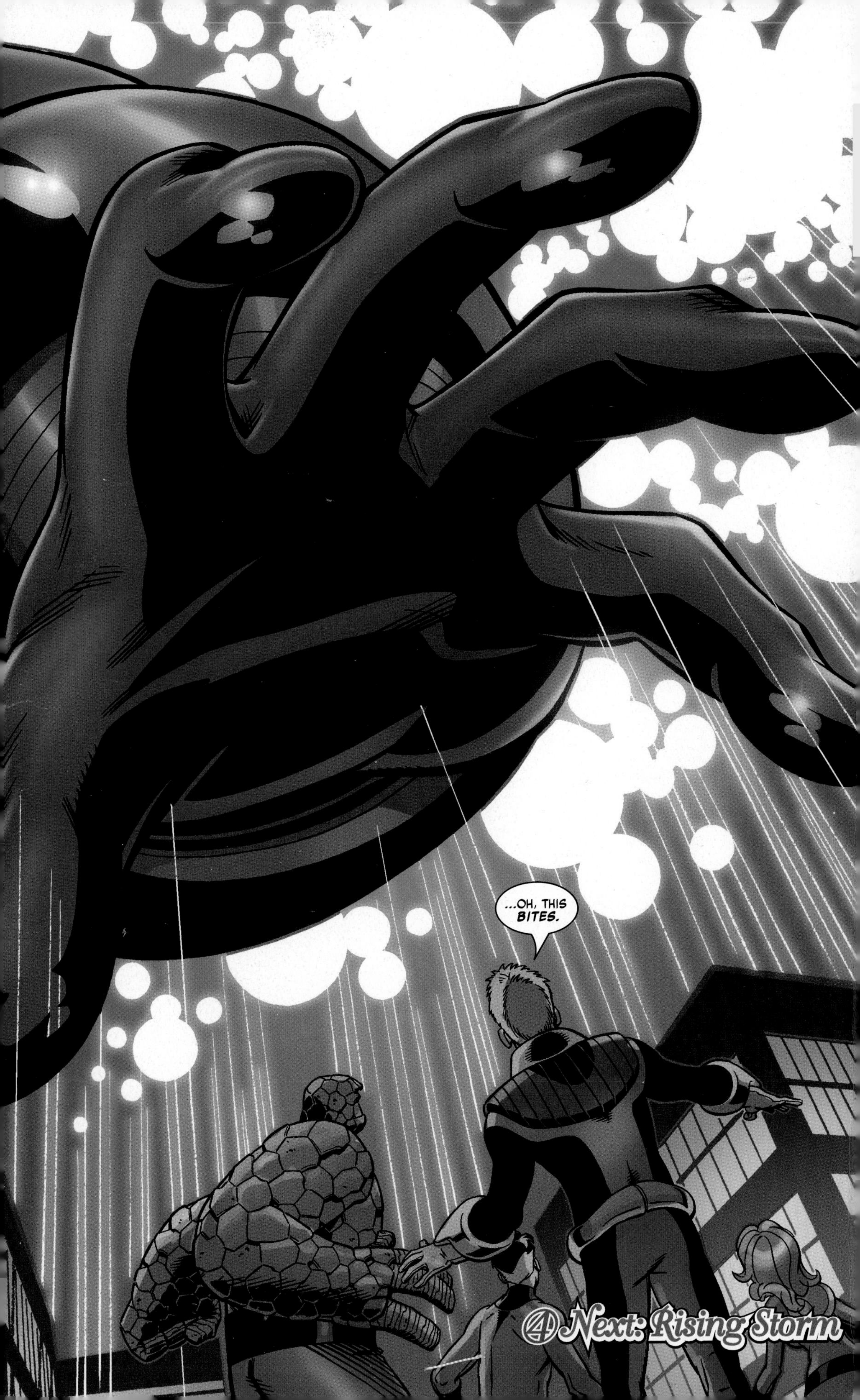
...OH, THIS BITES.
Next: Rising Storm

Fantastic Four

DISASSEMBLED

DYSFUNCTIONAL

WRITERS: Mark Waid & Karl Kesel
PENCILS: Paco Medina
INKS: Juan Vlasco
COVERS: Gene Ha & Morry Hollowell

FOURTITUDE

WRITER: Mark Waid
PENCILS: Mike Wieringo
INKS: Karl Kesel
COVERS: Mike Wieringo, Karl Kesel & Paul Mounts

COLORS: Paul Mounts
LETTERS: Virtual Calligraphy's Randy Gentile
COVER ART: Mike Wieringo, Karl Kesel & Richard Isanove
ASSISTANT EDITORS: Andy Schmidt, Nicole Wiley & Molly Lazer
EDITOR: Tom Brevoort
IMAGINAUTS: Stan Lee & Jack Kirby

COLLECTIONS EDITOR: Jeff Youngquist
ASSISTANT EDITOR: Jennifer Grünwald
BOOK DESIGNER: Patrick McGrath
CREATIVE DIRECTOR: Tom Marvelli

EDITOR IN CHIEF: Joe Quesada
PUBLISHER: Dan Buckley

Fantastic Four

DISASSEMBLED

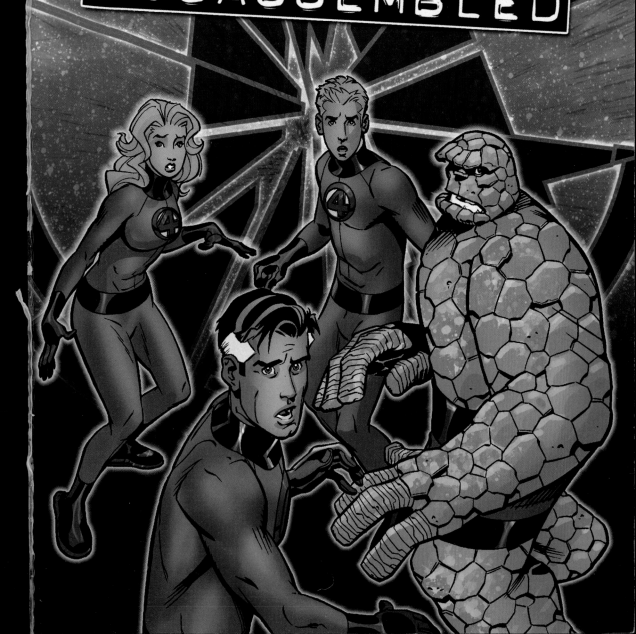